Palgrave Studies in Democracy, Innovation, and Entrepreneurship for Growth

Series Editor
Elias G. Carayannis
The George Washington University
Washington, DC, USA

The central theme of this series is to explore why some areas grow and others stagnate, and to measure the effects and implications in a trans-disciplinary context that takes both historical evolution and geographical location into account. In other words, when, how and why does the nature and dynamics of a political regime inform and shape the drivers of growth and especially innovation and entrepreneurship? In this socio-economic and socio-technical context, how could we best achieve growth, financially and environmentally?

This series aims to address such issues as:

- How does technological advance occur, and what are the strategic processes and institutions involved?
- How are new businesses created? To what extent is intellectual property protected?
- Which cultural characteristics serve to promote or impede innovation? In what ways is wealth distributed or concentrated?

These are among the key questions framing policy and strategic decision-making at firm, industry, national, and regional levels.

A primary feature of the series is to consider the dynamics of innovation and entrepreneurship in the context of globalization, with particular respect to emerging markets, such as China, India, Russia, and Latin America. (For example, what are the implications of China's rapid transition from providing low-cost manufacturing and services to becoming an innovation powerhouse?

How do the perspectives of history and geography explain this phenomenon?)

Contributions from researchers in a wide variety of fields will connect and relate the relationships and inter-dependencies among (1) Innovation, (2) Political Regime, and (3) Economic and Social Development. We will consider whether innovation is demonstrated differently across sectors (e.g., health, education, technology) and disciplines (e.g., social sciences, physical sciences), with an emphasis on discovering emerging patterns, factors, triggers, catalysts, and accelerators to innovation, and their impact on future research, practice, and policy.

This series will delve into what are the sustainable and sufficient growth mechanisms for the foreseeable future for developed, knowledge-based economies and societies (such as the EU and the US) in the context of multiple, concurrent and inter-connected "tipping-point" effects with short (MENA) as well as long (China, India) term effects from a geo-strategic, geo-economic, geo-political and geo-technological set of perspectives.

This conceptualization lies at the heart of the series, and offers to explore the correlation between democracy, innovation and growth.

More information about this series at
http://www.palgrave.com/gp/series/14635

Spyros Vliamos • Michel S. Zouboulakis
Editors

Institutionalist Perspectives on Development

A Multidisciplinary Approach

Editors
Spyros Vliamos
Neapolis University Pafos
Pafos, Cyprus

Michel S. Zouboulakis
University of Thessaly
Volos, Greece

Palgrave Studies in Democracy, Innovation, and Entrepreneurship for Growth
ISBN 978-3-319-98493-3   ISBN 978-3-319-98494-0   (eBook)
https://doi.org/10.1007/978-3-319-98494-0

Library of Congress Control Number: 2018959446

Cover image © Gerard Puigmal/Moment/Getty
Cover design by Akihiro Nakayama

This Palgrave Macmillan imprint is published by the registered company Springer Nature Switzerland AG
The registered company address is: Gewerbestrasse 11, 6330 Cham, Switzerland

CONTENTS

Notes on Contributors

Emmanuel D. Adamides is Associate Professor of Operations and Technology Management in the Division of Management and Organisation Studies at the Faculty of Engineering of the University of Patras, Greece. He holds degrees from the universities of Sussex and Manchester in the U.K., and a doctorate degree from Democritus University of Thrace in Greece. Before joining the University of Patras, Dr. Adamides has worked as a manager and consultant to the private and public sectors, and acted as lecturer and researcher to a number of universities in Greece. From 1991 to 1995. he was a Research Associate at École Polytechnique Fédérale de Lausanne (EPFL) in Switzerland. His current research interests are in the application of social practice theories under a critical realist perspective for studying transition processes concerning technology and innovation in organizations and institutions. Dr. Adamides has published two books and many articles in scientific journals that include International Journal of Production Economics, Technological Forecasting and Social Change, Technovation, Journal of Cleaner Production and Journal of the Operational Research Society.

Paschalis Arvanitidis, MEng, MLE, PgC, PhD Associate Professor of Institutional Economics at the Department of Economics, University of Thessaly. He is an engineer (Aristotle University of Thessaloniki) with postgraduate and doctoral studies in urban economics and property markets (University of Aberdeen). His specialization is on institutional economics, urban economics, urban development and real estate markets. His current research interests focus on issues of urban commons, social capital, user-based management of pubic space and the application of ICTs on these matters. He holds membership in seven professional organizations and over the last years he has participated in many EU and Greek funded research projects related to urban and regional development. Paschalis Arvanitidis is the author of a research monograph publish by Routledge, titled The Economics of Urban Property Markets: An Institutional Economics Analysis, co-author of two other books and he has published a number of research papers in collective volumes and peer reviewed journals, such as Public Choice, Peace Economics, Peace Science, and Public Policy, Journal of Economic Studies, Contributions to Political Economy and Bulletin of Political Economy.

Sławomir Czech holds a PhD in economics and works in the Department of Economics at the University of Economics in Katowice, Poland. His field of research includes political economy and comparative economic systems. Moreover he finds economic history and institutional economics as very inspiring areas of study. Currently he works on a book committed to explaining institutional change through the category of interest employing Swedish economic policy as a case study.

Yadollah Dadgar is a Professor of economics at the Economics Department, Beheshty University, Tehran. He is teaching public sector economics and economic methodology at Beheshty University (1992–present) and also Economic systems in other Iranian universities (1995–present). In the past he has taught Political Economy in the University of Illinois (2014–2015), and he was Visiting professor at Berkeley University (2008–2009) as well in University College Dublin (2010–2011). He is the Editor in chief of *The journal of economic research* (2006–present), Editor in chief, *Journal of economics and politics* (starting 2018). He has presented papers in more than 30 international conferences, and published five books in public sector economics, new development, methodology of economics and economic systems. He has also published more than 70 papers in economic journals including *Journal of European law and economics.*

Guy Féaux de la Croix was born in Berlin in 1948, but he grew up in Bonn. After his law studies in Bonn and Geneva he entered the German foreign service in 1978 to then serve in the German Embassies in Tokyo, The Hague, Paris, Warsaw, Athens and finally at the Holy see in Rome. He is the author of numerous essays on historical, cultural and European issues. He initiated and curated art exhibitions and other cultural events; for example in Paris, Cracow, Berlin, Brussels, Athens, Luxemburg, Shanghai and Beijing. His own works were shown in solo exhibitions in Paris, Warsaw, Munich, Athens and elsewhere. His paintings, which he calls peinture fraîche, is often fluid and surrealistic, his sculptures often hyper-realistic, a neo-Pop-art exploration of the relevance of the Ancient Greek experience for the culture of our own times and for our human identity. With Greece Guy Féaux de la Croix has been deeply connected ever since his time as Minister of the German Embassy (2005–2012) and his capacity of founding chairman of the Marathon Friends International Association and the Friends of Greece Society. In June 2014 the University of Thessaly in Volos honoured his achievements for friendship in Europe with the title of a Doctor honoris causa.

Konstantinos Gravas is a capital markets professional and a PhD candidate in the field of Global Political Economy. He is also a visiting lecturer at the Hellenic Air Force (HAF) Academy, where he teaches in the Hellenic Air Force Command and Staff College since 2015. He holds a 5-year MEng Degree in Chemical Engineering from the National Technical University of Athens (NTUA) and a two-year full-time MBA from the Athens University of Economics and Business (AUEB). He attended the Rotterdam School of Management, Erasmus Universiteit. He holds a second Master of Science in Mathematical Economics, obtained from the National Technical University of Athens (NTUA) in 2012. He is a frequent contributor to one of the top Greek financial websites (Capital.gr) regarding Politics & Economy since 2012. His main areas of interest include Monetary Economics and Economic History. He holds the professional certification of Xetra equity trader from Frankfurt Stock Exchange (Deutsche Boerse). He is also a certified Derivatives Market Maker/Trader from the Athens Derivatives Exchange (ADEX) and a certified Market Analyst and Portfolio Manager from the Hellenic Capital Market Commission and the Bank of Greece.

Geoffrey M. Hodgson is a Professor in Management at Loughborough University London. He is the author of sixteen books including *Wrong Turnings: How the Left Got Lost* (2018), *Conceptualizing Capitalism: Institutions, Evolution, Future* (2015), *From Pleasure Machines to Moral Communities* (2013). Conceptualizing Capitalism won the Joseph Schumpeter Prize in 2014. He has published over 150 articles in academic journals and played a leading role in the development of modern institutional economics. He is editor-in-chief of the *Journal of Institutional Economics* and a fellow of the Academy for Social Science and the Royal Society of Arts.

Ilias Kouskouvelis is a Professor of International Relations, Department of International and European Studies, University of Macedonia, Thessaloniki, Greece. He is the Director of the "Institute of International, European and Defense Analysis" (idea.uom.gr) and holder of the "Thucydides HNDGS Chair in Strategic Studies". His publications include the authoring of seven books, the editing of another thirteen, as well as many journal articles and book chapters. He is the author of Theory of Decision Making in Thucydides (2015—in Greek), and is currently working on the book's English edition under contract with Lexington Books.

Joanna Kuczewska is an Assistant Professor at the Faculty of Economics at the University of Gdansk, Chair of European Integration Economics. She graduated from the University of Gdańsk, with a degree in Economics (1997), from Corvinus University of Budapest intensive executive MBA course (2009), and holds a PhD in Economics at the University of Gdańsk. Her thesis' title was "European benchmarking procedure—instrument of Polish competitiveness improvement in the light of the European Integration process". Her main area of interest include the economics of European integration, enterprises strategies within the European internal market, international management and the European project management. She has also strong experience in the European project management being a coordinator of the following projects: (1996–1998) Tempus Project—College of Europe Natolin and Research Centre on European Integration, University of Gdańsk; (1998–1999) Jean Monnet doctoral research project—Benchmarking of enterprises—the instrument of improving the Polish economy competitiveness in the process of integration with the EU; (2000–2001) PHARE TACIS, "Urban System and Urban Networking in the Baltic Sea Region—the South Baltic Case Study"—Pomeranian Voivodeship, City Sopot and City Lębork; (2009–2011) Project "Improving the qualifications of employees in the automotive sector"—the European Social Fund.

Agnieszka Joanna Legutko, MSc is a PhD candidate since 2014, at the University of Economics in Krakow at the Faculty of Economics and International Relations with specialization in Economy and Public Administration. Her career is connected with work in an international environment and academia, especially within the Nordic region. In 2009, she started her BA studies at the University of Economics in Krakow at the Faculty of Economics and International Relations in the field of International Relations. In 2011 as an international exchange student, she completed a semester at Haskolinn and Bifrost in Iceland, where she received the Rector's award for the best group project about Viral Marketing. In 2012, she was awarded with BA diploma after defending her thesis—Multilateral diplomacy—the example of the activities of the Permanent Representations of the Republic of Poland. In 2014 she obtained her Master's degree at the University of Economics in Krakow at the Faculty of Economics and International Relations with the specializations in International Management. Her master thesis title was "Arctic in crossfire—climate change in the High North and their impact on the economy, politics and indigenous people", supervised by Professor Kazimierz Lankosz.

Kyriakos Mikelis is an Assistant Professor at the University of Macedonia/ Department of International & European Studies, specializing in International Relations. He completed his (post-)graduate studies at Panteion University (Athens, PhD) and the University of Kent at Canterbury (MA). His particular academic interests relate to International Relations theory, the field's history, international politics and European integration. He has published in both Greek and international journals and he has participated in several international scientific conferences. His recent publications include: Mikelis, K., & Stroikos, D. (2017) Hierarchies, Civilization and the Eurozone Crisis: The Greek Financial Crisis. In Marangos, J. (ed.) The Internal Impact and External Influence of the Greek Financial Crisis, 125–142, Palgrave Macmillan and Mikelis, K. (2017) The Long Road to a Democratic Networked European Union. In Bitros, G. & Kyriazis, N. (eds.), Democracy and an Open Economy World Order, 209–222, Springer International Publishing.

Sylwia Morawska is an Assistant professor at the Department of Administrative and Financial Law of Enterprises at the Collegium of Business Administration at the Warsaw School of Economics and the Prosecutor. She obtained the Habilitation in the institutional economy from the Warsaw School of Economics, thesis' title: "The Entrepreneur in face of bankruptcy. Diagnosis of proposals for changes of the institutional system in Poland". Her main area of research interest are: restructuring and bankruptcy of entrepreneurs, management of public organizations including courts. She also participates in scientific and research projects, including those of an international nature: Assessment of the actual level of protection of creditors' rights in Poland in 2004/2012—transaction costs of contract rights—grant Narodowe Centrum Nauki UMO-2013/09/ B / HS4 /03605; Building the organizational efficiency of justice units for the development of entrepreneurship, College of Business Sciences, Warsaw School of Economics No. 32771 and Increasing instability in the global economy and its impact on the competitiveness of enterprises in Poland. Part III. Knop/S15/01/15. The role of the judiciary and reducing instability in the economy.

Fotini Nasioka, BSc, MSc is a PhD candidate at the Department of Economics (University of Thessaly). She is an economist with specialization on applied and institutional economics. Her major research interests include institutional economics with emphasis on the analysis of institutional change in the context of common pool resource management. Her doctoral thesis focuses on the concept of community governance of urban commons, searching for those characteristics seen as significant for the successful management of a community-based system.

Rouhollah Nazari is a PhD candidate in Economics at Ferdowsi University, Mashhad Iran. He holds a Master degree in economics from Mufid University. His research interests include Public sector economics, Economic Development, Iranian economy. He teaches at Eilam University: Money and banking, Public economics and he has published about 20 papers in different scientific Journals. He is an Economic advisor in many economic institutions.

Andreas Stergiou is Assistant Professor at the Department of Economics (European Politics and History), University of Thessaly and Teaching Fellow at the Open University of Greece. Degrees: BA, History (Department of History, Ionian University) 1995 (Greek State Scholarship Foundation and Minor Asia Refugees Foundation). Magister and PhD (with distinction), Contemporary History and Political Science (University of Mannheim) 1996–2001 (Greek State Scholarship Foundation, Alexander Onassis Public Benefit Foundation, Kölner Foundation, Hermann Weber Foundation Germany). He has received a Postdoc grant in History of International relations (Department of History, Ionian University) 2004–2006 funded by the EU. He attended a Postdoctoral seminar on American Politics and Political Thought, Donahue Institute, University of

Massachusetts, Amherst (Summer 2010). He was Visiting Research Fellow at the Press Information Office (Cyprus), at the Truman Institute for advancement of Peace in the Hebrew University in 2013 and Research Affiliate 2014–2015 at the same Institute, at the Institute of World Economy and International Relations of the Russian Academy of Sciences (IMEMO) in Moscow (2015) as well as in Azerbaijan Diplomatic Academy (ADA University 2017). He has been Teaching Fellow at the University of Mannheim, Heidelberg and at the Diplomatic Academy of the Greek Ministry of Foreign Affairs. He has published in French, English, Greek and German, Portuguese and Russian.

Spyros Vliamos Professor Emeritus (Honorary) of Political Economy at the National and Kapodistrian University of Athens, specializing in *Institutional Economics and Entrepreneurship*. In 2015, he was appointed Dean of the Business School of Neapolis University Pafos in Cyprus.

He holds a PhD in Economics from the University of London, a MA in Economics from Manchester University, and a BSc in Economics from the University of Athens. Also, been member of the Senate at the University of Thessaly and Head of the Department of Economics and of the Department of Regional and Urban Planning. He has taught as Visiting Professor at the Graduate Institute of Regional Development of the Panteion University, at the National University of Nagoya-Japan and at the Economics University of Prague. Been also the co-founder and Director of the first and biggest private university in Czech Republic, under the name University of New York in Prague (UNYP).

He has also been (1) National Expert with the Joint Research Centre (JRC) of the European Commission in Ispra, Italy, (2) Secretary General for the Management of European Funds with the Greek Government (2004–2007), (3) Advisor to the Government of the Hellenic Bank of Industrial Development (1983–1991), (4) member of the Board of Directors of The Athens Stock Exchange and (5) member of the Board of Directors of The Hellenic Telecommunications Organization S.A. (OTE).

He has been co-founder and since then (2002) a Visiting Scholar of the *Pan – European Entrepreneurship Research Group (PEER-Group)* at the Université de Paris, Dauphine. Also he has been member of the Scientific Committee and the Faculty of the European Doctoral Program of the *European University Network on Entrepreneurship Research—ESU*.

His professional experience includes areas of specialized knowledge in: Entrepreneurship, Institutions and Economic Policy, Regional development, Local government, Economic analysis and policy, Investment appraisal.

Anna Ząbkowicz is Professor of economic sciences, chair of Institutional Economics and Economic Policies, at the Jagiellonian University in Cracow. She is also a professor in the Institute of Economic Sciences, Polish Academy of Sciences. She was a visiting fellow at University of Sussex and University of Cambridge, as well as a DAAD-supported researcher at Wilhelm-Westfaellicher Universitaet Muenster. She is an alumnus of PMD at Harvard Business School. The field of her special interest is policy formulation and economic advise, public choice theory and public policy, as well as international competition. Her contributions are made from various perspectives including comparative studies, cross-country perspectives, and historical assessments. She has published about one hundred articles in professional journals.

Jerzy Ząbkowicz Associate professor of international economic relations and economic policy at the Helena Chodkowska University of Technology and Economics in Warsaw (till 2015). He is Guest lecturer at the Jagiellonian University in Cracow, co-founder of the Forum for Institutional Thought and editorial member of the *Economics World* (David Publishing Company, New York). JZ is the author of the book *Rynkowe usługi użyteczności publicznej w Unii Europejskiej. W poszukiwaniu konsensu i pewności prawnej* (Market services of general interest in the European Union. In search of consensus and legal certainty, C.H.Beck 2017). He wrote over of 40 articles and book chapters on European economics and international economic relations, including "The Single Market and the 'bicycle theory' of the European Union politics. Does it still work?" (*Economics and Law* 2015) and Governance of the Single Market. How to Win Allies for a New Opening? (*Sustainable Growth in the EU. Challenges and Solutions*, Springer International Publishing AG 2017). Member of the management boards of several foreign trade enterprises. Research interests: the Single Market, the EU competition rules, services of general economic interest in the EU, the EU procurement rules, compensation of public service obligations under state aid rules (the EU framework), Public-Private Partnership within the EU (compatibility with the rules of the EU).

Vasilis Zervos is a member of the Economics Department of the University of Strasbourg (France) and as an associate professor leads the Policy-Economics-Law and Business & Management departments of the International Space University (Strasbourg). His background is in Economics and has studies and worked extensively in Greece, the UK and France. He holds a BA in Economics, MSc in Economics with his thesis on Monetary Policy and the European Central Bank and a DPhil in Industrial Economics (Space Industry). His areas of interest cover a wide scope with applications in areas like the analysis of strategic industries and their economic implications, economics of procurement, innovation and technological change, foreign direct investment, project management. He is widely published in peer-reviewed journals, books and collective volumes and regularly contributes to projects of defence and space interest. He advises space agencies, government institutions and intergovernmental organizations on strategic security and economic aspects.

Michel S. Zouboulakis PhD (Economics) and MSc (DEA in History and Philosophy of Economics) University of Paris 1, BSc (Economics) Aristotelian University of Thessaloniki, is a Professor in the History and Methodology of Economics, in the Department of Economics at the University of Thessaly. He is the author of *La science économique à la recherche de ses fondements. La tradition épistémologique ricardienne, 1826–1891* (Paris: Presses Universitaires de France, 1993), of a textbook on Economic Methodology (Volos: University of Thessaly Press, 2007) and of a recent book *The varieties of economic rationality: from Adam Smith to contemporary behavioural and evolutionary economics* (London: Routledge 2014). He has published articles in international peer reviewed Journals such as *The European Journal of the History of Economic Thought, Journal of the History of Economic Thought, Journal of Economic Methodology, Economies et Sociétés, History of economic ideas, Cahiers d'economie Politique, Revue Economique, Journal of Institutional Economics,* and *European journal of Law and Economics.* He served as Vice-Rector of Economic and Student affairs, Public and International Relations (elected) from 2008 to 2012, Vice-President of the University Council (elected) from 2013 to 2015 and Head of the Department of Economics from 2004 to 2009 and from 2015 until 2019.

LIST OF FIGURES

Public Goods, Club Goods and Specialization in Evolving Collaborative Entities

Amendments to Legal Regulations in the Field of the Enterprises Restructuring Procedures in Poland

LIST OF TABLES

Public Goods, Club Goods and Specialization in Evolving Collaborative Entities

Amendments to Legal Regulations in the Field of the Enterprises Restructuring Procedures in Poland

Editors' Introduction

Spyros Vliamos and Michel S. Zouboulakis

This volume includes selected chapters presented in the *5th International Conference "INSTITUTIONS & DEVELOPMENT"* held in the new premises of the Department of Economics of the University of Thessaly in Volos, Greece, from May, 17th to 19th, 2017. The main objective of the Conference was to depict the role of both formal and informal institutions in achieving long-term economic efficiency and development. As both the recent global financial crisis and the subsequent sovereign debt crisis within the Eurozone have shown, sustainable development is a combination of human, social and institutional factors that interact with each other and go beyond the strictly economic conditions of each country. As put elsewhere, '*Political Economy recognizes the fact that the performance of the economy depends only for a small part on nature factors, i.e. natural resources, and largely upon the institutional mechanisms that society chooses to use, as a matter of Policy, to motivate and to co-ordinate the participation of resources,*

S. Vliamos (✉)
Neapolis University Pafos, Pafos, Cyprus
e-mail: s.vliamos@nup.ac.cy

M. S. Zouboulakis
University of Thessaly, Volos, Greece
e-mail: mzoub@uth.gr

© The Author(s) 2018
S. Vliamos, M. S. Zouboulakis (eds.), *Institutionalist Perspectives on Development*, Palgrave Studies in Democracy, Innovation, and Entrepreneurship for Growth,
https://doi.org/10.1007/978-3-319-98494-0_1

1

in the social economy' Vliamos (1992: 5). Economics is first and foremost a social science. Skidelsky (2016) reminds us of John Stuart Mill, the great nineteenth-century economist and philosopher, *who 'believed that nobody can be a good economist if he or she is just an economist. (…) What unites the great economists, and many other good ones, is a broad education and outlook. This gives them access to many different ways of understanding the economy.'*

Academic literature during the last three decades offers a growing number of theoretical and empirical studies devoted to the interaction between institutions, on the one hand, and the economic conditions which stimulate growth and prosperity, on the other. Hence, North (1990: 112) asserted that *'the polity and the economy are inextricably interlinked in any understanding of the performance of an economy'*. In that sense, formal institutional constraints *'specify and enforce property rights that shape the basic incentive structure of an economy'* but also impose the rules of law that are most favourable to economic growth. Furubotn and Richter (1998: 293–5) defined the constitutional and operational rules of an efficient private ownership economy. In the former rules, they comprise the principles of private property, freedom of contract and individual liability to fulfil its respective obligations, while among the latter rules they include specific regulations for conducting and enforcing contracts. Furthermore, North (2005: 159) held that sustained growth is not a simple function of knowledge and technology; *'the key is the incentive structure … for productivity-improving activities'* provided by the institutional matrix. Efficient government is an essential part of the institutional matrix as it embraces both the creation of rules and their enforcement within an order of law. As he explained, for market institutions to work the state should respect the property and personal rights of its citizens; only then, *'all members of society have an incentive to obey and enforce the rules'* (North, ib. 107–8). The adequate institutional rules and appropriate allocation of property rights influence the alignment or not with the technological systems employed (Ménard 2014: 583). Additionally, a crucial element for economic performance and sustainable development is the quality of informal rules and social norms exemplified by the level of social capital and the variations of trustworthiness in business transactions: where social norms prescribing cooperation and trustworthiness prevail, formal regulations are far more efficient (cf. Keefer and Shirley 2000; Keefer and Knack 2005: 709).

Yet, according to King (2006: 1) '*constitutions can be rewritten, property rights revoked, and revolutions have been known to occur, illustrating the point that, as a society, we can never commit future generations—or even our future selves—to collective decisions.*' Although there is no way of enforcing that commitment, we can try to find ways of making it more or less credible; '*that we will, collectively, act in a way that is conducive to our long-run prosperity.*' King argues that '*one of the most important ingredients of a successful market economy is the set of institutions that constrain our future collective behaviour. Such institutions have cultural and political roots, but they have economic effects.*'

From the empirical standpoint, Acemoglu, Johnson and Robinson (2005) using the analytical tools of economic growth theory, asserted that '*differences in economic institutions are the fundamental cause of differences in economic development*'. In their thorough study, they claim that a given set of economic institutions may have very different implications for economic growth depending on the distribution of political power in society. Inefficient economic institutions have distributional consequences leading to more concentration of political power. Elsewhere, Acemoglu and Johnson (2005) provided robust evidence that '*property rights institutions have a major influence on long-run economic growth, investment, and financial development, while contracting institutions appear to affect the form of financial intermediation but have a more limited impact on growth, investment, and the total amount of credit in the economy*'. Interestingly, recent academic literature critically evaluates the dominant discourse on the relationship between institutions and economic development. As Chang (2011: 494–5) critically argues, '*institutional economists need to pay more attention to the real world, both of the present and historical—not the fairy-tale retelling of the history of the world that has come to characterize mainstream institutional economics today (...) but capitalism as it really has been.*' Chang observes that institutional economic theories have been very often developed '*on the basis of rather stylized understanding of reality (...) reality is often stranger than fiction and therefore our theories need to be more richly informed by real-world experiences—both history and modern-day events.*'

This volume is organized in three parts. The first part contains five chapters that deal with the historical and political roots that sustain the institutions favorable to development. Geoffrey Hodgson (University of Hertfordshire), in his official speech for the honorary degree presented the institutional changes introduced by the British "Glorious Revolution" in 1688 that were at the origin of the rise of capitalism and the unprecedented rise in production and innovation during the eighteenth century. Hodgson argues convincingly that it was mainly the growth of finance and the building of a new state administration that lies behind these changes and not the 'security of property rights' which were established long ago. If Hodgson deals with the early age of capitalism, Anna Ząbkowicz (Institute of Economics, Poland) and Sławomir Czech (University of Katowice) are facing its mature age and show the way in which the contemporary debtor state becomes critically dependent on international financial capital. Through an historical exegesis the authors explain how the role of the state has dramatically changed in the long term evolution of capitalism and offer a comprehensive framework that aims to reveal the matrix of conflictual interests that rule over contemporary capitalism. One possible actor having significant countervailing power in modern day capitalism comes from the Non-governmental organizations. Agnieszka Joanna Legutko (Cracow University) examines the growing role of NGO's in the modern state in innovation and sustainable development that allows both the economy and the democracy to flourish. Significantly, the former German Ambassador Guy Féaux de la Croix debates on crucial matters concerning the state of Democracy in Western developed countries using the Ancient Greek legacy as a source of inspiration for the renewal of democracy in those countries. In their thorough and original research Yadollah Dadgar and Rouhollah Nazari (Beheshty and Ferdowsi Universities) present a much less known case study, the Iranian economy and its institutional impediments to growth. The Iranian colleagues offer a genuine insider view of the evolution of the Iranian economy during the last two decades and suggest a theoretical model that captures the relation between institutions and economic development.

In the second part, some theoretical perceptions of immaterial institutions are attempted. Emmanuel D. Adamides (University of Patras) analyses the way that National Innovation Systems contribute to the development and diffusion of innovations. Adamides focuses on the relationship between universities and research centres on the one hand, and industry on the other. Assuming that the performance of a particular NIS is the emergent result of the behaviour of structures of organisations and institutions participating in it, the author reveals the underlying mechanism of this relationship that allows him to suggest the interventions that are needed to enhance productive innovations. In their contribution, Paschalis Arvanitidis and Fotini Nasioka (University of Thessaly) take in hand the problem of common pool resources which by their nature give rise to the social dilemma 'efficiency vs sustainability'. To apprehend this problem the authors made a laboratory experiment with 77 final-year undergraduates in Volos-Greece and show that individuals in commons dilemmas are not always confined to their narrow self-interest. On the contrary, small-group, face-to-face communication enables them to articulate cooperation-facilitating institutions and achieve outcomes that are socially efficient. In the next chapter, Vasilis Zervos (Strasbourg) is also concerned about cooperation. Specialization in collaborative entities is a historically efficient economic mechanism for achievement of common objectives. Using as a benchmark the aerospace sector Zervos suggests an illustrative model showing that economies of scale and scope in areas of inter-partnership contributions involving governments and the provision of public goods has a positive impact upon the respective relative national industrial performance in competitive commercial markets.

The third and last part explores how the various official institutions—such as international organizations—interrelate with the process of development. In the first chapter, which examines the evolution of central banks as powerful institutions within the global economic system, Spyros Vliamos and Konstantinos Gravas (Neapolis University at Pafos and National and Kapodistrian University of Athens) review the concept of international policy cooperation, starting from the first age of globalization in 1870s and comparing the two great financial crises of our age; the *Great Depression* of 1930s and the *Great Recession* of 2007–9. The authors offer a unique view of the political and economic context that determined the institutional arrangements and shaped monetary policy in the aftermath of the 'Great 2007–9 Recession', leading to a new paradigm of '*monetary peace*', i.e. the successful coordinated action between the leading systematically important central banks of the world in order to preserve an existing currency *regime*, while achieving monetary and financial stability. Ilias Kouskouvelis and Kyriakos Mikelis (University of Macedonia) examine how the engagement of realism with institutional analysis and, namely, the concept of 'regime' has enabled the former to account for cooperative dynamics and mechanisms in the international system. Within the same international relations perspective, Andreas Stergiou (University of Thessaly) focuses on the energy sector (natural gas) as a parameter of the overall EU–Russia economic relationship and their antagonism in South-Eastern Europe. Stergiou holds that Russia has an advantage over EU, which is a huge bureaucratic institution plagued by the so-called lack of ownership handicap, i.e. the contradictory and opposing interests among its members. The specificities of the EU internal organization are thoroughly discussed also by Jerzy Ząbkowicz (Forum for Institutional Thought, Poland). The author claims that the decreasing volume of the Commission's legislative actions over the last years simply follows the Commission's new approach to ensure its effectiveness in a changing environment, and it is not a result of losing influence over the two other European Institutional bodies, the European Parliament and the Council. The problems of efficiency of the EU policies in the enterprise sector are furthermore exposed by Sylwia Morawska (Warsaw School of Economics) and Joanna Kuczewska (University of Gdańsk). The authors are assessing the amendments to the EU legal regulations in the field of the enterprises restructuring procedures in Poland. Despite the continuous efforts of the EU to ensure a friendly business environment, the evidence from Poland indicates that the implementation of the EU regulations concerning the restructuring procedures for enterprises experiencing financial difficulties is still very weak and not aligned with the entrepreneurs' requirements.

We are particularly thankful to all the authors who travelled from abroad and gave us the pleasure to enjoy their company and inspirational discussions. We are also thankful to the members of the Department and mostly to the members of the scientific committee who had to review over 70 proposals and about 25 final submissions to this collective volume. We extend our sincere appreciation to the Kyriazis Foundation for making the conference possible through its generous grants. Our final word goes to Dr. Emmanouil-Marios Economou who served bravely and tirelessly as an organisational secretary, careful reader and faithful collaborator throughout the organization of this conference.

References

Acemoglu, D., & Johnson, S. (2005). Unbundling institutions. *Journal of Political Economy, 113*(5), 949–995.

Acemoglu, D., Johnson, S., & Robinson, J. (2005). Institutions as a fundamental cause of long-run growth. In P. Aghion & S. Durlauf (Eds.), *Handbook of economic growth*. Amsterdam: Elsevier.

Chang, H. J. (2011). Institutions and economic development: Theory, policy and history. *Journal of Institutional Economics, 7*(4), 473–498.

Furubotn, E., & Richter, R. (1998). *Institutions and economic theory*. Ann Arbor: University of Michigan Press (2nd ed., 2005).

Keefer, P., & Knack, S. (2005). Social capital, social norms and the New Institutional Economics. In C. Ménard & M. Shirley (Eds.), *Handbook of new institutional economics*. Dordrecht: Springer.

Keefer, P., & Shirley, M. (2000). Formal versus informal institutions in economic development. In C. Ménard (Ed.), *Institutions, contracts and organizations*. Cheltenham: Elgar.

King, M. (2006). *Trusting in money: From Kirkcaldy to the MPC*. Speech at the Adam Smith Lecture. Bank of England. Retrieved from https://www.bis.org/review/r061031a.pdf.

Ménard, C. (2014). Embedding organizational arrangements: Towards a general model. *Journal of Institutional Economics, 10*(4), 567–589.

North, D. C. (1990). *Institutions, institutional change and economic performance*. Cambridge: Cambridge University Press.

North, D. C. (2005). *Understanding the process of economic change*. Princeton, NJ: Princeton University Press.

Skidelsky, R. (2016). Economists versus the Economy. *Project Syndicate*, December 23. Retrieved from https://www.project-syndicate.org/commentary/mathematical-economics-training-too-narrow-by-robert-skidelsky-2016-12?barrier=accessreg.

Vliamos, S. (1992). *Economic theorising and policy making*. International Economic Conflict Discussion Paper No. 56. Nagoya: Economic Research Center, Nagoya University.

PART I

Institutional Roots of Development

1688 and All That: Property Rights, the Glorious Revolution and the Rise of British Capitalism

Geoffrey M. Hodgson

1 INTRODUCTION

A key problem for economic historians is to explain the innovations, rises in productivity and increases in the average standard of living that became evident in Great Britain by the nineteenth century and spread to other countries in the world.[1] Sometime after 1700, GDP per capita began to take off in Europe, and accelerated further upwards. Western European

[1] This essay extends some arguments in Hodgson (2015a). The author thanks Benito Arruñada, Michael Bordo, David Donald, Goncalo Fonseca, Anne Murphy, Sheilagh Ogilvie, Mehrdad Vahabi, two anonymous referees and participants at presentations (at the World Interdisciplinary Network for Institutional Research Symposium on Property Rights in Bristol, UK, at the Chinese University of Hong Kong in April 2016 and at the First International Conference on Cliometrics and Complexity in Lyon, France in June 2016), for very helpful comments and suggestions.

G. M. Hodgson (✉)
Loughborough University London, London, UK
e-mail: g.m.hodgson@herts.ac.uk

GDP per capita was about twenty times larger in 2003 than it was in 1700. World GDP per capita in 2003 was about eleven times larger than it was in 1700 (Maddison 2007).

What enabled this unprecedented rise in production and innovation? This question was a major concern of the late Douglass C. North. Regarding Britain, North and Barry Weingast (1989) stressed the importance of institutional changes following the Glorious Revolution of 1688. They claimed that it increased the security of property rights. Their argument has been followed by several others. But North's account has been subject to criticism. In particular, as several historians have pointed out, 1688 did not lead to major changes in property rights. It did mean a change in the de facto balance of power between the monarch and Parliament, but this was not a result of any major de jure legislation in the political settlement of 1689.[2]

Rather than changes in the security of property rights, the alternative account here underlines how 1688 ruptured England's preceding international alliances and thrust the country into a series of wide-ranging wars against France and Spain, climaxing in the global Seven Years' War of 1755–1763. These wars prompted the Financial and Administrative Revolutions, which rested on the 1689 accord between King and Parliament. The need to protect and maintain a growing trading empire pressured the British state to reform its finances, gather more taxes, and purchase industrial, agricultural and service outputs destined for its army and navy. The development of the financial system created new incentives and later possibilities for the use of landed property as collateral to finance investments infrastructure and industry.

Section 2 outlines the arguments of North and others concerning the alleged impact of the Glorious Revolution on the security of property rights. As a number of historians have pointed out, this revolution was essentially protective and conservative, and it involved few major legal changes.

Section 3 considers the evolution of property rights in England. Property rights, particularly in land, were relatively secure from the thirteenth century. A major problem for capitalist development was the feudal nature of those rights. But the most rapid progress in the reform of landed

---

[2] From 1603, England, Wales and Scotland were ruled by the same monarch. Hence the invasion and accession of William of Orange in 1688 affected all three nations of Great Britain. But Scotland retained a partially separate legal system, even after the Act of Union of 1707 that created a single British parliament.

property began in the 1750s, when much land became usable as collateral to finance loans for other projects. Similarly, a marked rise in patents—an important type of intellectual property—did not occur until the 1760s. Some property rights were made insecure, such as legislation to abolish heritable jurisdictions in the early 1700s.

Section 4 examines economic growth in the seventeenth and eighteenth centuries and concomitant changes in occupational patterns. Economic growth picked up around 1650 (long before 1688) but it remained steady until it began to accelerate after about 1760 (long after 1688). Evidence on the growth of social strata involved in industry and commerce shows that their percentage contribution to national income rose only slightly from 1688 to 1759. Hence there is no evidence of a strong shift of the balance of class power in favour of the bourgeoisie from 1650 to 1760.

Section 5 looks at the Financial and Administrative Revolutions lasting from 1689 to the early decades of the eighteenth century. By contrast to aforementioned indicators, immediately after 1689 there is clear evidence of a growing state administration, increased taxation, and major developments in financial institutions. These changes were pressured by the growing needs of defence and war. In turn, these Financial and Administrative Revolutions extended the foundation for a capitalist system based on collateralizable property, negotiable debt, global trade, and state power.

Section 6 summarizes the argument—with its different chain of events connecting 1688 and the Industrial Revolution—and concludes the essay.

2   1688, THE BALANCE OF POWER AND PROPERTY RIGHTS

North and Weingast (1989: 803) argued that the development of Britain's modern economy depended on 'secure property rights' and the 'elimination of confiscatory government'. The Glorious Revolution was allegedly crucial in this process, including the constitutional settlement of 1689 between the Crown and Parliament, where the Declaration of Right made the king subject to Parliament on matters of legislation and taxation.

Hence 'reducing the arbitrary powers of the Crown resulted not only in more secure economic liberties and property rights, but in political liberties and rights as well' (North and Weingast 1989: 816). Accordingly, 'the credible commitment by the government to honor its financial agreements was part of a larger commitment to secure private rights' (North and Weingast 1989: 824).

North and Weingast (1989: 825–28) pointed to a number of subsequent changes in the financial system, including the formation of the Bank of England in 1694, reductions in interest rates, rising trade in stocks and in securities, and the growth and development of banks. They cited these financial developments as the major confirmation of their claim that the settlement of 1689 helped to secure property rights and laid the foundations of eighteenth-century economic growth.

Similarly, Daron Acemoglu et al. (2005a: 393) suggested that in the English Middle Ages there was a 'lack of property rights for landowners, merchants and proto-industrialists' and that their 'development' first occurred in the late seventeenth century, when 'strengthening the property rights of both land and capital owners ... spurred a process of financial and commercial expansion.' They highlighted the settlement of 1689, which limited the power of the monarch and facilitated 'the development of property rights'.[3]

But crucial elements in this argument have been criticised by historians. Leading scholars have played down the extent of the constitutional settlement of 1689 by stressing its 'conservative' nature: it was aimed at the restoration of established rights, it salvaged previous constitutional arrangements after the turmoil of the Civil War and the Stuarts, and it was 'defensive' rather than innovative (Western 1972; Scott 1991; Jones 1992; Morrill 1992; Trevor-Roper 1992; Nenner 1997; Pincus 2009; Ogilvie and Carus 2014).

The settlement of 1689 ostensibly reinforced the de facto power of Parliament against the monarchy, but there was little rewriting of the rules. Although Parliament met more regularly after the Glorious Revolution, the Declaration of Right of 1689 was vague on this matter, and other legislation calling for frequent parliaments had been passed as early as the fourteenth century (Pincus and Robinson 2014: 197). 'There was also no new legislation enjoining the supremacy of the common law' after the Glorious Revolution (Pincus and Robinson 2014: 198). Steven Pincus and James Robinson (2014: 198) argued that legislation immediately following the Glorious Revolution was hardly innovative, and was preceded in 1624, 1644 and 1677 by other legislation attempting parliamentary oversight of state finances. Pincus and Robinson (2014: 201) summed up their critique: 'While North and Weingast were right to insist on a radical change in English political

---

[3] For similar arguments see Olson (1993, 2000) and Acemoglu and Robinson (2012).

behaviour after 1688 ... the mechanisms they have highlighted cannot have been the cause. ... The causes of England's revolutionary transformation must be sought elsewhere.'

Nevertheless, while the constitutional effects of 1689 may have been exaggerated by North and Weingast, there were important new controls by Parliament over sovereign powers and revenues. Generally, Parliament placed sovereign promises under its control (Cox 2012, 2016). Financial legislation in 1690 ended most lifetime grants for the King and replaced them by time-limited stipends (Roberts 1977). The Mutiny Act of 1689 made Parliament indispensable for the monarch in times of war. Overall, the King became more dependent on Parliament than before.

But it has not been shown that this constitutional shift affected property rights. This remains a major problem with the North-Weingast thesis. Some scholars have pointed out that property rights were already relatively secure before 1688, by 1600 or even earlier (Clark 1996, 2007; Sussman and Yafeh 2006; McCloskey 2010; Angeles 2011; Ogilvie and Carus 2014). Other historians have suggested that the effects of 1688–89 on the security of public and private financial activity were neither obvious nor immediate. Anne Murphy (2009: 5) pointed out that 'the financial promises of the post-Glorious Revolution were no more credible than those of previous Stuart monarchs.' Murphy (2013) also argued that post-1689 'credible commitment' to protect property was demanded from below by financial investors, and it was not offered from above.

Explicitly against North and others, Julian Hoppit (2011) and Sheilagh Ogilvie and André Carus (2014) argued that property was no more secure *after* the Glorious Revolution: the very fact that Parliament met more often posed greater legislative risks to property. Hoppit (2011: 108) noted forms of property that became more insecure after 1688: 'Heritable jurisdictions were courts and offices granted by the Crown to individuals and effectively owned as freeholds to be passed on by inheritance, gift or sale as they chose.' Although jealously guarded as sources of revenue and prestige, heritable jurisdictions began to be phased out in the early eighteenth century, leaving such offices to be filled by salaried appointments. The 1833 British abolition of property in slaves is a dramatic later example of property made insecure.[4]

---

[4] British slave-owners, however, did receive compensation. Much of this capital was invested in the railway boom of the 1840s.

Whatever the chain of causation, Britain's industrial development gathered pace much later. As Gregory Clark (1996: 588) put it: 'Institutionalists were stretching a point when forging the link between the institutional changes of 1688 and the Industrial Revolution beginning in 1760.' Robert Allen (2009) questioned similarly: if the outcome of the Glorious Revolution was so crucial for property and business, then why did England have to wait the major part of a century for the surges in innovation and productivity in the Industrial Revolution?[5]

This controversy concerns both facts and analysis. Economic history depends on the use and interpretation of empirical data. But the questions asked by economic historians, and the types and interpretations of the data employed, depend crucial on judgements informed by economic and social theory. Much of the discussion concerning the economic consequences of the Glorious Revolution has been guided by an unsatisfactory notion of property rights and views of monetary and financial institutions that underplay their conjunction with collateralizable property and debt. The aim here is to illustrate the plausibility of a new argument, based on an enriched conception of property, while stressing underestimated aspects of finance. Once property and finance are better understood, a new solution to the puzzle concerning 1688 appears.

This essay does not challenge the importance of property rights in economic development, but focuses on their deeper legal substance and their evolving, multi-faceted nature. Because, surprisingly, the very notion of 'property rights' is undeveloped in much institutional economics, these important nuances and changes have been often overlooked in debates about the role of property rights in development (De Soto 2000; Cole and Grossman 2002; Steiger 2008; Heinsohn and Steiger 2013; Hodgson 2014, 2015a, 2015b, 2015c; Cole 2015).[6]

In England, property rights (of a kind) existed and were relatively secure long before 1688. Slowly the nature of those rights changed,

---

[5] These apparent deficiencies in the timing and substance of institutional explanations led Deirdre McCloskey (2010, 2016) to emphasize instead the role of ideas in Britain's take-off from the late 18th century.

[6] If (economic) 'property rights' are defined in terms of possession or control (Alchian 1965; Barzel 1989), then evidence of their distinctive importance in promoting economic development is more elusive. But it would be mistaken to follow Angeles (2011) and others and eschew the general importance of 'property rights' in this context. Instead, 'property rights' need to be much better understood. This basic injunction flows from the approach dubbed as 'legal institutionalism' (Hodgson 2015a; Deakin et al. 2017).

enlarging possibilities for the use of land and other property as collateral to finance business ventures. This does not necessarily diminish the politico-economic importance of the Glorious Revolution, but it shifts the analytical emphasis. It establishes a stronger connection between the growing use of property as collateral and the development of financial institutions, particularly in the Financial Revolution of the early 1700s. Developments concerning property and finance are intimately conjoined. North and Weingast claimed that 1688 secured property rights led to the rise of finance; instead it is stressed here that the rise of finance stimulated the greater use of property as collateral for borrowing and financing investment.

The establishment of the Bank of England in 1694 was prompted by the need to finance a major war that broke out in 1688, as a result of the Glorious Revolution and England's new foreign alliances. It was part of a chain of institutional events that led to the development of a modern financial system in Britain, with the crucial role of the state in gathering taxes, issuing bonds and loans, buttressing private banks, and acting as lender of last resort. Hence it is important to understand the nature of modern financial systems (Mitchell, 1914; Keynes 1930; Moore 1988; Carruthers 1996; Ingham 2004, 2008; Wray 2012; Hodgson 2015a).

Unfortunately, there is a paucity of processed data in the period concerning the extent to which property was used as collateral, the scale of loans and investment, and the growth in the market for debt. By contrast, key legislative steps concerning changes to property rights and finance are known. Nevertheless, the central argument here must be considered as a hypothesis, awaiting further detailed empirical confirmation.

3   BAD TIMING: THE EVOLUTION OF PROPERTY RIGHTS IN ENGLAND

Were property rights insecure in medieval times? European countries were not uniform in this regard. We should not overlook the relatively advanced legal developments in England, compared to most other European countries.

Acemoglu et al. (2005a: 394) cited John M. Veitch (1986) to assert that there were 'numerous financial defaults by medieval kings.' Veitch (1986: 31) himself wrote: 'Property confiscation and debt repudiation were common in medieval Europe.' From this, Acemoglu and his colleagues infer that such insecurity was rife in England as well. But Veitch gave only four examples of property confiscation or debt default applying to medieval England. In particular, he noted that Edward I expelled the Jews and confiscated their property, and that Edward I, Edward II and Edward III all defaulted on Italian debts. These events occurred from 1290 to 1340 and targeted very few English property owners.

There were several confiscations after the medieval period. Henry VIII seized monastic lands in 1536–41; in 1638 Charles I appropriated £200,000 in coin and bullion from the London Mint to finance a war against Scotland; and Charles II defaulted on his debts in 1672. As North and Weingast (1989: 819–20) pointed out, from 1604 to 1628 James I and Charles I extracted a number of forced loans from English lenders. Of course, if a landowner committed treason or supported the wrong side in a civil war, then he would likely forfeit his lands. Otherwise, English kings sometimes seized property or defaulted on contracts, but compared with much of Continental Europe, these were less frequent events.

In the twelfth and thirteenth centuries, new legal systems were developed in England, and to some extent in other parts of Northern Europe, under the influence of the new canon law of the church, and the discovery of Justinian Roman law (Berman 1983, 2003). Consequently, with its long-established system of property, contract and criminal law, property rights for the wealthy were quite well entrenched in England, at least since the thirteenth century.

Of course, justice was much less accessible by the poor and the legal system was often subject to corruption and inefficiencies. The many surviving letters of the Paston family—who were rising landed gentry in Norfolk in the fifteenth century—illustrate the tedious complications and corruptions of laws concerning the ownership of land (Castor 2006). But the main problem for them was not the threat of confiscation by a powerful monarch.

The standard focus by North and others on 'secure property rights' points to events that are too early and too late. Property rights in England were relatively secure for the minority by the thirteenth century, but legal rights for the majority were insecure even during the Industrial Revolution. In addition, this standard view fails to distinguish between multiple types of property right, including the differences between rights to use, rights to sell, inheritance rights, and rights to use property as collateral (Honoré 1961).

Before the Industrial Revolution, by far the most important type of wealth was in land. A foremost obstacle to the development of commerce was not the insecurity of property rights, but the feudal nature of landed rights. Long after the decline of classical feudalism in England, enduring and well-defined rights often carried feudal obligations that limited the use of this wealth for investment and constrained the growth of markets, finance and capitalism.

While landholding had been subject to important legislation, including the 1660 abolition of military tenures by Charles II (which in most cases replaced the obligation of tenant farmers to military service by rental payments). land remained a major source and symbol of power for the families that owned it.

In particular, there were enduring restrictions on landed property, known as entails. Many entails enforced primogeniture, ensuring that a landed estate passed from one generation to another through the eldest son. This limitation on a right for the living owner of the estate became an enhanced right for his future heirs. But even when the courts limited the scope of entails in 1614, these were replaced by voluntary and widespread 'strict settlements' that had similar effects, and prevailed until the nineteenth century (English and Saville 1983; North et al. 2009: 89–9; Allen 2012: 65).

Entails and strict settlements 'restricted the uses to which land could be put. ... Holders could seldom sell, swap, or mortgage property under their control. Holders could not alter property, even if they considered the alterations to be an improvement, without risking legal suits ... [and] conducting transactions and enforcing contracts on settled land could be costly, uncertain, and insecure' (Bogart and Richardson 2011: 245).

It required much ongoing legislation to remove entails and strict settlements. They stubbornly endured, largely because the wealthy elite endorsed them. Owners were disinclined to sell or mortgage buildings or land that had been in their family for generations. Loss of land meant loss of status, influence, titles and privileges.[7]

---

[7] Feudal restrictions on landed property existed in pre-1789 France. But France was different from England in other crucial respects. There was a massive state bureaucracy, surmounted by a powerful King: lacking were adequate political checks and balances. Unlike England and the Netherlands in the 18th century, there 'was no developed capital market upon which the state could market its debt. Rather, France raised money through a complex and cumbersome system of tax farms, private bankers and venal offices' (Carruthers 1996: 23).

Much land was set aside as commons, for the shared use of villagers. It has been estimated that at the beginning of the eighteenth century about one-quarter of arable land in England was held as commons, where villagers shared rights to the use of pastures, water sources, or woods (Bogart and Richardson 2011: 247). This common land could not be sold or mortgaged.

These restrictions on the saleability of property were important not simply because they held back the development of English agriculture, which could release labour for growing industry once agricultural productivity increased. In addition, commons, entails and strict settlements greatly inhibited the use of land as collateral for loans, which could be invested in mercantile, industrial and infrastructural ventures.

The potential role of property as collateral is neglected in much of 'the economics of property rights' (Alchian 1965; Barzel 1989), which often focuses on the matter of de facto control, rather than on the importance of de jure legal title, granted by a juridical authority (Cole and Grossman 2002; Hodgson 2015a, 2015b, 2015c; Arruñada 2016). North (1981: 17, 1994: 361) himself made it clear that 'the state specifies the property rights structure' and 'property-rights dimensions are defined in legal terms' but he did not explore the key aspect of legal property as possible collateral.

Barriers to the commodification of land and its use as collateral did not disappear spontaneously or easily, despite the political convulsions of the fifteenth, sixteenth and seventeenth centuries. They were defended by strong and enduring vested interests. It took numerous varied Acts of Parliament to remove them, lasting well into the nineteenth century.

Every enclosure of common lands meant the appointment of commissioners and surveyors, the holding of village meetings, and adjudication in cases of dispute. Enclosures in England date back to the thirteenth century, but these were countered by anti-enclosure acts in 1489 and 1516. Enclosures accelerated thereafter, sometimes provoking rural revolts. Some enclosures were imposed arbitrarily, some were agreed voluntarily and some were imposed by Acts of Parliament. We have reliable data for Acts of Parliament only.[8]

---

[8] It is unnecessary for the purposes of this argument to assess whether enclosures improved agricultural productivity or not. This has been a matter of some empirical investigation and dispute (Turner 1986). Ostrom (1990) showed that collective arrangements remained viable in many diverse circumstances. The more important point here is that enclosures made land saleable and usable as collateral.

Estate acts undid strict settlements and statutory authority acts were used to develop infrastructure, including improvements to roads, rivers and the construction of canals (and later railways). Estate, statutory authority and enclosure acts all had a common theme: they relaxed constraints on the use of land and resources. Procedures for passing these acts were standardized in the early eighteenth century and operated with minor adjustments through the nineteenth century (Bogart and Richardson 2011: 248).

Dan Bogart and Gary Richardson (2011: 249–50) gathered parliamentary data on the numbers of estate, statutory authority and enclosure acts from 1700 to 1830. Figure 1 depicts the key trends. There was also a small spurt of such legislation between 1688 and 1700, which is omitted from the data, but this upturn was small compared to the post-1750 increases (Pincus and Robinson 2014: 203; Bogart 2011). The clear conclusion from these data is that legislative reform of landed property rights was sluggish from 1700 until about 1750 and then took off dramatically, with the strongest growth trends coming from enclosure and statutory authority acts. The all-important erosion of entails and strict settlements was a slow and steady process, lasting well into the nineteenth century.

Overall, the release of land for sale or collateralization, through the combined effects of estate and enclosure acts, was a process that extended

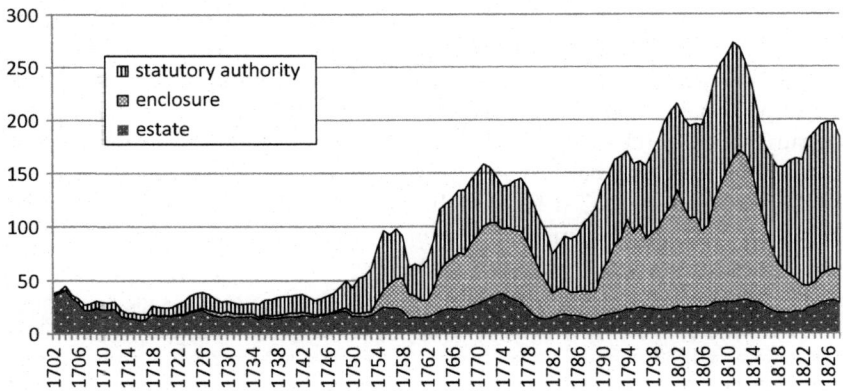

Fig. 1 Parliamentary Acts Reorganizing Landed Property Rights, 1700–1830. Source: Five-year moving averages, in a vertically cumulative presentation, using annual data from Bogart and Richardson (2011: 250)

well into the era of industrialization after 1760. The removal of feudal elements in property law was a lengthy process, beginning before 1688 and continuing long afterwards.

Many of these changes were instigated by local interest groups. Others were instigated by Parliament itself. Many property owners or users received compensation. Overall the effects were enormous. As Hoppit (2011: 100) reported, legislation on landed property, 'between 1750 and 1830, not only redistributed some property rights, but redefined or clarified the meaning of others in ways which many villagers disputed. Over 5200 acts were passed, involving up to 6.8 million acres, some 21 per cent of England's surface area.'

Bogart and Richardson (2011: 270) argued that the 1689 Declaration of Right and subsequent more regular meetings of Parliament 'encouraged the expansion of legislative activity'. But the dismantling of entails and strict settlements, and the enclosures of common lands, met significant enduring resistance from higher and lower strata of society. The 1689 settlement may have *enabled* such legislation, but it does not explain why people became incentivized to promote it, and how conservative vested interests in the status quo were overcome.[9]

Patents are an important form of intellectual property and loose indicators of the pace of industrial innovation. Notably, patenting was very expensive, and numerous innovations were not patented. Patents are highly imperfect indicators of overall innovation. Nevertheless, unlike unregistered innovations, patents are saleable and collateralizable property, and are important to consider, at least for that reason.

Patents gradually evolved from seventeenth-century instruments of royal patronage into the intellectual property of the inventors and manufacturers of the Industrial Revolution (MacLeod 2002). The British patent system was systematized and became more accessible during the reign of Queen Anne (1702–14). But the annual number of patents awarded remained low, until a marked rise in about 1760, with an acceleration thereafter (Dutton 1984; Sullivan 1989).

---

[9] Pincus and Robinson (2014: 203) and Bogart (2011) pointed out that the immediate effects of post-1688 statutory authority acts led to surges in investment in road and river improvements from about 1690 to 1730. But Bogart's (2005) own data show clearly that this early upturn of activity was minor compared with the much larger expenditures on infrastructural developments after 1730. Expenditure on turnpike roads alone tripled from 1730 to 1760, and grew impressively thereafter. Overall, while there were some infrastructural developments from 1690 to 1730, much more remarkable progress was made in later years.

In summary, the North-inspired 'secure property rights' argument has four major flaws—historical, analytical, motivational and distributional. Historically, property rights were mostly secure in England for the landed nobility from the thirteenth century, with relatively few debt defaults or confiscations of wealth by medieval monarchs. Furthermore, particular kinds of property right were made less secure by increasing parliamentary powers, including the enforced removal of entails.

Analytically, to enable the rise of capitalism, a major problem with older property rights was not their insecurity, but their entangled, feudal nature. In particular, the property rights of an heir to his father's estate prevented the sale of such property or its use as collateral for loans. In a sense, the problem was not that there were too few property rights, but too many.[10]

Motivationally, it is overlooked that strong vested interests protected the feudal nature of landed property rights. The nobility enjoyed huge wealth and power. Much of the nobility and landed gentry resisted the reforms to landed property rights including the removal of entails and strict settlements. These vested interests were not immediately diminished by the events of 1688–89. Major institutional changes were required to provide incentives for the commercialization of land and to enhance a money-making culture, over and above matters of status based on landed property. These changes did not occur until sometime after 1689.

Distributionally, the full flowering of capitalism required the extension of real and enforceable legal rights, from a narrow elite to a much bigger slice of the population. Such extensions often compromised the rights of existing property owners, and were often resisted for that reason. Nineteenth-century examples of ending property rights for some, in favour of the rights of many others, included the abolition of slavery and the removal of the automatic right of a husband to the property of his wife upon marriage (Hoppit 2011; Hodgson 2015a: 120–22).

Some accounts concerning the role of 'secure property rights' suggest that, once these were in place, institutions would largely be ready to support investment and entrepreneurship. This is mistaken. At least in the English case, a major problem was to reform well-established and secure property rights, not to establish them. Furthermore, the evidence suggests that the more dramatic changes in the nature of property rights came after 1750.

---

[10] Thickets of property claims were the feudal version of the 'anti-commons' problem of multiple entangled rights in modern capitalism (Heller 2008).

4   ECONOMIC GROWTH AND THE BALANCE OF CLASS POWER

The change in the balance of power between the sovereign and parliament, and the increased frequency of parliaments, may have increased *possibilities* for the development of commercial institutions; they do not explain the rise and empowerment of vested interests that could lobby for these changes and *make them real*. Crucial were the development of the bourgeois class, engaged in business and manufacturing, and a commercially-minded landed gentry, oriented more to trade and profit than to feudal power and status.[11] It was in the interests of these groups to support financial, administrative and property reforms, which helped expanding business and trade. When did these classes begin to exert greater economic weight and potential influence?

Acemoglu et al. (2005b) argued that economic development in Britain and elsewhere was partly stimulated by rising Atlantic Trade from the sixteenth century. This strengthened the political power of the bourgeoisie and stimulated a cumulative process of institutional reform. Earlier arguments along similar lines are found in works by Carlo Cipolla (1965), and Fernand Braudel (1984). These analyses point to positive feedbacks and processes of cumulative causation, leading to rises in bourgeois power.

Britain's involvement in global trade increased hugely in the second half of the seventeenth century. Between 1640 and 1700 its exports roughly doubled. By 1688 Britain had the largest merchant marine fleet in Europe, which had increased from 2 million tonnes in 1660 to 3.4 million in 1686 (O'Gorman 1997, ch. 1). The slave trade expanded massively. The numbers of slaves transported by British traders from Africa to the Caribbean and North America increased from 243,300 in 1676–1700, to 380,900 in 1701–1725, to 490,500 in 1726–1750 and to 859,100 in 1751–1775 (Eltis 2001: 43). But all these expansions began before 1688.

Because of the Civil War and other disturbances, English GDP per capita grew slowly in the first half of the seventeenth century. But economic growth had picked up substantially after the end of the Civil War in 1649. Data calculated by Stephen Broadberry et al. (2015: 199) suggest that GDP per capita grew from 1650 to 1700 at an average rate of 0.74 per

---

[11] Marx (1976: 875–6) argued that the development of wage labour was the 'starting point' of capitalism. He saw this development as taking hold in the 16th century. In fact, wage labour was prominent in England by the 15th century (Hodgson 2015a).

cent per annum. From 1700 to 1760 the growth figure is slightly lower at 0.67 per cent. After 1760, GDP per capita growth rose: from 1760 to 1780 the rate was 0.85 per cent, from 1780 to 1801 it was 1.46 per cent, and from 1801 to 1830 it was 1.64 per cent per annum. These data suggest that the most dramatic acceleration of growth began around 1760, and not immediately after 1688.[12]

Consider the rising strata of financiers, merchants, manufacturers, and commercial farmers. Giving evidence of changes in the relative importance of different occupations and social classes in the seventeenth and eighteenth centuries, Peter Lindert and Jeffrey Williamson (1982: 393–401) reported and adjusted data from three pioneering social surveys, by Gregory King in 1688, Joseph Massie in 1759 and Patrick Colquhoun in 1801–1803.

Table 1 the proportion of families in two important groups of socio-economic classes, and the contributions to national income by each of these groups, from 1688 to 1803. The landowning group consisted of the lords, nobility and gentry. This evidence suggests that their social presence and proportion of income did not change greatly in this period, except for a small decline in their proportion of income from 1759 to 1803. We may

Table 1   Landowners versus traders and manufacturers

	Landowners		Traders and manufacturers	
	Lords, esquires and gentlemen		Merchants, tradesmen, manufacturers, builders and miners	
Survey date	Per cent of families (%)	Per cent of national income (%)	Per cent of families (%)	Per cent of national income (%)
1688	1.4	16.2	27.7	37.6
1759	1.2	17.6	36.8	38.5
1801–1803	1.2	13.9	34.0	45.5

Percentages of Families and National Income from 1688 to 1803

Source: Lindert and Williamson's (1982: 393–401) data for England and Wales

[12] Other data series for this period paint slightly different pictures, but concur in finding no discernible acceleration of growth after 1689. Ogilvie and Carus (2014) review the evidence on growth in Britain in the 17th and 18th centuries.

conclude that the politico-economic influence of these landowning social classes remained high, long after 1688.[13]

The second group reported here consisted of those classes engaged in mercantile, trading, manufacturing, building and mining activity. It includes employers, employees and self-employed engaged in these activities. It indicates the social weight and revenues of the commercial and industrial sectors.

According to these data, by 1688 over a quarter of families were occupied in commerce and industry and they generated over a third of national income. Table 1 shows that these developing social strata were on the rise long before 1688. The bourgeoisie was already of economic significance in 1688, albeit with less power and influence than the nobility. Subsequently, from 1688 to 1759, the number of families involved in commerce and industry increased, but their percentage contribution to the national income swelled only slightly. Their contribution to national income increased more substantially after 1759.[14]

These social surveys show that while the bourgeoisie were already of economic significance in 1688, their economic presence did not increase greatly for the next 70 years, but they became more important thereafter. Again the data point to decisive economic changes occurring in the 1750s or after.

If the security of property rights was a major problem for commerce and industry before 1688, and that problem was alleviated by the political settlement of 1689, then we should expect a big increase in the proportion of the economy devoted to commerce and industry in the years that immediately followed. The data from these social surveys do not tally with this. Furthermore, if the insecurity of property rights was a major impediment to economic growth before the Glorious Revolution, then how do we explain the substantial weight, growth and economic importance of commerce and industry before 1688?

By this point the reader may be persuaded that the evidence undermines the claims of North and others concerning the economic consequences of the Glorious Revolution. But this would be a step too far. The

---

[13] Before the Reform Act of 1832, the franchise for parliamentary elections was confined to male property owners only—estimated at about 400,000 men (about 10 per cent of the adult male population) in England and Wales (Phillips and Wetherell 1995: 413).

[14] As Lindert and Williamson (1982) pointed out, the three surveys differed in their methodologies and rigour. Hence comparisons should be treated with caution, particularly when the reported differences are small.

remainder of this article shows how 1688 triggered a series of events that prepared the ground for the take-off after 1760.

We must examine events from the 1690s to the 1750s. We need to identify a chain of causation that connects the already-emergent bourgeoisie of 1688 with several later changes around the 1750s, including a marked quickening of economic growth, an increasing pace of reform of landed property rights, and a big increase in the pace of innovation. Such a causal chain would link 1688 to the Industrial Revolution that began around 1760.

5 The Financial and Administrative Revolutions

In the seventeenth century, the Netherlands developed a relatively sophisticated system of public and private finance. The state was able to raise a steady supply of funds through taxation, on the basis of which the government was able to borrow. The Dutch developed a range of innovative institutional devices for investment in trade, industry and infrastructure. Among these were public bonds, issued by governments on national, provincial, and municipal levels, and shares in publicly traded companies such as the Dutch East India Company. Financial markets, including the Amsterdam stock exchange, facilitated investment. Stock markets permitted smaller fractional shareholdings in mercantile and manufacturing enterprises. During the seventeenth century, about half of all ocean-going vessels worldwide were from the Netherlands. This tiny country dominated the international capital market, until successive political crises led to the collapse of the Dutch Republic in 1795 (Israel 1989; de Vries and van der Woude 1997).

Britain's Glorious Revolution of 1688 was in fact a Dutch-led invasion, albeit preceded by an invitation from a bishop and six members of the aristocracy. It had a religious motivation: James II was suspected of trying to restore Catholicism. The invading army of William of Orange involved 500 ships, 20,000 trained soldiers, and 20,000 mariners and support staff; it was similar in scale to the ill-fated Spanish Armada of a century earlier. William's army included English and Scottish exiles, plus mercenaries from Germany, Switzerland, Sweden and elsewhere. It received widespread support from a predominantly Protestant population.

This invasion shifted English allegiances from France to the Netherlands and led to an influx of Dutch merchants and financiers, as well as artists and scientists (Jardine 2008). Dutch businessmen brought knowledge of

Dutch financial institutions and helped establish London as the world's leading financial centre (Dickson 1967). Among Dutch innovations in public finance was the systematic dedication of revenues to the service and amortization of the public debt. Although Britain did not slavishly follow the Dutch, and it had made pre-1688 institutional innovations of its own (Murphy 2009), the ultimate impact of the Glorious Revolution on financial institutions was dramatic. Unsuccessful opponents of the 1694 formation of the Bank of England reportedly said that 'this project came from Holland and therefore would not hear of it, since we had too many Dutch things already' (Bank of England 1970: 6). In the decades after 1688, partly but not wholly as a result of the Dutch invasion, the institutional infrastructure of British finance was revolutionized.

North and Weingast (1989) argued that the diminished risks of debt default by the monarch lowered risk premiums and put downward pressure on rates of interest. By contrast, Clark (1996, 2007) argued that the evidence of falling interest rates is less clear. In any case, interest rates are determined by many factors, in addition to political risk, including the supply and demand for funds. These in turn are affected by institutionally-backed opportunities for the collateralization of wealth and expectations of profit from investment. We may concur with Peter Temin and Hans-Joachim Voth (2005: 325), and with Pincus and Robinson (2014: 205), that a narrow empirical focus on interest rates is 'fundamentally misguided' and 'a red herring'.

Stephen R. Epstein (2000: 211) argued that the constitutional restrictions on the power of the monarch in 1689 were less significant than England's 'belated catch up' with continental Europe's most developed financial systems: 'the result of the country's financial revolution rather than a revolution in political freedom and rights.' The new financial practices transplanted from the Netherlands were crucial (Powell 1915; Bagehot 1919; Dickson 1967; Kindleberger 1984; Neal 1990; Roseveare 1991; Carruthers 1996; Wennerlind 2011).

A boom in demand for stocks was underway in the 1690s, even before the Bank of England was formed (Murphy 2009). Financed by London merchants, the Bank of England issued loans to the royal treasury at 8 percent interest, the payments of which were in turn funded by taxes and custom duties. For the Bank of England these royal debts were its monetary assets, which in turn were buttressed by a renewed public faith in sovereign integrity. These assets became the basis of a further massive loan issue by the bank. The government borrowed widely, cementing together the interests of aristocrats, gentry, manufacturers and merchants.

Market information became more available. By 1698, stock price quotes were regularly published in London (Morgan and Thomas 1962). Also after 1688 'came a flurry of joint-stock company formations ... By 1695 100 new companies had been formed with a capital of £4.5 million in all' (Kindleberger 1984: 196). The Bank of England was followed by the establishment of several other London banks, about 25 in number by the 1720s and 50 in 1770. Numerous banks began to appear in the provinces after 1750 (North and Weingast 1989: 826).

Stephen Quinn's (2001: 613) study of the accounts of a prominent London banker showed how from 1680 to 1705 'the mechanics of private debt were transformed by the dual revolutions in England's systems of constitutional power and public finance. Bankers and their customers began to use the improved financial instruments of the government to facilitate private lending.'

In 1690 the prescient economist Nicholas Barbon helped to found the National Land Bank, which issued mortgages against real estate. By 1696 the Land Bank was so successful that it threatened to usurp the Bank of England. Also opposed by the Treasury and Parliament, this scheme eventually foundered. John Clapham (1966: 33–34) puts this failure down to the underdeveloped state of the money and bond markets at the time. It took several decades to build up financial institutions under which available land could be readily mortgaged. In addition, as shown in Sect. 2 above, much land at that time could not yet be used as collateral. Further changes in the nature of land ownership were necessary, and these were slow in coming until the 1750s.

Much of the impetus for the heavy involvement of the state in the development of the British financial system in the eighteenth century was the need to finance wars abroad (Mann 1986: 485–6; Bowen 1995: 5; Carruthers 1996). Because of its new international alliances and enemies, England was plunged into a long period of war, requiring major reform of its fiscal and administrative arrangements. The Nine Years' War (1688–97) was quickly followed by the long War of Spanish Succession (1701–13). The overthrow of the Stuarts in 1688 led within Britain to the Jacobite Rebellions of 1715 and 1745. There was the War of the Quadruple Alliance (1718–1720), the Anglo-Spanish War (1727–1729), the War of the Austrian Succession (1740–1748) and the global Seven Years' War of

(1756–1763). Britain was involved in war, with at least one other major power, in 45 of the 76 years from 1688 to 1763 inclusive.

Finance and war were intimately connected. As Bruce Carruthers (1996: 8) noted, in 1672, although there were trading in stocks, there was no organized stock market in London, and 'England was a weak nation-state and a second-rate military power. In 1712, only forty years later, the shares of many joint-stock companies were traded on an active and highly organized capital market that had emerged in London. Furthermore, Great Britain had become one of the major military powers in Europe and had successfully checked French expansion'.

Contrary to the claim of North and Weingast (1989) that the political settlement of 1689 made government more stable, Pincus and Robinson (2014: 199) wrote: 'Far from making government more predictable, the Revolution of 1688 instantiated one of the most intensely polarized and unstable periods in English and British history.' The litany of war and revolt from 1688 to 1763 underlines this.

Of course, there were many wars before 1688. For example, in the years after the Restoration, there were the Second (1665–1667) and Third (1672–1674) Anglo-Dutch Wars. But the sovereign often had difficulty raising money to finance these ventures. What changed in 1689 was the practical accord between the sovereign and Parliament, which ultimately locked them together in common cause, especially when dealing with enemies abroad, despite no shortage of fractious internal disputes in those difficult times. 1689 secured the compliance of both King and Commons in meeting the needs of war. North and Weingast (1989) were right about the importance of the Glorious Revolution, but for the wrong reasons. It had little immediate effect on the security of property rights.

By accident or design, some measures indirectly made regular parliaments more likely, especially in the context of war. The 1689 Declaration of Right required that no standing army may be maintained during peacetime without the consent of Parliament. In the same year, the Mutiny Act was passed to deal with some rebellious Scottish troops who had remained loyal to James II. This Act allowed the sovereign to maintain a standing army in war or peace, for one year, but no longer. Consequently, if the country were to be kept on a war footing, parliament had to meet annually and renew the Mutiny Act (Winthrop 1920: 19–20). A new Mutiny Act was passed each year until 1879. In addition, the financial settlement of

1690 put time-limits on funds for the monarch, which had previously been granted for life (Roberts 1977). Again this reinforced the sovereign's dependence of regular parliaments.

Parliament became more able to put the king on a shorter financial leash, to control government debt, and to control its executive (Cox 2012, 2016). Military and financial needs also helped Parliament keep the monarch under control.

The state continued to play an important role in stimulating corporate activity overseas. The Crown organized groups of creditors into companies, including the New East India Company (1698), the United East India Company (1708), and the South Sea Company (1708). The South Sea Bubble of 1720 led to a severe crash, but the financial system as a whole recovered.

This period saw expansion of the British Empire. Before 1688 England had major colonies in North America, the Caribbean and West Africa. By 1763 Britain had gained more territory in India and North America and it had established a strategic Mediterranean base in Gibraltar. The growth of slavery was another part of Britain's increased trading activity from the 1690s to the 1760s. More broadly, as Patrick O'Brien (2006: 14) pointed out: 'Already by the close of the Seven Years' War, something like half of the nation's workforce (de-linked from agriculture) depended directly and indirectly on markets overseas for its livelihood.'

From 1687 to 1703 the number of workers employed in naval yards more than quadrupled. Daniel Defoe remarked at the time that 'in some respects the navy is largest industry in the country' (Hill 1961: 230). More people were required to administer the growing war machine and to raise taxes to finance it.

The needs of war and the combined pressures of global and domestic commerce were major forces behind the development and reform of financial institutions and state administration (O'Brien 2011). The Glorious Revolution and subsequent international conflicts led to major transformations of the state apparatus, including the Act of Union with Scotland in 1707. As Henry G. Roseveare (1991: 4) pointed out, accompanying the political and fiscal changes after 1688 there was 'an administrative revolution—or, at least, a striking growth in the power and effectiveness of the state which manifested itself not merely in war but in the subtler tasks of peace.'

Fig. 2   Full-Time Employees in the State Fiscal Bureaucracy, 1690–1783. Source: Data from Brewer (1988: 66)

Figure 2 shows the growth of the number of full-time employees involved in the fiscal bureaucracy, including those in customs, excise, the post office and the Treasury. It shows a remarkable rise from 1690 to the 1720s, when the bureaucracy more than doubled in size.

The state administration established a stronger fiscal base and empowered a growth in tax revenues, particularly to finance wars. The settlement of 1689 strengthened the political consensus, creating the foundation of an effective fiscal state (Roseveare 1991). In 1692 Parliament introduced a national land tax. A window tax was introduced in 1696. But the major part of state revenue was through customs and excise charges, which increased with the growth of Britain's power and trade abroad (Mathias 1983: 428).

Figure 3 shows the total tax revenue as a proportion of national income from 1670 to 1810. There is a marked rise from 1680 to 1690, and thereafter to 1700. Consequently, impelled by the outbreak of war in 1688, and as a result of the settlement of 1689, the government was able to ramp up tax revenues, more than doubling the tax-take as a percentage of national income. Ironically, the most obvious and immediate effects of 1688 were not a growth in free enterprise, but a considerable expansion in state bureaucracy and taxation.

The Financial Revolution was a protracted affair, lasting decades. It involved several legislative steps, including changes to laws concerning usury and the sale of debt, and the development of new organizational structures and business habits. The growing use of debt led to instability

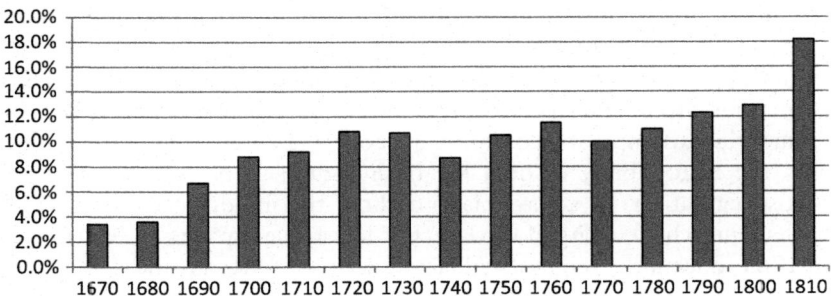

Fig. 3 Total Tax Revenue as a Proportion of National Income, 1670–1810. Source: Data from O'Brien (1988: 3). See also O'Brien (2011: 428) and Cox (2012: 576)

as well as growth (as exhibited in the South Sea Bubble of 1720) and Temin and Voth (2005) have provided evidence to argue that wartime government borrowing crowded out private lending. Nevertheless, the overall effect of the Financial Revolution was positive. Above all, it enlarged possibilities for borrowing and investment, by establishing a modern banking system. These institutional changes bore fruit in the Industrial Revolution.

Addressing the evolution of finance in Italy, the Netherlands and Britain, Geoffrey Ingham (2008: 70) concluded that 'the capitalist monetary system developed from the integration of private networks of mercantile trade credit-money with public currency—that is, state money.' For Ingham (2008: 74) and others, crucial to this system was the role of debt: 'Capitalism is distinctive in that it contains a social mechanism by which privately contracted debtor-creditor relations ... are routinely monetized.'

Vital to the development of a modern banking system was the emergence of institutions making debt itself saleable or 'negotiable.' A promise to pay could then be sold to another, who would then take on the legal obligation of payment. A key problem is effective legal enforceability. For general negotiability, the transfer of obligations also had to be recognized and enforced by the legal system. Contracts ordinarily involve legal obligations to deliver goods or services in exchange for money. Exchanges of promissory notes involve instead the purchase of a promise, and originally this was not recognized as a valid contract in law: the selling of debt was not sanctioned by legal recognition of the transfer of the obligation to its purchaser. Major legislative changes were necessary to make this possible.

In the seventeenth century, commercial cases shifted from the law merchant courts to common law courts (Baker 1979; Berman 1983). But the 'blundering attempts' by common law courts (Beutel 1938: 840) to deal with the negotiability of debt led businessmen to press Parliament for robust legislation. In a way this underlines the importance of the 1689 settlement, which enlarged the effective legislative capacity of Parliament. In 1704, during the reign of William's successor Queen Anne, Parliament passed 'An Act for giving like Remedy upon Promissory Notes, as is now used upon Bills of Exchange, and for the better Payment of Inland Bills of Exchange.' Significant further legislation, including another Act as late as 1758, was required to consolidate negotiability (Beutel 1938; Lawrence 2002). Once negotiability was established, the capitalist genie was out of the bottle. As Henry Dunning MacLeod (1872: 481) wrote:

If we were asked—Who made the discovery which has most deeply affected the fortunes of the human race? We think, after full consideration, we might safely answer—The man who first discovered that a Debt is a Saleable Commodity.[15]

The use of this 'discovery' required firm legal foundations and consolidation through more than one Act of Parliament. But eventually, through these means, the emerging capitalist financial system empowered economic development on a massive scale.

Capitalist finance involves a complex web of contractual obligations. Commercial banks since the fourteenth century operated increasingly by keeping only a fraction of their deposits in reserve as cash or gold. Fractional-reserve banking has a cumulative effect on money creation by commercial banks as it expands the money supply beyond the scale of the deposits alone. Any debt is funded by current assets, or by claims owed by a third party. The purchaser of debt receives the right to an asset that itself can be used as collateral to borrow (Veblen 1904: 113, 149). Credit money thus feeds on itself: commercial bank money is created endogenously (Moore 1988; Wray 2012). As if in defiance of the conservation laws of physics, banks can thus create more money 'out of nothing' (Schumpeter 1934: 73).

---

[15] MacLeod (1858: 476–8) coined the term 'Gresham's Law.' Mitchell Innes (Mitchell 1914: 9) credited him as the originator of the state theory of money. Commons (1934: 394) described him as 'the first lawyer-economist.' Schumpeter (1954: 718) judged him the only contemporary of Marx to make a systematic advance towards a credit theory of money.

But this depends on a legal structure of enforceability, a fractional reserve system backed by private and state assurances, and sufficient confidence that debt can be redeemed. In Britain, once legal institutions supporting collateralizable property, credit money, and the sale of debt were in place, a new dynamic was unleashed.

The argument in brief is this. The evolution of the financial system in the first half of the eighteenth century facilitated more and more industrial and infrastructural projects based on large-scale borrowing. They triggered another process of cumulative causation and positive feedback, which became evident by the 1750s. As the profitability of larger-scale investments was demonstrated, wealthy landowners and other investors were enticed by further commercial ventures. Growing opportunities for profit eroded longstanding, sentimental, family commitments to their estates. This impelled the removal of entails and strict settlements, so that land could be used as collateral for loans. Hence the major capitalist reforms to property rights in land followed rather than preceded the Financial Revolution.

Consequently, institutional changes in the eighteenth century increased the stock of property that was usable as collateral, creating the opportunity for increased loans. The growth of incentives and opportunities for borrowing, alongside the development of post-1694 arrangements in a debt-based monetary system based on negotiable paper, enlarged the market for debt, fuelling further speculation and investment. A modern financial system developed, which rested on the pillars of collateralizable property, negotiable debt, global trade, and state power.

6   Conclusion: From Critique to Reconstruction

The Glorious Revolution made no laws concerning property and few edicts on the role of Parliament. It did not increase the security of property rights, and it did not lead to an immediate acceleration in the pace of economic growth or of a growth in the economic weight of the bourgeoisie. But it did have two major portentous effects.

First, as evidenced by the nature and pace of legislation after 1689, there was a shift in the de facto balance of power between the sovereign and Parliament. As North and others emphasized, this countervailing power placed important checks on the powers of the monarch. Nevertheless, this shift is insufficient to account for the reforms to property and finance that were necessary to sustain a rising capitalist economy.

The power and motivation of a rising bourgeois class were necessary to overcome the vested interests in existing, semi-feudal landed property rights. This did not happen until long after 1688.

Second, 1688 meant a major shift in foreign alliances and prompted a number of major wars, up to the Seven Years' War of 1755–1763. Facilitated by the enhanced de facto role of Parliament, international conflict forced reform upon the British state, and required it to raise funds to finance war. The Financial and Administrative Revolutions of the early eighteenth century were the most immediate outcomes of 1688. Hence it was the financial and military needs of the state, more than the rising bourgeoisie, which provided the main impetus for change from 1688 to 1750.

But institutional changes, particularly in the spheres of law and politics, combined with the demands of war upon industrial production, eventually facilitated a rise in the weight and influence of the industrial and commercial classes, which in turn benefitted from expanding British trade and Empire. These socio-economic results were discernible by 1760.

As the industrial take-off gathered pace after 1760, it increased the pressure to reform property rights in land, so that it could be used as collateral for industrial and commercial investments. New pecuniary opportunities overcame the resistance to reform by conservative landowners. While much industrial investment came out of existing profits, such sources were sometimes inadequate or unreliable. Some firms issued shares. Other finance for investment in industrial ventures was obtained via relatives, friends, intermediaries or banks, sometimes requiring land or other collateral to secure the loan (Heaton 1937; Mathias 1983: 130–36; Crouzet 1990, ch. 5; King and Timmins 2001: 114–20).

Writing of the early phase of the Industrial Revolution, T. S. Ashton (1955: 26) concluded: 'It is true that self-financing was a marked feature of the period, but it would be an error to consider it as universal or to think of the markets for capital as circumscribed.' As Peter Mathias (1983: 135) noted: 'Freehold property remained the best security extant in eighteenth-century England, and the mortgage market was one of the most efficiently organized sides of the capital market.'

For example, the firm of Boulton and Watt—founded in 1775 and famous for the manufacture of steam engines—took out mortgages on land and other assets to secure loans for their budding enterprise (Roll 1930: 105–7). Similarly, around that time, mortgages were sometimes used to help finance canal construction, alongside the issue of shares (Ward 1974: 35, 116).[16]

The account here puts the growth of finance at the centre in the explanation of the rise of capitalism. Neither the establishment of secure property rights (North), nor the rise of a capitalist class employing waged labour (Marx), accurately characterize the period from 1688 to 1750. While secure property rights, trade and wage labour may be taken as necessary features of capitalism, they are insufficient to define that system. At the core of capitalism—as it emerged in the eighteenth century—is a set of financial institutions based on collateralizable property and credit creation. These institutions and the monetary system are typically buttressed by the state (Ingham 2008; Hodgson 2015a).

As Joseph Schumpeter (1939: 223) pointed out, 'capitalism is that form of private property economy in which innovations are carried out by means of borrowed money, which in general ... implies credit creation.' Money is borrowed on the basis of collateral. Yet this aspect of property is neglected in much of the 'economics of property rights', which concentrates instead on property in terms of control. Schumpeter (1954: 78 n.) also emphasized 'the importance of the financial complement of capitalist production and trade'. Hence 'the development of the law and the practice of negotiable paper and of "created" deposits afford perhaps the best indication we have for dating the rise of capitalism.'

This article has located key developments in financial institutions in the opening decades of the eighteenth century. These institutional changes, tied up with reformed financial and administrative functions for the state, provide the missing causal links between the Glorious Revolution of 1688, the rise of capitalist financial institutions, and the beginnings of the Industrial Revolution around 1760.

If this analysis applies to the development of capitalism in countries beyond Britain, then it would suggest that the building of a state administration, which can sustain a modern monetary system and secure the use of private property as collateral, is an important precondition of rapid

---

[16] A more comprehensive account of the extent of the use of collateral to finance industrial projects in the late 18th and early 19th centuries is a matter for further research. Insufficient attention has been devoted to this topic, because of the inadequate recognition of the importance of collateralization and because of the widespread conflation by economists of 'capital' as things (such as machinery) with 'capital' as finance (which can be a means to purchase machinery, or the value of machinery which can be used as collateral to obtain further loans) (Veblen 1908; Hodgson 2014, 2015a, 2015b).

economic growth. Hence a stress on the 'security of property rights' would be insufficient in developing countries. The nature of property, and its connection with finance and politics, have to be better understood.

REFERENCES

Acemoglu, D., & Robinson, J. A. (2012). *Why nations fail: The origins of power, prosperity, and poverty*. New York and Profile, London: Random House.

Acemoglu, D., Johnson, S., & Robinson, J. A. (2005a). Institutions as a fundamental cause of long-run growth. In P. Aghion & S. V. Durlauf (Eds.), *Handbook of economic growth* (Vol. Vol. 1A, pp. 385–472). North Holland: Elsevier.

Acemoglu, D., Johnson, S., & Robinson, J. A. (2005b). The rise of Europe: Atlantic trade, institutional change and economic growth. *American Economic Review, 95*(3), 546–579.

Alchian, A. A. (1965). Some economics of property rights. *Il Politico, 30*: 816–829. Reprinted in Alchian, A. A., ed. (1977). *Economic forces at work* (pp. 127–149). Indianapolis: Liberty Press.

Allen, R. C. (2009). *The British industrial revolution in global perspective*. Cambridge and New York: Cambridge University Press.

Allen, D. W. (2012). *The institutional revolution: Measurement and the economic emergence of the modern world*. Chicago: University of Chicago Press.

Angeles, L. (2011). Institutions, property rights, and economic development in historical perspective. *Kyklos, 64*(2), 157–177.

Arruñada, B. (2016). Coase and the departure from property. In C. Ménard & B. Elodie (Eds.), *The Elgar companion to Ronald H. Coase* (pp. 305–319). Cheltenham, UK and Northampton, MA: Edward Elgar.

Ashton, T. S. (1955). *An economic history of England: The eighteenth century*. London: Methuen.

Bagehot, W. (1919). *Lombard street: A description of the money market (first edition 1873)*. London: Murray.

Baker, J. H. (1979). The law merchant and the common law before 1700. *Cambridge Law Journal, 38*(2), 295–322.

Bank of England. (1970). *The Bank of England: History and functions*. Debden: Gordon Chalmers Fortin.

Barzel, Y. (1989). *Economic analysis of property rights*. Cambridge: Cambridge University Press.

Berman, H. J. (1983). *Law and revolution: The formation of the western legal tradition*. Cambridge, MA: Harvard University Press.

Berman, H. J. (2003). *Law and evolution II: The impact of the protestant reformations on the western legal tradition*. Cambridge, MA: Harvard University Press.

Beutel, F. K. (1938). The development of negotiable instruments in early English law. *Harvard Law Review, 51*(5), 813–845.

Bogart, D. (2005). Did turnpike trusts increase transportation investment in eighteenth century England? *Journal of Economic History, 65*(2), 439–468.

Bogart, D. (2011). Did the Glorious Revolution contribute to the transport revolution? Evidence from investment in roads and rivers. *Economic History Review, 64*(4), 1073–1112.

Bogart, D., & Richardson, G. (2011). Property rights and parliament in industrializing Britain. *Journal of Law and Economics, 54*(2), 241–274.

Bowen, H. V. (1995). The Bank of England during the long eighteenth century: 1694–1815. In R. Roberts & D. Kynaston (Eds.), *The Bank of England* (pp. 1–18). Oxford and New York: Oxford University Press.

Braudel, F. (1984). *Civilization and capitalism, 15th–18th century, Vol. 3, The perspective of the world.* London: Collins.

Brewer, J. (1988). *The sinews of power: War, money and the English state, 1688–783.* New York: Knopf.

Broadberry, S. N., Campbell, B. M. S., Klein, A., Overton, M., & van Leeuwen, B. (2015). *British economic growth 1270–1870: An output-based approach.* Cambridge and New York: Cambridge University Press.

Carruthers, B. G. (1996). *City of capital: Politics and markets in the English financial revolution.* Princeton, NJ, Chichester, UK: Princeton University Press.

Castor, H. (2006). *Blood and roses: One family's struggle and triumph during the tumultuous Wars of the Roses.* New York: Harper Collins.

Cipolla, C. M. (1965). *Guns, sails and empires: technological innovation and the early phases of European expansion, 1400–1700.* New York: Pantheon.

Clapham, J. H. (1966). *The Bank of England: A history. Volume One, 1694–1797.* Cambridge: Cambridge University Press.

Clark, G. (1996). The political foundations of modern economic growth: England, 1540–1800. *Journal of Interdisciplinary History, 26*(4), 563–588.

Clark, G. (2007). *A farewell to alms: A brief economic history of the World.* Princeton: Princeton University Press.

Cole, D H. (2015). "Economic property rights" as "Nonsense upon stilts": A comment on Hodgson's article. *Journal of Institutional Economics, 11*(4), 725–730.

Cole, D H., & Grossman, P. Z. (2002). The meaning of property rights: Law versus economics? *Land Economics, 78*(3), 317–330.

Commons, J. R. (1934). *Institutional Economics – its place in Political Economy.* New York: Macmillan.

Cox, G. W. (2012). Was the Glorious Revolution a constitutional watershed. *Journal of Economic History, 72*(3), 567–600.

Cox, G. W. (2016). *Marketing sovereign promises: Monopoly brokerage and the growth of the English state.* Cambridge and New York: Cambridge University Press

Crouzet, F. (1990). *Britain ascendant: Comparative studies in Franco-British economic history.* Cambridge and New York: Cambridge University Press.

De Soto, H. (2000). *The mystery of capital: Why capitalism triumphs in the west and fails everywhere else.* New York: Basic Books.

Deakin, S., Gindis, D., Hodgson, G. M., Huang, K., & Pistor, K. (2017). Legal institutionalism: Capitalism and the constitutive role of law. *Journal of Comparative Economics, 45*(1), 188–200.

Dickson, P. G. M. (1967). *The financial revolution in England: A study in the development of public credit, 1688–1756.* London: Macmillan.

Dutton, H. I. (1984). *The patent system and inventive activity during the Industrial Revolution, 1750–1852.* Manchester: Manchester University Press.

Eltis, D. (2001). The volume and structure of the transatlantic slave trade: A reassessment. *William and Mary Quarterly, 58*(1), 17–46.

English, B., & Saville, J. (1983). *Strict settlement: A guide for historians.* Hull: University of Hull Press.

Epstein, S. R. (2000). *Freedom and growth: The rise of states and markets in Europe, 1300–1750.* London and New York: Routledge.

Heaton, H. (1937). Financing the industrial revolution. *Bulletin of the Business Historical Society, 11*(1), 1–10.

Heinsohn, G., & Steiger, O. (2013). *Ownership economics: On the foundations of interest, money, markets, business cycles and economic development, translated and edited by Frank Decker.* London and New York: Routledge.

Heller, M. A. (2008). *The gridlock economy: How too much ownership wrecks markets, stops innovation, and costs lives.* New York: Basic Books.

Hill, C. (1961). *The century of revolution 1603–1714.* London: Van Nostrand Reinhold.

Hodgson, G. M. (2014). What is capital? Economists and sociologists have changed its meaning – should it be changed back? *Cambridge Journal of Economics, 38*(5), 1063–1086.

Hodgson, G. M. (2015a). *Conceptualizing capitalism: Institutions, evolution, future.* Chicago: University of Chicago Press.

Hodgson, G. M. (2015b). Much of the "economics of property rights" devalues property and legal rights. *Journal of Institutional Economics, 11*(4), 683–709.

Hodgson, G. M. (2015c). What Humpty Dumpty might have said about property rights – and the need to put them back together again: A response to critics. *Journal of Institutional Economics, 11*(4), 731–747.

Honoré, A. M. (1961). Ownership. In A. G. Guest (Ed.), *Oxford essays in jurisprudence* (pp. 107–147). Oxford: Oxford University Press. Reprinted in the *Journal of Institutional Economics 9*(2): 2013, 227–255.

Hoppit, J. (2011). Compulsion, compensation and property rights in Britain, 1688–1833. *Past and Present, 210*(1), 93–128.

Ingham, G. (2004). *The nature of money.* Cambridge: Polity Press.

Ingham, G. (2008). *Capitalism*. Cambridge: Polity Press.

Israel, J. I. (1989). *Dutch primacy in world trade 1585–1740*. Oxford and New York: Oxford University Press.

Jardine, L. (2008). *Going Dutch: How England plundered Holland's glory*. London: Harper.

Jones, J. R. (Ed.). (1992). *Liberty secured? Britain before and after 1688*. Stanford, CA: Stanford University Press.

Keynes, J. M. (1930). *A Treatise on money, Vol. 1: The pure theory of money, Vol. 2: The applied theory of money*. London: Macmillan.

Kindleberger, C. P. (1984). *A financial history of Western Europe*. London: George Allen and Unwin.

King, S., & Timmins, G. (2001). *Making sense of the industrial revolution: English economy and society 1700–1850*. Manchester: Manchester University Press.

Lawrence, W. H. (2002). *Understanding negotiable instruments and payment systems*. Newark, NJ: Matthew Bender.

Lindert, P. H., & Williamson, J. G. (1982). Revising England's social tables, 1688–1812. *Explorations in Economic History, 19*(4), 385–408.

MacLeod, H. D. (1858). *Elements of political economy*. London: Longmans Green.

MacLeod, H. D. (1872). *The principles of economic philosophy* (2nd ed.). London: Longmans Green.

MacLeod, C. (2002). *Inventing the industrial revolution: The English patent system, 1660–1800*. Cambridge and New York: Cambridge University Press.

Maddison, A. (2007). *Contours of the world economy, 1–2030 AD: Essays in macroeconomic history*. Oxford and New York: Oxford University Press.

Mann, M. (1986). *The sources of social power, Vol. 1: A history of power from the beginning to A.D. 1760*. Cambridge: Cambridge University Press.

Marx, K. (1976). *Capital., Vol. 1, translated from the fourth German edition of 1890*. Harmondsworth: Pelican.

Mathias, P. (1983). *The first industrial nation: An economic history of Britain 1700–1914*. London and New York: Routledge.

McCloskey, D. N. (2010). *Bourgeois Dignity: Why economics can't explain the modern world*. Chicago: University of Chicago Press.

McCloskey, D. N. (2016). Max U vs. humanomics: A critique of Neo-Institutionalism. *Journal of Institutional Economics, 12*(1), 1–27.

Mitchell, I. A. (1914). The credit theory of money. *The Banking Law Journal, 31*, 151–168.

Moore, B. (1988). *Horizontalists and verticalists: The macroeconomics of credit money*. Cambridge: Cambridge University Press.

Morgan, E. V., & Thomas, W. A. (1962). *The stock exchange, its history and functions*. London: Elek Books.

Morrill, J. (1992). The sensible revolution. In J. I. Israel (Ed.), *The Anglo-Dutch moment: Essays on the Glorious Revolution and its world impact* (pp. 73–104). Cambridge and New York: Cambridge University Press.

Murphy, A. L. (2009). *The origins of English financial markets: Investment and speculation before the South Sea bubble.* Cambridge and New York: Cambridge University Press.

Murphy, A. L. (2013). Demanding "credible commitment": Public reactions to the failures of the early financial revolution. *Economic History Review, 66*(1), 178–197.

Neal, L. (1990). *The rise of financial capitalism: International capital markets in the age of reason.* Cambridge and New York: Cambridge University Press.

Nenner, H. (Ed.). (1997). *Politics and political imagination in Later Stuart Britain.* Rochester, NY: University of Rochester Press.

North, D. C. (1981). *Structure and change in economic history.* New York: Norton.

North, D. C. (1994). Economic performance through time. *American Economic Review, 84*(3), 359–367.

North, D. C., & Weingast, B. R. (1989). Constitutions and commitment: The evolution of institutions governing public choice in seventeenth-century England. *Journal of Economic History, 49*(4), 803–832.

North, D. C., Wallis, J. J., & Weingast, B. R. (2009). *Violence and social orders: A conceptual framework for interpreting recorded human history.* Cambridge: Cambridge University Press.

O'Brien, P. K. (1988). The Political Economy of British taxation, 1660–1815. *Economic History Review, New Series, 41*(1), 1–32.

O'Brien, P. K. (2006). Provincializing the first industrial revolution. Working paper 17/06, Global Economic History Network (GEHN), London School of Economics, January 2006. Retrieved February 20, 2016, from http://eprints.lse.ac.uk/22474/1/wp17.pdf.

O'Brien, P. K. (2011). The nature and historical evolution of an exceptional fiscal state and its possible significance for the precocious commercialization and industrialization of the British economy from Cromwell to Nelson. *Economic History Review, 64*(2), 408–446.

O'Gorman, F. (1997). *The long eighteenth century: British political and social history 1688–1832.* New York: Arnold Press.

Ogilvie, S., & Carus, A. W. (2014). Institutions and economic growth in historical perspective. In P. Aghion & S. Durlauf (Eds.), *Handbook of Economic Growth* (Vol. 2A, pp. 403–513). Amsterdam: Elsevier.

Olson Jr., M. (1993). Dictatorship, democracy, and development. *American Political Science Review, 87*(3), 567–576.

Olson Jr., M. (2000). *Power and prosperity: Outgrowing communist and capitalist dictatorships.* New York: Basic Books.

Ostrom, E. (1990). *Governing the commons: The evolution of institutions for collective action.* Cambridge: Cambridge University Press.

Phillips, J. A., & Wetherell, C. (1995). The Great Reform Act of 1832 and the political modernization of England. *American Historical Review, 100*(2), 411–436.

Pincus, S. C. A. (2009). *1688: The first modern revolution*. New Haven: Yale University Press.

Pincus, S. C. A., & Robinson, J. A. (2014). What really happened during the Glorious Revolution? In S. Galiani & I. Sened (Eds.), *Institutions, Property rights, and economic growth: The legacy of Douglass North* (pp. 192–222). Cambridge and New York: Cambridge University Press.

Powell, E. T. (1915). *The evolution of the money market (1385–1915): An historical and analytical study of the rise and development of finance as a centralised, coordinated force*. London: Financial Press.

Quinn, S. (2001). The Glorious Revolution's effect on English private finance: A microhistory 1680–1705. *Journal of Economic History, 61*(3), 593–615.

Roberts, C. (1977). The constitutional significance of the financial settlement of 1690. *The Historical Journal, 20*(1), 59–76.

Roll, E. (1930). *An early experiment in industrial organisation: Being a history of the firm of Boulton and Watt 1775–1805*. Abingdon: Frank Cass.

Roseveare, H. G. (1991). *The financial revolution. 1660-1760*. Harlow: Longman.

Schumpeter, J. A. (1934). *The theory of economic development: An inquiry into profits, capital, credit, interest, and the business cycle*. Cambridge, MA: Harvard University Press.

Schumpeter, J. A. (1939). *Business cycles: A theoretical statistical and historical analysis of the capitalist process* (Vol. 2 vols). New York: McGraw-Hill.

Schumpeter, J. A. (1954). *History of economic analysis*. Oxford and New York: Oxford University Press.

Scott, J. (1991). *Algernon Sydney and the restoration crisis, 1677–1683*. Cambridge and New York: Cambridge University Press.

Steiger, O. (Ed.). (2008). *Property economics: property rights, creditor's money and the foundations of the economy*. Marburg: Metropolis.

Sullivan, R. J. (1989). England's "age of invention": The acceleration of patents and of patentable invention during the Industrial Revolution. *Explorations in Economic History, 26*(4), 424–452.

Sussman, N., & Yafeh, Y. (2006). Institutional reforms, financial development and sovereign debt: Britain 1690-1790. *Journal of Economic History, 66*(4), 906–935.

Temin, P., & Voth, H. J. (2005). Credit rationing and crowding out during the Industrial Revolution: Evidence from Hoare's Bank, 1702–1862. *Explorations in Economic History, 42*, 325–348.

Trevor-Roper, H. (1992). *Counter-reformation to Glorious Revolution*. Chicago: University of Chicago Press.

Turner, M. (1986). English open fields and enclosures: Retardation or productivity improvements. *Journal of Economic History, 46*(3), 669–692.

Veblen, T. B. (1904). *The theory of business enterprise*. New York: Charles Scribners.

Veblen, T. B. (1908). Professor Clark's Economics. *Quarterly Journal of Economics, 22*(2), 147–195.

Veitch, J. M. (1986). Repudiations and confiscations by the medieval state. *Journal of Economic History, 46*(1), 31–36.

de Vries, J., & van der Woude, A. (1997). *The first modern economy. Success, failure, and perseverance of the Dutch economy, 1500–1815.* Cambridge and New York: Cambridge University Press.

Ward, J. R. (1974). *The finance of canal building in eighteenth-century England.* Oxford: Oxford University Press.

Wennerlind, C. (2011). *Casualties of credit: The English financial revolution 1620–1720.* Cambridge, MA: Harvard University Press.

Western, J. R. (1972). *Monarchy and revolution: The English state in the 1680s.* London: Blandford.

Winthrop, W. (1920). *Military law and precedents* (2nd ed.). Washington, DC: Government Printing Office.

Wray, L. R. (2012). *Modern money theory: A primer on macroeconomics for sovereign monetary systems.* London and New York: Palgrave Macmillan.

The Contemporary State and Interests: A Framework of Analysis

Anna Ząbkowicz and Sławomir Czech

1   INTRODUCTION

Capitalism is a system based on internal conflicts and contradictions. The agreements between labor and capital that took place in the past in many Western countries allowed for expressing optimism that it could adopt more civilized form mitigating these conflicts and their outcomes. Unfortunately, the contemporary stage of capitalism has dispelled these hopes. The institutions adopted by most advanced economies have lead to the financial crisis marking the end of neo-liberal accumulation period and thus pushing world economy into the phase of interregnum in which we are aware of the deficiencies of the current institutional order, but a new order still needs to be forged. There is little doubt that the financial crisis

A. Ząbkowicz
Jagiellonian University in Cracow, Kraków, Poland
e-mail: anna.zabkowicz@uj.edu.pl

S. Czech (✉)
University of Economics in Katowice, Katowice, Poland
e-mail: slawomir.czech@ue.katowice.pl

S. Vliamos, M. S. Zouboulakis (eds.), *Institutionalist Perspectives on Development*, Palgrave Studies in Democracy, Innovation, and Entrepreneurship for Growth, https://doi.org/10.1007/978-3-319-98494-0_3

of 2008+ has been a systemic crisis. Otherwise, it would be possibly resolved by standard measures of bailouts, new regulations and stimulus programs. Alas, these measures proved to be insufficient: economic growth remains sluggish, whereas social and economic tensions keep rising. A more radical change is required, but apparently abandoning the existing policy paradigm is a grave challenge. It is not that there is no alternative, but the existing institutional order is backed by powerful interest groups which tend to benefit on it either in terms of wealth accumulation or wielding political powers.

The interest-centered perspective largely explains the systemic resistance to change and institutional inertia that we could have witnessed for the last few years. The 'neoliberal' capitalism seems to reduce the idea of institutional order down to a framework of profit-making with 'free market' as a label. This is accompanied by the revival of conservative policies and a tide of concepts and values once linked with right-wing politics, all of which increasingly influence implemented institutional arrangements on national level. The traditionally perceived state is put under great stress in this situation as its long-established functions of social mediator and provider of public services begin to crumble. Moreover, the reasons of power and macroeconomic contraction aggravated budget deficits as well as domestic and external public debts. The recent sovereign debt crisis in Europe, and the Greek crisis in particular, revealed indebted democratic state in a trapped position trying to satisfy conflicting interests of domestic and global actors. These phenomena are, however, hardly understandable under standard economic analysis. This is why we approach this issue from the institutionalist political economy perspective that is considering interests and power to be basic factors of institutional and economic outcomes. We share the view that politics and power relations have governed and still govern what kind of and how transactions are made, they influence the distribution of economic power, and they often determine winners and losers of economic game (Galbraith 1983; Acemoglu and Robinson 2006).

The starting point of this article is the finding that contemporary debtor state becomes critically dependent on international financial capital (Ząbkowicz and Czech 2016). The question posed is whether reconfiguration of the democratic state's trapped position is possible by loosening this addiction.

The goal of this paper is to introduce a framework of analysis which would provide new insights into the political economy of contemporary capitalism. We begin with brief inspection of historical differentiation between market economy and capitalism as described by historian Fernand Braudel and then we move to more contemporary socio-economic readings referring to interests and power. In the second section we introduce the matrix of interests seen in contemporary capitalism, discriminating between national market economy, international financial capital and the democratic state. The final section concludes.

2   A Historical Perspective on Market Economy and Capitalism

As Fernand Braudel showed in his seminal works (1983, 2008 [1985]), market economy and capitalism belong to different levels of trade and economic activity and as such they should be perceived as different categories. In a historical perspective, market economy referred basically to exchange developed between production and consumption. It was closely bounded to the place of exchange—local markets, bazaars, periodic fairs, cities, and eventually regional and national markets. Yet the main feature of this level of 'economic life' was that market economy was a 'world of transparence and regularity, in which everyone could be sure in advance, with the benefit of common experience, how the process of exchange would operate' (Braudel 1983, p. 455). Agents were thus able to largely calculate outcomes of their actions as these were repetitious in certain time intervals and concerned the exchange of everyday goods delivered through rather stable supply chains. One could then predict with decent probability such variables like prices, volume of exchange or profits. Small-scale speculation was of course possible, but had very limited impact on the economy as a whole.

In contrast to market economy thus perceived, the essence of capitalism lied not in simple, almost routine exchange of goods and services, but in financial profits gained from a variety of operations which were usually of large-scale character and burdened with high risk and unpredictability of outcomes. As Braudel puts it in relation to trade transactions (1983, p. 456): 'the capitalist game only concerned the unusual, the very special, or the very long distance connection—sometimes lasting months or even years'. The involvement of capital was not limited to any particular commodity, place or territory. If shipping of spices and textiles from India to Europe provided higher profits than participation in local production, the involvement of capital shifted. When a development of textile industry seemed more promising than spice trading, the capital shifted again with no respect to former business relations and consequences for local partners and societies. The same happened when any other kind of activity enabled by technological or institutional change allowed for gaining comparatively higher financial returns. Links to national markets and geographical boundaries were thus of secondary meaning; they mattered only for legal and logistic reasons. Capital does not commit itself to a persistent production of a specific good or to repetitive trade transactions; its ontology should be rather portrayed by a constant movement and hunt for opportunities. The heart of capital consists not of emotional or national bounds, but of mobility and profit seeking. It is thus no wonder that the 'core' of capitalism has so far shifted at least eight times starting from Bruges through Venice, Anvers, Genoa, Amsterdam, London, Boston, New York to Los Angeles always moving to those places which offered best opportunities for reaping high profits. Capitalism has been rather detached from its market economy base, but paradoxically enough could not exist without its customers, suppliers, and production base.

Braudel investigated how these two levels of economic activity developed and coexisted in pre-modern Europe. However, a straightforward transposition of his idea to modern times reveals an essential deficiency of omitting the role of the state without which one cannot imagine performing an analysis of contemporary institutional economic order. In times studied by Braudel state's role was negligible when it came to mediating between the interests of early capitalists versus interests of folk and local communities. Rulers were rather interested in securing the former as they got their share in rents and taxes. It was not until the twentieth century when, due to political alliance with labor, the state happened to change into a referee in labor-capital conflicts and a provider of legal and institutional framework for domestic economy.

An essential contribution to economic theory in the field of interests was made by John R. Commons and John K. Galbraith. Instead of concentrating on the exchange of goods and creation of value they preferred to focus on analyzing conflicts of interests and the ways of overcoming them in order to build effective social and economic institutions. Commons (1936, 2012 [1924]) maintained that a reasonable social order needed a careful design of institutions rather than their spontaneous creation in a process of laissez-faire competition. Moreover, the infamous interest groups, with the term usually referring to unions, were crucial for reforming capitalism, because by exerting pressure on politicians and keeping capital owners in check they contributed to a rise of more just and fair socioeconomic system. Commons' approach was continued by Galbraith who in his famous work on American capitalism (1993 [1952]) elaborated on the concept of countervailing powers formed by labor unions and employers' organizations. His very idea was that in the face of dominating economic power of employers, workers decided to form their own counter-monopoly which controlled the supply of labor. Galbraith realized that in modern times 'since competition had disappeared, all effective restraint on private power had disappeared' (p. 111).

The world was no longer characterized by competitive relations between buyers and sellers which used to constrain the exertion of power similarly to the model of perfect competition, but evolved into concentrated power on one or both sides. So in order to provide stability and in fact to save the future of the capitalist system, 'private economic power [was] held in check by the countervailing power of those who [were] subject to it' (p. 111). The counterbalance was thus a result of self-generating phenomenon of collective action, which proved crucial for capitalism's dynamics and eventual survival. Still, the conflict between workers and employers was unable to reach permanent and credible solutions without engaging a third party, that is the state, which would ensure the agreements were respected by both sides. Spontaneous struggles between labor and capital became with time monitored and arbitrated by the state, which heavily contributed to long-lasting social peace and creation of systems of welfare.

Today the landscape has changed much further. Capitalism has gone global leaving national boundaries behind and challenging the historical role of the state. After a period of divergence between the state and capital in the era of welfare capitalism, we are witnessing a restoration of the preceding alliance, which had been critically analyzed inter alia by Karl Marx, Walter Eucken or Joseph Schumpeter. Since the 1970s new relations of power is to be seen between governments, financiers with increasing control both over governments and non-financial corporations, and rather disorganized trade unions (Ingham 2011, pp. 249–250; Streeck 2009). As we intend to show in next section, the state-capital relations seem to have been restored not in a form of mutual cooperation between the two, but rather with the state on instrumental position and with internationalized financial capital taking advantage of state's political assets.

We believe the Galbraithian concept of countervailing powers of labor and capital, which contributed to the creation of welfare capitalism in postwar times, to be no longer valid. We would rather reconsider the Braudelian idea of discriminating between market economy and capitalism. He perceived the former as predictable local activities, and the latter as an engine of ongoing internationalization and risk taking by means of detaching accumulated capital from local markets. Respectively, in times more contemporary than those studied by Braudel we recognize the successors in national market economy and in internationalized (mostly financial) capital.

The scope of their actions as well as their features have naturally changed. Local markets have evolved into national economies and merchant capital turned into sophisticated internationalized finance. The risk level of economic activities has grown on both sides. Their basic logic has, however, remained the same. Economy is busy with production and consumption in contrast to monetary capitalism which is not concerned with utility but with financial profits alone (Ingham 2011, p. 261).

There are tensions not only between domestic economy and internationalized capital, but also in their relations with the state that put democratic values and institutions under growing threat. The recent international financial crisis revealed a peculiar contract between the state and financial capital in troubled water. This 'tacit' but binding agreement assumed that gains from the risky but lucrative operations on financial assets would be privatized while costs and losses would be socialized. All reforms initiated recently seem to strive for a new equilibrium between capitalist state on the one hand and securities markets on the other (Ingham 2011, p. 251).

3   THE MATRIX OF INTERESTS IN CONTEMPORARY STAGE OF CAPITALISM

Braudel's discrimination between market economy and capitalism proves to be surprisingly useful when theorizing on contemporary capitalism. We are going to argue that it is the differentiation of interests of capitalism's agents and those of market economy's that adequately explains modern capitalistic social order and delineates the scope of social interactions overstepping national boundaries. Having Braudel's observation of historically supranational and limitless nature of capitalism in mind, we pinpoint and define three groups of actors which constitute the essence of contemporary socioeconomic order. These groups not only compete between themselves pursuing their economic interests within a given framework, but try to influence national and global politics in order to change the rules of the game in their own favor thus seeking for political rents as well. Their interests are often of contradictory nature and the scope of potential cooperation is put nowadays under growing threat.

National market economy (NME) actors. By this category we mean agents that are entirely or almost entirely involved *domestically* in production, exchange and consumption of goods and services. It thus includes small firms and medium companies, households in their dual role of consumers and wage or salary earners, financial intermediaries like local banks or other companies which provide financial services to domestic actors and have their profits depending on customers' performance and solvency. What all actors mentioned have in common is that they are embedded within national economy on which their survival and well-being depends. Households' earnings and spending capacities, firms' production and expansion perspectives, financial sector's soundness, they all hinge on stability, performance, and subjectively perceived expectations toward the future of domestic economy. This group of actors can thus be reduced to three subgroups which could well function within a relatively closed economy as they mostly did in the post-war regime of welfare capitalism. These subgroups are: (1) democratic electorate, i.e. roughly labor and welfare recipients, (2) production-linked domestic capital, (3) nationally vested financial capital, whereas both (2) and (3) are interested in acting on local and/or national markets.

In the relations between NME agents themselves the question of power is of great importance as the era of industrial and monopolist capitalism showed. Bargaining power of an individual is negligible against the concentration of power on both labor and goods markets. As a matter of fact, since nineteenth century creating or joining an interest group has been rather a question of subsistence and survival than of pursuing economic aims of wants and desires. Thus, countervailing powers emerged in the form of labor unions and later of consumer cooperatives which confronted monopoly of employer and monopoly of seller. In response many corporations created their own employers' organizations. All of these pursued collective goals of their members through even more power concentration and rising political pressure capacities.

This picture of countervailing powers was well portrayed in the already mentioned Galbraith's classic work. Our point is, however, that even though these actors have struggled against each other in the process of economic and political competition, in contemporary perspective they articulate quite common interests toward the state. The latter is perceived as a creator and administrator of legal and institutional framework, a likely protector of national branches against tough international competitors, a supplier of public goods (including legislation, law enforcement, social order, basic infrastructure, sound currency etc.), and possibly an arbiter and mediator in social and economic conflicts. The state is thus supposed to provide stable, predictable, and transparent economic and legal order that serves best public interest, even though many interest groups do try to change the rules of the game in their own favor. The state is then to some extent a kind of 'external' agent in relation to NME actors (with the exception of public employment and government purchases naturally), which stands above the economy though monitoring its development and protecting national interests against foreign competitors. For this reason we believe that locally embedded labor and capital may be seen as a whole in peculiar sense. These forces, though often being in opposition, nowadays share similar expectations toward the state and experience anxiety facing globalizing economy and ruthless international actors.

International financial capital (IFC) actors vel internationalized capital. The second group of actors include companies or groups of companies interrelated on financial and functional basis doing business globally in production, trade, banking, and other operations, usually finance-related. We have qualified both financial international corporations like investment funds, insurance companies, brokers etc. and huge multinationals like GM or Siemens into this group due to their massive accumulation of capital and perspective in doing business. Moreover, as recent research on non-financial companies (mostly those originating from the US) shows, their activities tend toward financialization (Krippner 2005; Crotty 2003) which is another reason for associating them with international financial capital. In short, our focus is principally on actors that are rather loosely involved in real sector operations or happen to be exclusively committed to financial operations. All these actors constitute, in our opinion, the very essence of boundless and borderless capital, which characterizes capitalism and is the source of main threats posed against societies and traditional markets. Was it not a largely irresponsible behavior of global banks and insurers that caused the crisis of 2008+? This group of actors enjoys the highest potential of capital mobility and is rather loosely bound to national economies; their main goal is to make profits on purely financial operations thus seeking for attractive opportunities throughout the world and not hesitating to shift the allocation of capital on a day-to-day basis.

IFC actors enjoy vast economic power in the sense that complex networks as well as scope of their operations make states succumb to their demands thus marking a contemporary stage of capitalism. Internationalized financial capital is, however, not omnipotent. Profiting on operations on international markets of financial assets involves risk, which can be noticeably limited with the help of relevant legislation and exercising political channels of pressure. For achieving this, internationalized capital must be assisted by the state that wields democratic legitimization and appropriate institutional measures. This is why IFC agents have interest in subordinating the state in such a manner that their expectations are secured, yet obligations remain rather limited.

We are aware of the fact that this classification may bring up doubts of being imprecise and leaky. Our principal caveat here is that the division between financial corporations doing business globally and locally is rather unclear. The former often register their subsidiaries in certain countries with the perspective of doing business locally. On the other hand, there are national banks that decide to go global, but keep in touch with their local ties and identity. However, we proceed with this simplification to make the presentation transparent in academic terms. To sum up, our perspective discriminates across financial companies with their interests oriented globally thus belonging to the contemporary international superstructure of capitalism versus financial intermediaries that act and make profits mostly on local markets thus being a part of national market economy domain.

The democratic state. We understand the democratic state as a social structure that wields law-making and coercive power over certain territory and population which has been given to it by political legitimization stemming from the very society by democratic vote. We focus on the key functions of the state which include creating and managing legal-institutional order as well as addressing society's preferences. Nevertheless, by no means we see the state as both impersonal and impartial administrative unit which acts in favor of vaguely defined general welfare. We share the public choice approach being aware that the state consists of individuals with their own expectations and interests.

The state is a complex structure—it is not a centralized monolith organized in a single location and is not represented by central government or by central bank nor by parliament or by supreme court alone, but consists of numerous agencies, civil service, public institutions, local governments etc. Nonetheless, we can roughly reduce the state's agents into two groups, namely politicians and bureaucracy. The public choice approach conceives them as actors pursuing their own particular goals that do not necessarily comply with the preferences of society or people they represent and serve. In the democratic state politicians are mostly interested in keeping their political power and winning elections, whereas bureaucrats strive for maximizing budgets under their control (Buchanan and Tullock 1997 [1965]). However, recent developments have made it clearer than ever that politicians and bureaucracy share a common goal of protecting financial stability of the state. Firstly, because it enables financing state's expenditure on public goods which is of great help for politicians to gain popularity among voters, and second, because individual welfare of bureaucrats in terms of employment and salaries depends on it.

The three groups identified above form a matrix of interests which in our opinion is critical for understanding the challenges which contemporary capitalism poses to the future of democratic societies. National-market-economy group historically was and still remains interested in the state's roles of a coordinator and an enforcer of social order as well as a provider of public goods. Respectively, the democratic state is interested in votes of NME actors which translate into political legitimization and power. In order to gain them (never ignoring bureaucrats' aims mentioned above) it badly needs a financial stabilization and capabilities which can result from tax contributions and loans. For political reasons the state is more interested in the latter kind of inflows and therefore it has interest in maintaining correct relations with financial intermediaries, many of them operating internationally. As far as internationalized capital is concerned, the state can be supportive to it in terms of exerting political pressures on foreign or domestic debtors or by encouraging other countries to welcome financial players. Yet more importantly, when international financial markets become turbulent, like they did after 2008, the state is suddenly perceived as an insurer of last resort in terms of bailouts, easy credit or favorable legislation.

In the new matrix of interests we can see the state torn apart between serving the national economy as a provider of public goods and supervisor of legal and institutional framework on the one hand and responding to the demands of international financial markets on the other hand. The state's position is less that of coordinator of events standing above the actors and more like a bewildered agent sitting on a fence trying to satisfy conflicting interests. As a matter of fact the state seems to be trapped. It should address the expectations of NME agents which provide it with political legitimization, yet it feels obliged to listen to IFC due to financial dependency reasons. The exchange between the state and NME actors concerns a provision of public and social services in return for votes and public support. However, to meet voters' expectations the state needs to be financially solvent and so debts need to be sustainable. Alas, when the accumulation of debt begins to threaten the financial stability of the state, the interests of voters suddenly find themselves in opposition of creditors' interests. As Tomz and Wright (2013, p. 22) put it: 'when governments appropriate funds to service the foreign debt, they are making a political decision to prioritize foreign obligations over alternative goals that might be more popular with domestic constituents'. A likelihood thus appears that outlays for public services may be dramatically constrained for the sake of paying back the creditors, which in turn translates to shrinking capability of meeting the expectations of voters and other domestic actors.

A risk of social discontent arises, but the fear of shaking the 'state of confidence'[1] of state's creditors often prevails over the obligations toward the society. Politicians are afraid of discontenting financial markets because it could escalate into political and economic crisis. Thus IFC can exercise an indirect power over governmental policies and the state becomes a hostage of their 'state of confidence'. Once indebted in foreign currencies the state is on the string of capital inflows. States need to assure their 'state of confidence' with relevant preferential conditions of business-making or adequate measures in the field of public finance. The example of 2008+ crisis is very revealing in this matter. Many IFC agents benefited on bail-outs and/or tax reductions which resulted in sharp rise in public debt in some countries. This outcome provided them with even greater opportunities to exert pressure on states.

---

[1] We borrow this concept from Michał Kalecki, who in his famous paper on full employment (Kalecki 1943) mentioned that a 'state of confidence' is a very promising way of keeping governments in check by 'captains of industry'. He remarked that capitalists had 'a powerful indirect control over government policy: everything which may shake the state of confidence must be carefully avoided because it would cause an economic crisis. (...) The social function of the doctrine of 'sound finance' is to make the level of employment dependent on the state of confidence' (p. 325). Analogous mechanism works today.

4   Concluding Comments

Reconsidering the state in this context invites to a discussion on the durability of links in the matrix of interests. Drawing on inspiration from Braudel's works, we have pointed to a significant gap between the interests of huge international financial corporations, constituting modern capital, and domestically-linked, locally engaged companies, being a part of market economy. This gap could be well employed in forging a new alliance between the state and domestic constituents to counterbalance the power of internationalized capital.

However, the change in mental and cultural patterns is needed. Namely, the concept of self-regulating market is still welcomed by the public and policy-makers. The states have to abandon rhetoric of "there is no alternative" first. Cultural patterns which constitute foundations of society need to remain repressed and shaped by free-market utopia no more. It is very often just the thinking patterns that prevent us from doing things that are allegedly impossible. The disappointing progress of reforms in the face of current crisis suggests that careful redesign of the system is insufficient for changing the course of events in the long run. Failures to introduce unanimously Tobin tax or to hit "too-big-to-fail" banks via European banking union did not have their causes so much in technical details, but in thinking patterns that followed the already beaten tracks. What indeed needs to change are institutions understood not only as 'rules of the game' of typical Northian approach (North 1991), but more of 'a system of shared beliefs about how the game is played' (Aoki 2001, p. 26). It is a question of cognition first that induces us to change our minds and, consequently, to modify the formal rules of the game.

The recent crisis revealed the strings of subordination to capital which have been developed under neo-liberal policies and reforms. The latter enabled the IFCs to become a formidable player on national and supranational levels. The indebted democratic state has become subordinated to international financial capital with the latter continuously creating the narrative of state's dependency on financial markets' benevolence. The contemporary matrix of interests presents the indebted state in a trapped position trying to satisfy conflicting interests of domestic and global actors. This poses a threat of state's rising dependency on internationalized capital and neglecting its commitments toward society. There is a possibility, however, that realization of community of interests of the state and national-economy actors may change the balance of power and allow for developing new political institutions that would bring about a widely accepted equilibrium. Strategic political alliance is never an easy task, yet the era of industrial capitalism witnessed an emergence of countervailing power successful enough to keep capital in check.

REFERENCES

Acemoglu, D., & Robinson, J. A. (2006). Paths of economic and political development. In B. Weingast & D. A. Wittman (Eds.), *The Oxford handbook of political economy* (pp. 673–692). Oxford: Oxford University Press.

Aoki, M. (2001). *Toward a comparative institutional analysis*. Cambridge: MIT Press.

Braudel, F. (1983). *Civilization and capitalism, 15th–18th century. Volume II: The wheels of commerce*. London: Book Club Associates.

Braudel, F. (2008 [1985]). *La dynamique du capitalism*. Paris: Flammarion.

Buchanan, J. M., & Tullock, G. (1997 [1965]). *The calculus of consent. Logical foundations of constitutional democracy*. Ann Arbor: The University of Michigan Press.

Commons, J. R. (1936). Institutional economics. *American Economic Review, 26*(1), 237–249.

Commons, J. R. (2012 [1924]). *Legal foundations of capitalism*. Whitefish, MT: Literary Licencing LLC.

Crotty, J. (2003). The neoliberal paradox: The impact of destructive product market competition and impatient finance on nonfinancial corporations in the Neoliberal Era. *Review of Radical Political Economics, 35*(3), 271–279. https://doi.org/10.1177/0486613403255533.

Galbraith, J. K. (1983). *The anatomy of power*. Boston: Houghton Mifflin.

Galbraith, J. K. (1993 [1952]). *American capitalism. The concept of countervailing power*. New Brunswick, NJ: Transaction Publishers.

Ingham, G. (2011). *Capitalism*. Cambridge: Polity Press.

Kalecki, M. (1943). Political aspects of full employment. *Pol Quart, 14*(4), 322–330.

Krippner, G. (2005). The financialization of the American economy. *Socio-Economic Review, 3*(2), 173–208. https://doi.org/10.1093/SER/mwi008.

North, D. C. (1991). Institutions. *Journal of Economic Perspectives, 5*(1), 97–112.

Streeck, W. (2009). *Re-forming capitalism. Institutional change in the German Political Economy*. Oxford and New York: Oxford University Press.

Tomz, M., & Wright, M. J. L. (2013). Empirical research on sovereign debt and default. NBER Working Paper 18855. Retrieved from http://www.nber.org/papers/w18855. https://doi.org/10.3386/w18855.

Ząbkowicz, A., & Czech, S. (2016). Revisiting conventional wisdom: Does financialization have to make sovereigns subordinated. *Ekonomia: Rynek, gospodarka, społeczeństwo, 47*, 135–148. https://doi.org/10.17451/eko/47/2016/188.

NGO in the Modern State

Agnieszka Joanna Legutko

Non-governmental organizations (NGOs) are recently being recognized as key third sector actors covering work in various fields such as human rights, as well as social and environmental issues. Development of NGOs enabled the growth of civic awareness and the understanding of the concept of social dialogue and its recognition in practice. As Rymsza (2008) claims the essence of civil dialogue as an institutional solution is the socialization of public decision-making processes by enabling citizens (especially formalized bodies representing citizens, including non-governmental organizations) to systematically influence the law-making process and the preparation of state documents concerning those citizens directly. The complementary institutions of representative democracy (e.g. the elected public authority) through participatory democracies (direct involvement of citizens) are being promoted. The aim of this chapter is to analyze the changing role of NGO in globalized reality. The research question explored here is what is the role of NGOs in modern state. Document analysis method is applied to present essential role of NGO as a balancing factor between state and market. With the use of source analysis method, the definition of the NGO is sharpened. Many typologies concerning

A. J. Legutko (✉)
Cracow University of Economics, Kraków, Poland

© The Author(s) 2018
S. Vliamos, M. S. Zouboulakis (eds.), *Institutionalist Perspectives on Development*, Palgrave Studies in Democracy, Innovation, and Entrepreneurship for Growth, https://doi.org/10.1007/978-3-319-98494-0_4

development of 3rd sector are introduced, deepened on social and political situation. Changes in the role of NGO in many spheres are described. The article verifies the hypothesis whether the role of civil participation is a vital factor for smart development of the modern societies and is essential for economic and political affairs.

1   HISTORICAL OVERLOOK

Civil involvement in state affairs has existed in various forms for centuries, yet for the first time, NGOS has been recognized as potential consultative entities during the founding conference of United Nation in San Francisco in 1945 in the 71st Article of the Charter. That was the Act when one of the first definitions of such organizations has been created. Another statement concerning NGOs internationally was made in resolution 1996/31 of the Economic and Social Council (ECOSOC) in 1996. At that point, NGOs were recognized as the consultative bodies and were granted the access to attend in an open meeting of ECOCOS as the observers. Civil cooperation to achieve bigger influence has started in middle ages. Following the process of the formation of non-governmental organizations in modern Europe, **the universal Church** cannot be overlooked. It was perceived as a union of individuals linked by a unified social structure that allowed anyone to adhere to certain values. The Christian Church is often referred to as the first social organization, which was not based on primary relation (family, language, race, neighborhood proximity), but on a system of values that was represented by the Church's collective and transcended across borders. The medieval **Hansa**—the merchant corporation in Northern Europe—had a similar international character. The members belonged to Hansa because of the criterion of professional activity. Hansa not only fulfilled the functions of professional organizations, but also helped members in various fields staring cooperation in a new city. Referring to medieval systems, **guilds** are to be mentioned. In those merchants' associations of one craft that oversaw their practice in a particular area, features needed for of a non-governmental organization can be recognized. In spite of the lack of development of traits on a broader scale, they maintained close ties (e.g. journeys of the members all over the continent). A special place should also be attributed to **universities**, and to professional community of lecturers and students. Despite the multiplicity of subjects of the modern age, it was the state and public authority that obtained the exclusive right to act as an only actor of international relations. Due to the custom, but also the size of the community, the Catholic Church was tolerated, but its status in the sphere of law was determined by the public authority.

Only in the nineteenth century the revival of the sources of universalist institutions allowed people to build organizational connections above states borders. Although sources are not consistent in designating the very first modern non-governmental organization, academics mention three main entities. First is a non-intergovernmental conference which declared the World Convention against Slavery in 1840, second International Committee of the Red Cross established in 1863 and third is a parallel operation of the International Ornithological Committee (1863). What all these three entities have in common was the fact that their activities covered spheres outside of state jurisdiction. That was the main reason why they did not get into conflict with a state as it was previously observed with international entities or trade unions. Although, the mid-twentieth century is considered to be the period when the state monopoly over the international arena was over and the outgrowth of non-state formations flourished, it took a long time before the intergovernmental organizations were recognized as equal partners—even the League of Nations was not recognized as a subject of international law. In the twentieth century there was a sharp shift in the centre of gravity of international relations from bilateral to multilateral. This has increased the effectiveness of tackling international and global problems. After the expansion of intergovernmental organizations, the importance of social movements and non-governmental organizations has arose. Social movements emphasizing the fundamental problems and challenges common to Euro-Atlantic culture, including: human rights and freedoms (women's rights, the abolition of slavery), or environmental protection have marked their presence and accompanied the creation of law for centuries, often initiating law-making activities. The role of such movements was appreciated late, not until the late 1990s (Menkes and Wasilkowski 2014). Rising environmental awareness and concern about human rights, as well as the collapse of the USSR that caused liberation of Central and Eastern Europe, have led to increased social engagement, the need to rebuild the state in a new order with the voice of citizens being heard. NGOs become a bridge between the citizens and the public authority. It is the social movement that facilitates participation in the political system for organized entities better than individuals. As Hausner (2006) points out, *the development of the third sector is supported by all major doctrinal political orientations (social democratic, liberal, Christian) in democratic countries.*

In the end of twentieth century, one can clearly see severe growth in NGO engagement in participation with solving not only social but also economic issues. *It is difficult to know precisely how many NGOs there are, because few comprehensive or reliable statistics are kept. Some estimates put the figure at a million organizations, if both formal and informal organizations are included, while the number of registered NGOs receiving international aid is probably closer to "a few hundred thousand."* (Levis 2010). The ongoing processes of globalization and democratization that are being observed in the Western world are one of the reasons for changing the power structure in the global relations. Growing role is being played by non-state actors, especially by non-governmental organizations (NGO). Their involvement in a number of new, crucial tasks in various fields such as civil rights, environmental issues, cooperation between various groups and communities societies, innovation and entrepreneurship has resulted in their growing political role and stronger influence in international scene. Undoubtedly, it leads into presence of those organizations in cooperation with state administration as well as widening the spectre of their activities. Thanks to those circumstances NGOs' role in decision making processes is constantly increasing. *Currently, 4,507 NGOs enjoy active consultative status with ECOSOC* (ECOSOC 2017). In 1992 there were 700, and in the first year after granting the NGOs consultative status it was 41 organizations. Consultative status provides NGOs with access to not only ECOSOC, but also to its many subsidiary bodies, to the various human rights mechanisms of the United Nations, ad-hoc processes on small arms, as well as special events organized by the President of the General Assembly. Moreover, the notion of NGO diplomacy, so non-governmental diplomacy or diplomacy of non-governmental organizations, appears more and more frequently in academic publications. Such organizations are no longer just technical experts in the field but becoming equal partners in the decision-making process. NGO diplomacy is not affiliated with nationality, but shares common values, knowledge and interests such as ecological issues or sustainable development. NGOs have many of the same functions that professional diplomats—represent their members' interests, engage in information exchange, negotiate and provide political advice (Betsill and Corell 2008).

Challenges of the modern societies are so dynamic that their overcoming is not always a role of weakening state but more and more often non-state actors are taking over due to better flexibility and more direct forms of action omitting both bureaucracy and state apparatus. As Kwiatkowska

(2010) points out *it is inevitable to reformulate the relationship between the participants of socio-political life in the new conditions.* The new approach refers to issues such as partnership, diversity of actors or dispersion of power, thus rejecting classical analysis of vertical relationships, leaning towards perceiving reality in terms of network or loop. The importance of flexible attitudes grows as well as decisions based on consensus.

As Kafel (2014) claims, one can observe the process of decomposition of old political, economic and social structures, due to globalization. In such conditions, NGOs are useful in both—helping those who have difficulties to operate in new structures such as loops and in creating directions for the recomposition in the changed reality Thriving and trustworthy non-governmental sector and widely speaking, civil society is one of the most important factors nowadays that shape strong democracy in the Western countries. No bounds with political leader or source of income of businessmen strengthen trust in third sector entities and is inviting to be engaged in action. High level of civil participation easily leads to increasing awareness and deeper social involvement and responsibility. That creates a stable base for better development of 3rd sector and further the whole community.

Due to various factors influencing changes in the states such as globalization, economic integration, informatization and technological development the process of enlargement of the third sector affects modern democracies on different levels.

2   State, Market and Civil Society

In socioeconomic life we distinguish 3 sectors. The first one is the **public sector** that is represented by institutions, departments (also local government) which are part of the state authorities. The primary objective of the first sector is to execute the functions of the state. The second sector—**private** one, is the business sphere that aims to maximize profits. The third sector often called **civic or voluntary** consists of non-profit entities. The third sector in its the most general definition is a civic sphere that works together with the other two sectors complementing the deficiencies, that other two are not able to fill. Koźlicka (2000) distinguishes five features of the third sector: (1) formal structure, (2) institutional independence from public authorities, (3) non-for –profit, (4) self-governance and (5) voluntary. According to Gliński (2005), the civil sector refers to what is outside the government and becomes visible through social self-organization and civil activism. As Szacki (1997) points out, civil society more and more often become equal to the activity of the third sector.

The concept of modern democracy includes a specific model of relations between the state, and citizens. On one hand, it is based on setting the line that limits state's interference in the sphere of fundamental civil liberties, on the other on bilateral impact, so participation in political life of state by citizens.

More and more often, one can observe that neither the state itself nor the market are sufficient to sustain a strong democratic society since facing social needs create specific limitations for the market economy and state structures, such as imperfect competition, GDP and employment fluctuations or existence of public goods.

Creating an enduring social network of NGOs that mediate between the state and the people is vital to proper smart development of modern democracy where forces can cooperate and use advantages of specific segment and become complimentary towards each other instead of trying to achieve an artificial sense of substitution. NGOs act then as agents between citizens and state, and creating an area to debate, cooperate and provide better, faster solutions. The stronger the voice of the citizens, the fairer and the more responsible democracy can become and assets can be used wiser and get better allocation.

J. Sztumski (1993) points out civil society is *a society consisting of individuals aware of their rights and obligations resulting from their values and aspirations*. The measures of participation in civil society recognized by A. Sułek (2009) are both willingness of individuals to gather in organizations to pursue common goals, as well as the use of political rights expressed by political involvement in local communities, voting in elections, which translates into rights and decision-making According to Stuart Langton's (1979) classic proposal, civil participation encompasses four categories of citizens' participation in public life:

(1) public activity (activities that are initiated by citizens and controlled by them to influence decisions of authorities and voters),
(2) citizens' involvement (actions initiated by government during fulfilling their public and administrative tasks; the aim of those action is to enhance discussion processes and embetter quality of services so that citizens start to appreciate it),

(3) electoral participation (necessary actions to nominate candidate and choose representation to exercise decisional functions on different levels of governance),

(4) mandatory participation (citizens' actions are imposed by law to allow authorities to fulfill their statutory functions and tasks)

The more developed voluntary sector and good will initiatives are, the higher level of participation is visible. Presence of all four types of participation in democratic counties is crucial for system to function correctly.

Citizen participation is an idea narrower to civil society. This is a process where citizens' impact (indirectly control) decisions of public authorities, presuming direct or indirect influence on the citizens' interest. *Such participation differs from traditional one in the electoral process and is organized by other means. Citizens being able to affect regulations at the early stages of its creation are more likely to be involved in its implementation* (Długosz and Wygnański 2005). The basis is an interactions of authorities with civil organizations, so that communities can be engaged in shaping issues at an early stage that are directly relevant to them and proposing changes that are better understood on the local level than by the central units. Referring to the economics theory, the markets are the mechanism that provides an efficient allocation of resources (Pareto), assuming that markets are perfectly competitive, subjects are fully and uniformly rational, and information is complete. However, reality, market imperfections exist and, therefore, n inefficient (Pareto) allocation of resources occurs. Main sources of imperfection recognized by Stiglitz (1998) are public goods, imperfect competition (monopoly or oligopoly), external factors, economic imbalance, information deficiencies, an unjust distribution of income. The result of market failures is a deadweight loss, that leads to permanent loss of social well-being. As N. Acocello (2005) points out, if market failures are recognized, there is no need to automatically reject government intervention. *The interference of public authorities into the economy is justified by the need to remove the causes or effects of this disability.* The benefit of state intervention is (potentially) economic efficiency; on the other hand particular costs appear, such as tax burdens and state failures. As Krueger (1991) points out, the sum of the actions (of the state) or lack of them resulting in a non-optimal solution and lead to inefficient allocation of resources by public institutions. The main characteristics highlighted as state imperfections are limitations or lack of access to information, restrained control over the functioning of private markets, incomplete implementation, the pursuit of the particular interests of policy makers instead of the public interest, and lack of mechanisms to verify the efficiency of the public sector (Leszek 2010).

In such circumstances the NGOs can take over in some fields solving problems of the market such as unprofitability (social health care) or where benefits are to be seen in long term (ecological education) as well as state related issues such as not enough budget, high level of centralization and lack of qualified specialists. As J. Hausner (2006) claims *non-governmental organizations are the answer to the state and market failures, although they do not replace them, and they do not have such aspirations.* Non-governmental organization hold economic advantage in providing public services due to specialization in atypical cases, low cost as a result of volunteer work and financial support from donors. It should be emphasized that the third sector is not focused solely on fixing economic problems due to market and state imperfections. NGOs often act as an intermediary in solving political problems such as freedom of association as well as social e.g. the involvement of citizens.

3   The NGO: Definition Attempt

The first definition of the NGO appeared relatively late, only in the Charter of UN in Article 71. Most of the definitions referring to the third sector, especially those relating to the formal and legal sphere, have been negative for a long time. They defined what a NGO is **not** rather than focusing on what it really is. For example in 1950, the UN Economic and Social Council defined NGOs as an organization that was **not** established under an international agreement. However, a number of theoretical approaches to the third sector suggested by academics concern various aspects of non-governmental organizations. I cite some of the most important for further consideration in the paper. According to P. Drucker (2005), NGOs exist to bring change into society as well as individuals. It may be stated that a NGO is a third-sector party that has a specific structure, private character, operates not-for-profit (Krzyżanowska 2000), it is entitled to independent and sovereign decisions, is created voluntarily and is committed to a specific social mission (Górniak 2008). Evers and Laville (2004) claims that NGOs do not fill the gaps between the economy and the state, but they are a hybrid between organization and enterprise that use various resources to merge areas of their activities. M. Kaldor (Anheier et al. 2004), believes that the third sector is changing along with societies, so organizations are involved in negotiations with authorities and lawmakers. Researchers from the John

Hopkins Center of Civil Studies have launched a comparative project to analyze the scope, funding structure and various roles that the third sector conducts in countries around the world. According to the typology, the following characteristics of the organization of the third sector can be distinguished: (1) organized (institutionalized into some extent), (2) private (autonomy from the government), (3) self-governed, (4) non-profit (voluntary). A good summary is N. Akerstom's (2012) theory claiming that partnership between sectors is a response to the growing diversity of society that leads NGOs to the role of negotiators between citizens, political and economic forces. By observing the activities of the third sector in different countries, one can easily draw a conclusion that they are developing at different pace (Jordan and Tuijl 2006). The needs that arise in every society strongly influence the direction of NGO activities. In the societies where social sphere still need relatively high level of input, less advanced non-governmental structures continue to play the role of alternative social service providers, focusing on solving the economic problems of society resulting from the imperfection of the market and the state in service offer. This is a so-called **orientation to the citizens**. In many countries where the tradition of civil participation and the constructive cooperation of governmental administration and citizens are long established, there are more people-oriented organizations often called as **oriented from the citizens**. These can be defined as representatives of the society to public authority in various cases such as political issues, respect for civil and social rights, human capital such as workshops and trainings to provide better trained and educated citizens willing to spread the knowledge and of course in innovation as investing in newest technologies with a long term benefits (Fig. 1).

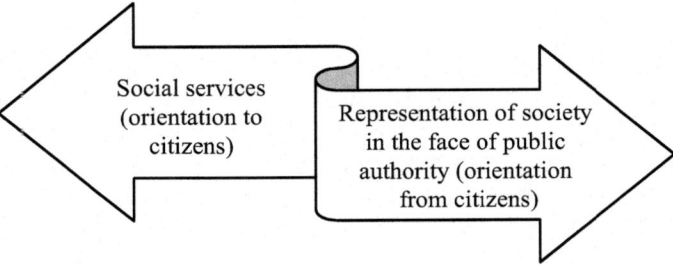

Fig. 1 Directions of the social organization according to Berger and Neuhaus. Source: Own elaboration based on Berger, P., Neuhaus, To Empower the People, Washington, DC 1975

4   PRESENT STAGE OF NGO DEVELOPMENT

The growing role of NGOs is a fact. Their influence on the regional, national and international scope differs. NGOs are the voice and exemplification of civil society in international relations. The rise of awareness thanks to new technologies and fast exchange of information allow entities to cooperate in real time manner not only within the state but also internationally. NGOs emphasize their independence from state and economy bounds, as they stress the fact that they belong to the sphere of freedom typical for modern democratic state cooperating within social, political and economic spheres and allowing citizens voice to be heard on equal level with both first and second sector. Discussion on NGOs, is a result of not only growing impact of these organizations but also various stages of their development, issues that they are involved in and level of impact they are able to gain. Academics look into them from the perspective how is the whole community affected by civil participation and what are the circumstances leading to certain stages of development. As B. Lowenkron (2007) pointed out that NGOs help to strengthen democracy in three ways:

(1) NGOs work to establish awareness of and respect for the right of individuals to exercise freedoms of expression, assembly and association, which is crucial to participatory democracy.
(2) They work to ensure that there is a level playing field upon which candidates for elective office can compete and that the entire elections process is free and fair.
(3) Finally, NGOs work to build and strengthen the rule of justice as well as responsive and accountable institutions of government so that the rights of individuals are protected regardless of which persons or parties may be in office at any given time.

As third sector is an answer for the imperfections of state and market. it has a unique ability to comprise various social groups and categories. It bases its actions not only on formal criteria but also analyzes particular situation in a micro scale trying to fit best solutions. A big share of NGO's actions are based on sympathy and social engagement as well as organization's mission and core values. Big advantage of NGO is broad based approach keeping the trust of all parties while operating in the spheres where neither state nor market want to be involved. The role of NGO is to raise engagement and promote dialogue between parties within a state.

They should provide various options being a consultation platform as well as enhance public responsibility and keep transparency of public debate.

There are various typologies and classifications of non-governmental organizations. Due to the functions that they play in the state and among citizens, it is possible to identify those that:

(1) control and correct the activities of the other two sectors,
(2) represent social needs and interests,
(3) complement deficiencies in the areas of need that the other remaining sectors are not willing (or able) to fulfill,
(4) create innovations in the social reality.

The first two types represent an alternative to the political system. The next two gather people into communities and are able to satisfy needs that individuals would not be able to on their own.

As suggested by Lasocik (1994) organizations can be also divided into groups based on their activity profile:

(1) self-help (taking care of the organization's members),
(2) welfare (services for all who need it or for particular groups in need),
(3) representative (represent interests of specific groups),
(4) ad hoc (created for the purpose of certain action),
(5) leisure (gathering of people interested in the same subject),
(6) task (perform tasks entrusted by the authorities),
(7) traditional (wide spectrum of activity).

Situation of the 3rd sector is very dynamic and stages of development, professionalization and thus impact vary depending on the region. There are many factors that allow and motivate NGOs to grow faster and being deeper enrooted into state affairs. Great share is taken by tradition of gatherings, association and cooperation between citizens as well as awareness of the society on existing challenges within communities. Other important ones are level of wealth, legal regulations and political system. Cultural factors such as main religion, tolerance and customs cannot be omitted. Those circumstances can be easily recognized in comparison of NGOs based in Eastern Europe and Nordic countries. Lower income and standard of living create a need of more social concerned organization helping with public health, care and inclusion of seniors or education whereas in

Nordic countries more attention is put into ecological issues, innovation and humanitarian help abroad. Scandinavia welfare state takes over many fields that are traditionally associated with third sector actions. Severe climate and low population density of small towns in Northern parts of Nordic countries coerced cooperation between of inhabitants. In Poland years of war and soviet influence did not allow for cooperation between citizens to flourish before 1989.

T. Kafel (2014) proposes to divide non-governmental organizations into 4 stages of development:

(1) spontaneous charity,
(2) building legal bases and establishing cooperation,
(3) professional action,
(4) full participation.

In turn, D. C Korten (1987) has named NGOs reaching the highest stage of development Third Generation NGOs. They have gained knowledge about system participants, which makes them able to build coalitions and agreements. They are not only a service provider, but a catalyst for development, thus fully cooperate in functioning with the other two sectors and actively influencing decision-making. They have the ability to manage sustainable development systems in a regional and even national scope while also having access to public funding on equal terms influencing economic and social development, environmental protection, preservation of culture and tradition, as well as security assurance in wide scope.

5   Conclusions

The following paper is an elaborate study on changing role of civil engagement and further non-governmental organization starting from associations in the Middle-Ages showing the evolution of civil movements up to evoking civil participation in modern state. It is a unique combination of theoretical approaches from literature and actual role and influence of NGO is modern societies and economies. Author attempts to fully define blurred area of non-governmental organization referring to various definitions, classifications and approaches blending it with examples of actual field work of those type of entities. Paper delivers study on complementarity of NGOs along with theory of imperfections of state and market and discussing present stage of NGO in global economy stressing possible usage e of specific features that organization of third sector carries.

For many centuries the state was the main power to set the rules and lead on international scene. Even though civil cooperation and signs of formalized structures can be observed since Middle Ages, NGOs have played a major role influencing national and international relations only in recent decades. Along with the development of democracy in Western countries, the role of non-governmental organizations in the international arena has grown significantly. The increased participation of NGOs reflects the broader changes in the nature of world politics. The term of NGO diplomacy has become a part of international rhetoric. Real democracy needs citizens that are aware of their rights and the processes they can influence. Increasing involvement of citizens in social life and participating in civil society is desired for better functioning of the state. As Putman (2002) suggests, civil engagement determines social and economic development and institutional efficiency is strongly determined by civil involvement so it provides for a solution for crisis and stagnation of the state.

I have positively verified the hypothesis that civil participation is vital factor for smart development of modern societies and essential for political and economic sphere letting three spheres to use strongest side of each by complementation one another. The advantage of multisectoral solutions is to use different sectors to meet social needs and to build such relationships that allow using strengths and the reducing constraints. Increasingly, non-governmental organizations are working with state and market to achieve greater efficiency in allocation of resources, which can lead to change not only in local community but up to international level of services. Non-governmental organizations are an integral part of the modern global reality and a medium of exchange between the state and the market. Unlike state institutions, in most cases NGOs have rather modest financial means, but they have many opportunities that the so-called official channels do not have at their disposal. Non-governmental sector connects diverse communities and different notions in various spheres, effecting changes on wide scope and having a large impact on society. NGOs have also contributed significantly in making the voice of the society hearable by making a difference at the local level that is extremely important to the citizens. Arising often from grassroots initiatives, they have better insight into internal issues than central authorities thus can initiate dialogue and find solutions more effectively into some extent taking over lead to prevent state imperfections.

Non-governmental organizations are a great help in transition of the modern system and form a platform between citizens and state. Thanks to multiple actions, 3rd sector plays crucial role in various spheres staring with alternative provider of social services, through civil engagement, political transparency, spreading economic knowledge and good practices up to leisure and sport and innovations, letting society being heard and using their positive power to brighten modern state. More involved society can easier overcome crisis due to optimized uses of resources, faster creating needed actions initiated from the bottom-up as well as preventing and overcoming market and state imperfection to some level. Trust of all parties allows keeping sector transparent, responsible and sustainable. Due to high level of awareness and knowledge, 3rd sector parties are able to launch fast, to the point solutions without resource waste and lowering the costs, since they know the insight of the situation. They provide services that can be not profitable for market or state. NGOs play vital role in innovation and sustainable development within the state that allows both economy and democracy flourish.

REFERENCES

Acocella, A. (2005). *Economic policy in the age of globalisation.* Cambridge: Cambridge Univeristy Press.

Akerstrøm, A. N. (Ed.). (2012). *Hybrid forms of governance self-suspension of power.* Basingstoke: Palgrave Macmillan.

Anheier, H. K., Kaldor, M., & Glasius, M. (Eds.). (2004). *Global civil society 2004/5.* London: Sage.

Betsill, M. M., & Corell, E. (2008). *NGO diplomacy: The influence of nongovernmental organizations in international environmental negotiations.* Cambridge, MA: MIT Press.

Długosz, D., & Wygnański, J. J. (2005). *Obywatele współdecydują, Przewodnik po partycypacji społecznej.* Warszawa: Stowarzyszenie na rzecz Forum Inicjatyw Pozarządowych.

Drucker, P. F. (2005). *Zarzadzanie organizacja pozarządową: teoria i praktyka.* Warszawa: Fundusz Współpracy: Program Phare Dialog Społeczny NGOs.

ECOSOC. (2017). *Giving civil society a voice* [online]. Retrieved August 2017, from https://www.un.org/development/desa/en/news/intergovernmental-coordination/giving-civil-society-voice-at-un.html.

ECOSOC NGO Branch. Retrieved July 15, 2017, from http://csonet.org/?menu=100.

Evers, A., & Laville, J. L. (Eds.). (2004). *The third sector in Europe globalization and welfare.* Cheltenham: Edward Elgar Publishing.

Gliński, P. (Ed.). (2005). *Samoorganizacja społeczeństwa polskiego III sektor i wspólnoty lokalne w jednoczącej się Europie.* Warszawa: Wydawnictwo IFiS PAN.

Górniak, K. (2008). *W poszukiwaniu sprawnej I skutecznej organziacji non profit "Trzeci Sektor"*, nr 13.

Hausner, J. (2006). *Organizacje pozarządowe–trzeci sektor współczesnego społeczeństwa*. Krakow: Zeszyty Naukowe Akademii Ekonomicznej w Krakowie.

Jordan, L., & Tuijl, P. (2006). *NGO accountability. Politics, principles and innovations*. Available via EarthScan, London. Retrieved August 19, 2017. from http://www.untag-smd.ac.id/files/Perpustakaan_Digital_2/NON%20 GOVERNMENT%20ORGANIZATION%20NGO%20Accountability%20 Politics,%20Principles%20and%20Innovations.pdf.

Kafel, T. (2014). *Metody profesjonalizacji organizacji pozarządowych*. Kraków: Wydawnictwo UEK.

Korten, D. C. (1987). *Third generation NGO strategies: A key to people centered development world development* (Vol. 15, s. 145–159). [Online]. Retrieved August 19, 2017, from http://livingeconomiesforum.org/sites/files/pdfs/ Korten%20Third%20Generation%20NGO%20Strategies.pdf.

Koźlicka, R. (2000). *Pozycja sektora pozarządowego w Unii Europejskiej*. Trzeci sektor w Unii. Przewodnik dla Organizacji pozarządowych, Klon/Jawor, Warszawa.

Krueger, A. O. (1991). *Government failures in development*. National Bureau of Economic Research [online]. Retrieved August 16, 2017, from http://www. nber.org/papers/w3340.pdf.

Krzyżanowska, M. (2000). *Marketing usług organizacji niekomercyjnych*. Warszwa: Wydaw. Wyższej Szkoły Przedsiębiorczości i Zarządzania im. L. Koźmińskiego.

Kwiatkowska, M. (2010). NGOs, a demokracja w świecie globalizacji. In A. Pawłowska (Ed.), *Niepaństwowi uczestnicy stosunków międzynarodowych*. Lublin: WSPA

Langton, S. (1979). *Citizen participation in America*. Lexinton: Lexinton Books.

Lasocik, Z. (1994). *Centrum Informacji dla Organizacji Pozarządowych BORDO*. Warszawa: Fundusz Współpracy.

Leszek, P. (2010). Koncepcje zawodności rynku: teoria a rzeczywistość. *Equilibrium, 1* (4).

Levis, D. (2010). Nongovernmental organizations, definition and history. In H. K. Anheier & S. Toepler (Eds.), *International Encyclopedia of civil society*. New York: Springer.

Lowenkron, F. B. (2007). Absurdist Republic. The Role of NGOs in the Development of Democracy. Available via NGO Pulse. Retrieved June 15, 2017, from http://www.ngopulse.org/article/role-ngos-development-democracy.

Menkes, J., & Wasilkowski, A. (2014). *Organizacje międzynarodowe. Prawo instytucjonalne*. Warszawa: Wolters Kluwer.

Putman, R. (2002). *Democracies In Flux. The Evolution of social capital in contemporary society*. New York: Oxford University Press.

Rymsza, M. (2008). *Organizacje pozarządowe. Dialog obywatelski.* Warszawa: Polityka państwa, Instytut Spraw Publicznych.

Stiglitz, J. (1998). *Redefining the role of the state.* World Bank.

Sułek, A. (2009). Doświadczenia i umiejętności obywatelskie Polaków. In P. Gliński & A. Kościanowski (Eds.), *Socjologia i Siciński – Style życia – społeczeństwo obywatelskie – studia nad przyszłością.* IFiS PAN: Warszawa.

Szacki, J. (Ed.). (1997). *Ani książę, ani kupiec: obywatel.* Kraków: Wydawnictwo Znak.

Sztumski, J. (1993). *Problemy teoretyczne związane z przyśpieszeniem zmian społeczno-gospodarczych w Polsce, w zbiorze, Społeczeństwo polskie w procesie demokratycznych przeobrażeń.* Katowice: Janusza Sztumskiego.

Freedom and Friendship: Some Thoughts on the Renewal of Our Democracy

Guy Féaux de la Croix

In our modern constitutions the freedom of the individual is regularly assumed to be the mother concept of democracy, its fundament and point of departure. The two institutions, freedom and democracy, seem to be in a chicken and egg relationship. It is true that democracy seems the one and only form of government in which the free remain free. Democracy is both the safeguard and engine of freedom. But when it comes to the question whether democracy bore the concept of freedom or if freedom brought forth democracy, the answer seems very clearly to lie in the precedence of freedom. How could a society of unfree have constituted itself as a democracy?

Historical experience seems to corroborates that sequence: at the beginning of a democracy we see in most instances the act of liberation from an undemocratic and unfree system. We see the free individual as being the result of the revolutionary deed, be their revolution violent or non-violent, before the liberated then, ideally, tackle the task of setting up a democratic society.

G. Féaux de la Croix (✉)
Ambassador, D, Bad Münstereifel, Germany

© The Author(s) 2018
S. Vliamos, M. S. Zouboulakis (eds.), *Institutionalist Perspectives on Development*, Palgrave Studies in Democracy, Innovation, and Entrepreneurship for Growth, https://doi.org/10.1007/978-3-319-98494-0_5

The American Revolution is a good case in point. But the founding fathers probably erred when they assumed that "all men are by nature equally free and independent", as they phrased it in the Virginia Declaration of Rights, adopted in 1776. The truth is that the experience of humankind stands against that assumption. The unfree individual has been the rule. In an overview of the thousands of years of human societies and the myriad of social systems which they brought forth, the society of free stands out as a rare exception. Freedom thus appears to be a social construct rather than the natural state of man.

Did the old Greeks then invent and construct freedom in the way the steam engine was invented and built by James Watt? Probably it is more correct to say that the ancient Greeks *discovered* freedom. I suggest that freedom is a result of a sort of institutional Darwinism, in that, in the competition of various societal models, the alliance of the free proved itself to be a very efficient society. The citizens experienced the state of the free as a system of governance which yielded the comparatively best economic results. It also proved at the time to be an effective military basis to defend a country against external enemies and to expand the territory of the state. The victories at Marathon and at Salamis are our cases in point and, less virtuous in our present-day perspective, also the success formula for the Athenian imperialism of the fifth century.

In the light of the Ancient Greek achievement, freedom is not so much the origin but rather the destination of the human individual, the morally ultimate destination of the human individual and of his community.

The great achievement of the Ancient Greeks then was to recognise the inherent ethical quality of freedom and to build up an institutional system which consolidated and reinforced the potentials of freedom, of free thinking, free speech, free arts, the competitive effectiveness of the free sciences. It is precisely this point on which I have an issue with Plato in that he did not fully grasp the grounds on which he himself stood. On freedom I hold Pericles to be the greater philosopher, however fragmentary the legacy of his political thinking known to us may be, but very clearly expressed in his funeral oratory, also in the conceptualisation of the Parthenon frieze.

Is the difference between the understanding of freedom as being a natural state or an evolutionary construct a distinction which matters in practice? Well, I think it does. It explains, for example, why so many people show in their deferential attitudes little of a creature born free, but one ready to fall back into the unfree state of the human being.

If a free society wishes to found its future on an alliance of free individuals, then it follows from all said here, that the evolutionary freedom process must be repeated in the upbringing of each individual. Education and culture are the prerequisites of a free society. It also goes to prove the importance of a massive investment in the education and culture of immigrants coming to us from unfree societies, lest a free society risks the very foundations on which it rests.

The anarchistic presumption of the born free, for whom society is by definition a state of alienation, is in the light of freedom as being a social construct preposterous and indefensible.

And finally, if freedom is the result of an institutional survival of the fittest rather than a natural state, its survival depends on remaining the economically most effective system of governance and of again and again proving itself to be that. The moment China shows itself clearly superior over the free societies in yielding the best economic results and possibly also bringing forth a more social and just society, a society which masters the ecological challenges of the new millennium better than others, then the universality of freedom and democracy will be at stake.

Civil society action seems to me to be a most important answer to the frustration of so many citizens about the impossibility for them, as they perceive it, for them to influence the course of the society.

For that, to be allowed to cast a vote once every four years is not enough indeed and especially not for the free individual. New experiments with direct democracy have proven more problematic than convincing to be a good answer to the shortcomings of a representative democracy. Problematic for the lack of the qualification which an informed participation in the making of important political decisions requires and without which the people easily and sometimes also quite willingly become the victims of the demagogues.

By contrast, for an NGO to be taken serious by the political establishment usually takes painstaking efforts to master the substance matter in question and to also impress public opinion. NGO involvement simply implies an awful lot of voluntary work. In terms of the ethical code of the classical Athenian polis the NGO volunteer, with no other personal aspiration but to see the cause he or she believes in succeed, represents the virtuous citizen. Whilst they called a person refusing to get involved with the affairs of the polis an *idiotis*, an idiot, the active citizen who devotes a fair share of his or her time to public affairs is the anti-idiot, the good citizen.

Spiritually speaking, academically, historically, my friendly relationship with the University of Thessaly in Volos began on September 11th of the year 490 BC. If this is a bit of a surprise to the reader let me remind you that this was the day on which the Athenians victoriously won the battle of Marathon. My dating the battle on the 11th September may no less surprise you. May it suffice here to say, and without having the time here to elaborate, we can in my opinion extrapolate the date from Herodotos' histories.

My involvement with 2500th Marathon anniversary began in 2010 when we established a group of friends, the Marathon International Friends Association, with a view to duly and internationally celebrating the event which has proven so constitutive for the development of democracy.

When the University of Thessaly troubled itself to pay tribute to my activities, it was especially with a view to the modest contribution I had been allowed to make to that initiative.

At the time of the anniversary we not only staged a number of events, but probably our most ambitious product was to formulate and publish the "Marathon 2500 Declaration". You might still read this as a charter of what we, in our group of friends, believed could be retained as lessons from the history of the Athenian democracy in its classical times. The chapters of the Declaration read, to name but a few of the altogether 21 chapters:

- the fraternity of the free citizens,
- the individual's self-investment in his society,
- the duties of the democrat,
- the praise of politics,
- responsible leadership,
- the education and culture of democrats,
- the democratic deficit of the European Union (EU).

But of course the reader will expect more from me in this paper rather than to just recite a declaration formulated seven years ago. And more than merely a rehash of my acceptance speech of 2014, in which I had focused on the idea that a bond of fraternity between the democrats, no matter which ideological or political interests they fight for in the democratic contest for power, is an indispensable prerequisite for the functioning of democracy.

This democratic essentiality of fraternity would in fact be my first point of actualisation. From here, and where I left it in 2014, I shall today put forward some ideas on the worrying state of democracy in Europe and beyond the borders of our little continent, worldwide. That democracy is in a precarious situation. I trust that will also be your perception of the state of the world, and hardly needs to be laid out here in detail: anti-democratic forces have gained in strength in more than just one country, or are being kept at bay only with a tremendous effort as we have seen in France. Elected leaders and governments which as soon as they have been voted into power by a majority of the electorate have nothing better to do than to lay fire to essential democratic institutions, to the constitutional courts, to the free media.

Obviously, the space which the editors allowed me for my observations will not nearly suffice to present you with a complete charter for the renewal of democracy. That would, indeed, be the high task of another European convent or for a worldwide democratic alliance. What I have to say to you today, are simply some fragmental observations on the problems which worry me and to lay out, more importantly, what I believe to be a new set of principles to help us to pave a way forward, to save democracy and to develop it as the challenges of our times warrant it.

1   THE FRATERNITY OF THE DEMOCRATS

Returning to the idea of the fraternity of the democrats, I am still pleased about a symposion which, just before Easter 2017, I had the honour to organise in Athens, on the occasion of my art project Edge. Piraeus as a fringe event of the documenta art festival. Our topic for the evening was the relevance or irrelevance of the ancient Greek legacy to the culture of our own times. Under the excellent symposiarchy of Nicos Kyriazis we had *inter alia* such speakers as Yanis Varoufakis and Petros Doukas.

Yanis Varoufakis may also be remembered by our reader as the motorbike riding first finance minister of the Syriza led Coalition. Petros Doukas, was minister in a number of conservative Nea Dimokratia cabinets and is generally considered to be a representative of liberal economic theories.

When I had informed our invitees that Varoufakis was coming, not a few said that in that case they would not attend, and others not if Doukas was coming. Finally a lot people did come and witnessed two wonderful performances, I would say, as it was an art event. Varoufakis brilliantly explained the principle of critical self-introspection as being a crucial element of Ancient Greek drama. Doukas pointed out the great contribution Sparta had made to the development of democracy. Unsurprisingly, he comes from a Spartan family. And Nicos Kyriazis, from a famous Athenian family, then had a bit of an argument with Doukas about the latter's Spartan thesis.

My point, however, is what a good moment it is in a democracy when people from such different ends of the political spectrum, people who have caused considerable bitterness in the ranks of their political adversaries, come together on other levels and on other issues. The conclusion of the symposion was that, in the conviction of all speakers, the Ancient Greek achievements remain highly relevant for addressing the problems of democracy in our times. That conviction to be a common ground for the democratic discourse should indeed please all phil-hellenists.

Our principle must indeed be that of inclusion rather than that of exclusion. To seek dialogue not only with the like-minded, which so often turns out not to be very fruitful, but to engage in a dialogue and even in controversy with those who in our democracies hold very different opinions.

There may be a red line of acceptance in who we associate with, a red line for not upgrading demagogues who very openly threaten the principles of democracy, not to speak of criminal enemies of our democracies and those ready to employ violence for their anti-democratic objectives. But where such individuals and movements place themselves not very clearly outside the democratic spectrum our attitude should be in *dubio pro dialogue*.

If my reader insisted on an empirical verification of my thesis of democratic fraternity, I could point to the societies here in Europe and elsewhere, where politicians and parties have come to consider each other as enemies, as opposed to political systems in which an atmosphere of mutual respect prevails. An atmosphere of animosity usually paves the way for the undermining of democracy. The situations in which we see various European countries speak for themselves.

In my country, Germany, and also in Greece, I am glad to say, we have not yet reached the point where the foundations of democracy seem at stake. Maybe, even though in very different ways, a certain immunization by the experience of tyranny is still having its effects. We still live in times in which much seems to divide our two peoples, or rather the governments and the atmosphere in the media. Today is not the time to discuss German-Greek controversies. What could, however, be helpful and important for all of Europe is for both countries to rediscover common ground in their commitment to the cause of democracy as such, a refreshened sense of community in the defense of democratic values.

2   THE RULE OF THE PEOPLE

Democracy is the rule of the people. It is not the rule of the majority. There is no specific morality in the rule of the majority other than being a practical need, a technique for coming to decisions.

In the late summer of the year 490 BC the Athenians decided by a very narrow majority to intercept the Persian invaders on the beach of Marathon. And those who in the vote had opposed the decision did not stay behind, but went to fight side by side with their comrades.

To obey the decisions of the majority is a tremendous and virtuous effort of the free and equal who find themselves in the minority. If follows from there that the minority deserves to be honoured and respected. About a year ago I was in a debate with the President of our Constitutional Court, Professor Vosskuhle. Asked if he could summarize the function of the Constitutional Court in a single phrase he answered, after a moment of reflection: "To protect the chances of the minority to become the majority".

This is the markstone then by which we can quite easily see what is going wrong in some countries here in Europe and elsewhere, where we see a lack of respect for the minority. We observe massive campaigns of those voted into power, and often by only narrow majorities to eternalize their rule by changing the mechanisms of democratic checks and balances and electoral processes.

For us here, I trust, an attitude of "the winner takes all" and "the winner is free to change the rules of the game", is incompatible with the principle of governance by *all* the people. We see however that the Europeans, and not only the Europeans, are divided on this quintessential principle of democracy. If we are not to fall apart over this question we must seek to reach a new and deeper understanding and agreement of the fundamental principles of democracy.

3   THE PEOPLE'S POLITICAL RESPONSIBILITY

In our Marathon Declaration we formulated a praise of politics: in Chapter IX paragraph 3 we wrote: "Contrary to the fact that politics tire and annoy the citizens of contemporary democracies, we still need more and not less politics". Good politics, hopefully. And we highlighted the political responsibility of the citizen.

Were we to revise and to amend our Declaration we would unfortunately have to take into account the experience of how morally ambiguous the will of the people may be. The Sicilian expedition, which in 414 BC for the Athenians ended in a war-decisive disaster, could not only be blamed on the demagogy of Alcibiades. It was the will of the people who would not listen to those warning against it. "Athenian history", we stated in our Marathon Declaration, "has proven how freedom and democracy can be jeopardized by foolish expeditions to distant foreign coasts".

The distant foreign coasts of our own times carry the name of Iraq and Afghanistan. They were, in their want of truthfulness and rational assessment, truly evil decisions by the standards of a virtuous democracy. George W. Bush, the Alcibiades of our times, but the people elected him twice!

If Donald Trump frightens us each day anew with his irrationality, with the red button to start an atomic Third World War any moment in his reach, then it is also true that millions of American people voted for him. These millions of Americans frighten me no less than the man, though they represented not even the majority of the electorate. Similarly the readiness frightens me of millions of British people, Turks, Poles, Hungarians, to let their electoral decisions be guided by xenophobia and by the politics of hatred. They worry me as much as their seducers.

How do we in modern democracies address the problem of the evil potential inherent in the people? As little as it proved true in Plato's *Politeia* that whatever the tyrant holds to be just is *per se* justice, is it true that whatever the people decide is *per se* just and virtuous. No less than the politicians may the people be vicious and evil.

4   Populism and Ethical Politics

We have a debate in Germany about the usefulness of the term "populism". Those putting it into question argue that listening to the will of the people is perfectly legitimate and normal in democracy. True, the word "populism" is misleading in that it suggests a genuine commitment to the people. In reality the essence of what is traditionally called populism is the politics of appealing to the lowest instincts of the people, their egotism, their xenophobia, their resentment against societal and political elites. Demagogy would probably be the better word.

The evil of populism is clearly recognized when we hold it against its opposite, the politics of ethics. This distinguishes the virtuous politician from the evil one. The virtuous politician distinguishes him or herself in appealing to the morally good potential of the people, to cultivate the goodness in the people, to bring to bear their social responsibility for the well-being of others and their readiness to make sacrifices. To respect Emmanuel Kant's categorical imperative.

It is this a distinction which we can clearly base on the principles of the classical Athenian polis. Plato's political thinking revolved around the question of what justice is. In his *Politeia* he makes it very clear when he opposes the position of Thrasymachos that whatever the ruler holds to be just is justice. For Plato there is an objective level of political virtue.

To extrapolate from Plato: In a democracy, not just anything which a majority of the people decide is per se just and virtuous. When the majority errs and votes for evil political intentions, it is our freedom and maybe also obligation to denounce their decisions as such.

What is the practical use of these distinctions? Firstly, to clearly denounce the evilness of populism. Secondly to cultivate in both the people but also in the politicians a sense of ethical obligation.

5   EDUCATION AND CULTURE

In the classical polis the answer to this need of political ethics was education and education by culture. The arts of the theatre, but no less the omnipresence of sculptures virtually standing for the values of the polis, were the ethical school of the nation.

What then are, in our times, the sources for an ethical orientation of the people and of their politicians? Is it not so, that whatever sources of morality we may have had in the past, the churches, public culture, non-partisan public television, newspapers, are being profoundly undermined by sources of orientation which in no way are obliged to an ethical education of the people?

How do we respond to that need of ethical education and the lack of it in our present day democracies? Our democracies will truly be at stake as long as we do not find ways to strengthen the ethical resources of our communities.

6   INTERESTS AND ETHICS

In the Marathon Declaration we said: "The wealthy by talent, industry or birth shall not pretend that what is beneficial to them is also good for the people".

We have become used to the politics of interests. We find it legitimate for the people to vote according to their own interests. And then the people are surprised that the politicians too act in the way of their own interests.

We see that a political system guided only by the politics of interests leads into a dead-end of frustration. The people, themselves guided by nothing but their interests or what they are made to believe to be in their interest, will finally be disappointed by the very people they voted into power. And finally they will reject the rule of the elites and those who pretend to more truly represent their interests.

Democracy will be an endangered species, if we do not succeed to bring the politics of interests and an ethical obligation of all politics, of the people as well as their politicians, into a new balance. For that balance we need a greater weight of the ethical determinant.

7   ELITES AND SOCIAL COHESION

In our Marathon Declaration, we stated that the key to a democratic governance of the polis lay in an equilibrium between the elites and the people. We wrote: "The elites were well aware that this newly founded cohesion depended on a social equilibrium and the state's procuration of the poorer citizens." Writing here in a publication of a Greek economic faculty, I would be pleased to learn how this thesis can be further corroborated by what we know of the socio-economics of the Athenian state, an issue to be considered for further research.

It is one of the lessons of the twentieth century indeed that modern democracy too depends on an economic equilibrium. It was the success formula of the newborn German state after the Nazi catastrophe. The idea of the "Sozialstaat" or social market economy, with similar convictions of the French, Italian and Benelux founding fathers, that became the fundament of the European integration process. Only that the principles of the free market economy were very strongly inscribed in the mission of the European institutions, but not by contrast a social dimension of the European integration. The mission of the EU is an unbalanced one.

The disaster of the Euro construction and the debt crisis are a direct consequence of this disequilibrium.

8   Democracy in the Times of Globalization

The gap between wealthy elites and normal people, not to talk of the poor, has obscenely widened. If globalization is blamed for it, we must be fair enough to add that the EU has not been a victim of galloping globalization, but that it has been its foremost driving force. The EU has been and still is a driving force of global globalization and of internal EU globalization alike. The expansion policies of the EU are part of this, the often unreflected and over-hastened enlargement rounds and association agreements.

Social justice therefore is not only a necessity for the sake of social justice, but an indispensable condition for the survival of democracy. To counter-argue that international competition in times of globalization does not allow for more social justice, is therefore tantamount to saying that democracy cannot be maintained in such times of globalization.

Let us act and respond to the socio-democratic challenge of globalization, with a policy of ethics before even more popular demagogues abuse the people for their evil intentions.

9   Digital Media and Democracy

The digital social media undermine democracy in restricting more and more an open exchange of diverging opinions. They favour the emergence of ego-spaces and echo-spaces which leads to a break-down of the democratic discourse and the radicalization of ideological positions.

Especially the younger generation experiences the digitalization of the media as being the ultimate realisation of their freedom. Little do they realise or care that in the exercise of their freedom they are fully in the hands of a capitalistic system, of digital capitalism.

The difficulties our governments encounter in fighting criminal abuses of new media, from child abuse to weapons dealing on the darknet, put before us the question if we shall have to resign ourselves to that situation. How can we possibly re-establish on a European and international level the prerogative of democratic politics.

To do this without infringing on the basic rights of freedom of expression seems like squaring the circle. It is nevertheless a challenge which must be tackled.

10   THE DEMOCRATIC DEFICIT OF THE EUROPEAN UNION

Already in our Marathon Declaration we drew attention to the democratic deficit of the EU. We pointed out the relative lack of democratic legitimation of the European institutions and the remoteness of the European Parliament from the European citizen.

In the Greek debt crisis, especially the "Troika", called "the institutions", stood for the lack of democratic legitimacy. It has been a particularly painful experience. The imbalance in their mission and lack of democratic legitimacy resulted in financial recovery strategies in which the well-being of the people, of the human individuals, played no role.

The British people have retaliated against the democratic deficit with their Brexit vote. In other European member states anti-European resentments have grown in importance. It is difficult to see that the European institutions have in any respectable way responded to these lessons and warnings. Resisting on all levels the arrogance of power must become a cornerstone of a new European alliance for democracy.

11   CONCLUSIONS

I could not possibly, in my short text, here address all the menaces to democracy and develop in full possible response strategies. I have made an effort here to show how the Greek legacy may serve as an inspiration for the renewal of democracy. In doing so I am full aware that this would need further study and debate. Let me, however, sum up my observations and recommendations as follows:

- On the state of democracy: Admit and identify the democratic deficit, favour a self-critical readiness of the elites.
- On the politics of ethics: Strengthen the ethical capacities of our societies, beginning with the individual citizen, work for a greater balance between the politics of interests and the politics of ethical values and virtues.
- On social transparency and orientation. Lay open the mechanisms which are the driving forces for an ever-greater social division; examine every policy with a view to its social effects.
- On social balance: Address the social imbalance in the constitutions, strengthen social responsibility in the rights of the elites and the social rights of the weaker members of society.

- On oppose the arrogance of power: Expose all manifestations of the arrogance of power, of Parliamentarians no longer feeling obliged to their electors, of the agents of the executive in their dealings with the people, formulate codes of conduct and install remedies to oppose arrogant attitudes.
- On the European Parliament: Lay open its remoteness from the citizen especially of the European Parliament, oblige MEPs to be adequately present in their constituencies, radically improve the public information work and instruments of the EU institutions.
- New alliance of democracy. Strengthen the ranks of the true democrats in Europe! Oppose the emergence of "echo spaces" by making room for new fora for public debate. Do not avoid political controversy but seek to engage in a fruitful debate, especially with those who are of a different ideology and political inclination.

Do we in Europe or the world have a platform where we can discuss, between academics, the citizens and the politicians, all these challenges and the necessary response strategies as the situation warrants it? No, we do not. The EU has established an Observatory on Anti-Semitism in Vienna, an Observatory on Minority Rights in Warsaw. We obviously need, urgently need, an observatory on democracy.

As a very concrete consequence of what I had to say to you today I propose to establish here in Greece—what other location could be more appropriate?—a European Institute for Democracy and Humanity.

And I invite you, the distinguished reader, to support this concrete proposal.

We still have four more years to prepare for the 2500th anniversary of the battle of Salamis. This time we should be well prepared to celebrate it on an international scale. I propose that, besides a tall ship parade and a film documentary, an important element should be a "Salamis 2500 declaration for freedom and democracy". And I suggest that our Marathon 2500 Declaration is a good basis for preparing such a document.

I sincerely hope that the celebrations of the Salamis victory will also mark the end of the Greek financial crisis, a victory for the Greek people and for the Europeans. And that Salamis 2500 will also mark a new start for a more socially just and balanced European democracy.

The Institutional Impact on Economic Development in Iran

Yadollah Dadgar and Rouhollah Nazari

1 INTRODUCTION

Investigating the roots of differences in the economic performance of different countries must of course take into account wider economic considerations. A key question is why some countries are well developed and others less so (Janine 2000). Unsurprisingly, some developing and even some of the least-developed countries have benefited from abundant natural resources, their geopolitical situation and even adequate human capital; yet they suffer from poor economic performance. It is pertinent to compare the such as Iran, with their actual performance. Middle Eastern countries own more than 62% of world gas reserves, and almost 65% of world oil reserves. Middle Eastern countries' share of global gross domestic product (GDP), however, is less than 7%. Iran (as the case study in this chapter

Y. Dadgar (✉)
Economic Department, Beheshty University, Tehran, Iran
e-mail: y_dadgar@sbu.ac.ir

R. Nazari
Ferdowsi University, Mashhad, Iran

© The Author(s) 2018
S. Vliamos, M. S. Zouboulakis (eds.), *Institutionalist Perspectives on Development*, Palgrave Studies in Democracy, Innovation, and Entrepreneurship for Growth, https://doi.org/10.1007/978-3-319-98494-0_6

shows) holds about 16% of world gas reserves and about 14% of oil reserves. But its share of world GDP is less than 1%. Thus, the developmental gap in Iran is much deeper than for some other developing countries. We can compare the potentialities and actual developmental situation of Iran with those of South Korea, Singapore, Malaysia and even Qatar. Iran started its developmental plan alongside those of Brazil, China and Turkey. The product of the plan, however, is very different in Iran as compared with those other nations. Therefore, the key question is why Iran has not succeeded in filling some parts of its developmental gap. What are main causes of this failure? Answers to this question are provided by external and exogenous factors on the one hand, and institutional and endogenous ones on the other. As far as the external factors are concerned, some argue that international sanctions, war in Iraq and natural disasters are responsible for the failure of the developmental plan in Iran. Notwithstanding the impact of the above factors on the unsuccessfulness of the Iranian developmental plan, though, they are not the main factors in this regard. By investigating more deeply we can see that institutional and endogenous factors are the main causes of underdevelopment in Iran. This is the case in some other countries as well (Romer 1990). We believe that the dominance of bad institutions and bad governance are major causes of underdevelopment in some Middle Eastern countries generally, and in Iran particularly. Providing good institutions and reforming public-sector structure could be construed as preconditions of better economic development in Iran. Protection of property rights, proper warranting of contract rights, facilitating business, accountability of the supreme leadership, effective corruption control and obeying the international rules of diplomacy and trade are basic first steps to providing sufficient ground for enhancing development in Iran. In other words, applying a package of optimum management is urgently required to standardize the Iranian economy and save it from its currently less-developed framework (Das and Paksha 2011). By considering these concerns, this chapter will analyze the relationship between development in the Iranian economy and its institutional performance. Here, economic growth has been chosen as a proxy for economic development. Moreover, as mentioned, reforming the institutional framework of the public sector is another surefire way to enhance development in Iran. Accordingly, in this chapter, promoting the crucial elements of good governance, economic freedom and democracy are selected as proxies for the institutional package. Sources of data include the central bank of Iran (CBI 2017), the World Bank and some other statistical centers (Marshal 2016), which are all used to test the hypothesis set out in this chapter.

2   THE DIFFERENT IMPACTS OF INSTITUTIONS ON DEVELOPMENT IN DIFFERENT COUNTRIES (EMPHASIS ON IRAN)

The reasons for and causes of underdevelopment have been debated in so many studies. The causes in question are seen to range from geographical and technical, to historical and cultural ones. Some researchers maintain the importance of the influence of historical and institutional elements on economic development. Others emphasize geographic factors above all; these include distance from the main markets, weather and climate. Yet others argue for the role of historical, cultural and democratic institutions in this regard (Acemoglu et al. 2004; Acemoglu and Robinson 2001, 2016; North 1990). Acemoglu (2009) stresses the role of beliefs as characteristic factors affecting economic growth in developed countries. Thus, different beliefs may produce different institutions, with different impacts on economic growth and development. The rational or ideological approach can have an effect on the institutional framework and ultimately on economic development too (Lessem 2017).

Comparison of developmental trends in North Korea and South Korea could be a brilliant case study in this connection. The influence of certain ideological and political beliefs on the mentality of the leaders in North Korea has created some very destructive institutions, which are responsible for the current poor economic performance in this country (Kim 2017). Conversely, the sovereignty of rational beliefs in South Korea enhances the productive trends in this country (Schwekendiek 2016). By applying good institutions and rational ethics, and benefiting from the experiences of developed countries, South Korea has been led to create efficient and sustainable development.

This in turn reminds us of the comprehensive statement of Michio Morishima (1982), the great Japanese economist, regarding the main causes of Japanese development: "Why has Japan succeeded? Western technology and Japanese ethos".[1] Some of the remarkable institutions behind economic development in South Korea include establishing private property rights, fiscal discipline, efficient market mechanism forces and so on. On the contrary, by abolishing private property rights and nationalizing the capital in North Korea, bad governance took over the whole economy, which destroyed the private sector and market mechanisms altogether.

---

[1] This is also the title of Morishima's famous book.

Unfortunately, in the Iranian economy, especially in the period 2005–2012, it was as of the North Korean administration had been chosen as a role model. By imposing a specific ideology, some pressure groups crowded out the private sector from the economy. Lack of an efficient tax system and the financing of government expenditure through selling crude oil have led to the sovereignty of a rentier government and to Dutch Disease in Iran. By contractual definition all countries which finance above 42 percent of thier public expenditure from non-tax revenue (and for instance and finance it from celling oil) are envolving in Dutch Diseaese. Overall, the Iranian economy suffers from a paucity of good management and from bad institutional frameworks (Dadgar 2017; Sariolghalam 2010).

3   The Interrelationship Between Institutions and Economic Growth

3.1   General Background

A traditional debate in developmental literature has been around the relationship between economic development and political development: which one is the cause and which one is the effect? Some studies (including Lipset 1959) maintain that political development is the main influencing factor for economic development. They indicate that providing democratic institutions is an essential prerequisite for any economic development. According to these findings, creating democratic institutions, and thereby controlling the power of government, could protect property rights and increase the efficacy of the economic system as a whole. The result of the above trend would be to enhance productivity and economic growth. Alternatively, other research argues for the leading role of economic development in achieving political and social development. Such studies maintain that the role of economic elements is to enhance the democratic environment. For instance, on the one hand Knack and Keefer (1995) suggest that there is a significant impact from good institutions on economic growth. Lipset (1959), on the other hand, contends that only the citizens of wealthier countries can participate effectively in political affairs. In this context, economic wellbeing would work as an influential factor in achieving political development.

Proponents of the latter approach argue that the high level of human capital (resulting from economic development) will lead to the application of good policies and so enhance political stability, which in turn will protect property rights and enhance economic growth. Advocates of the former approach promote the crucial influence of political institutions on economic growth and development (Bennedsen et al. 2005; Easterly and Mirvat 2002; Fioretos 2017). Lack of good institutions or the dominance of bad institutions exert a negative effect on economic growth and development. In sum, nowadays the significant impact of institutions on economic development has become too obvious to deny. Thus, the main point here is not about realizing the impact in question; the key debate is rather around "know-how" of its effects on economic development. Nevertheless, the impact of institutions on economic development is indirect and not necessarily clear at first. Institutions affect development in different ways; understanding these plays a central role in implementing the institutions in question. In the next sub-section we posit the ways in question (Glaeser et al. 2004; Hall and Jones 1999; Matsuo 2006; Jalilian et al. 2006).

3.2   Main Channels of Institutional Performance

In this chapter, we posit some good governance indices along with some democratic indices as proxies for the optimum working of institutions in the Iranian economy. The institutional package in this research includes voice and accountability, political stability, government effectiveness, regulatory quality, rule of law, control of corruption and economic freedom. Voice and accountability indicate that citizens have political rights, access to a free press, freedom of expression, freedom of association and so on. Voice itself refers the freedom of speech. Research reveals the significant relationship between democracy and economic growth (Barro 1999; Chen 2014; Laurent 2017). The absence of a standardized democracy in Iran could be partly responsible for the current low level of development in this country. Based on the findings of some studies (Barro 1999 as a typical one), political instability can be seen to worsen productive investment, which in turn detracts from economic growth. Thus there is a negative relationship between political instability and economic growth. Due to prevalence of terrorism in the Middle East, as well as engagement in regional wars, unrest and bad governance, Iran suffers from various kinds of political instability.

Government effectiveness is another sub-index for good governance and also a proxy for optimal management in Iran. Assessing government effectiveness captures perceptions of the quality of public services, the quality of civil services and the degree of their independence from political pressures, as well as the credibility of the government's commitment to such policies. This covers the level of bureaucracy and red tape too. Rule of law, regulatory quality

Table 1   Some empirical studies: Institutions and development

Researchers	Institutional indexes	Findings
Mauro (1995), Fosu (2002)	Political stability and democracy	Positive relationship
Knack and Keefer (1995)	Risk of expropriation and corruption	Significant negative relationship
Barro (1996, 2000)	Rule of law and democracy	Rule of law (positive), democracy (U shape)
	Government size, property rights	Government size (negative), property rights (positive)
Butkiewicz and Yanikkaya (2006)	Rule of law and democracy	Both positive relationships
Laurent (2017), Hilhorst and Weijs (2017)	Democracy	Positive relationship

and control of corruption are other proxies for optimal management and institutions helpful for good performance of the public sector. Inefficient rule of law leads to a decline in economic growth (Barro 1999; Bingham 2011; Carnoy and Shearer 2017). Regularity quality reflects the ability of the government to formulate and implement sound policies and regulations that promote private-sector development. According to Transparency International (TI 2017; World Bank 2016, 2017), corruption is the abuse of entrusted power for private gain. As Kaufman et al. (2006) correctly argue, corruption is a symptom of institutional failure, and it has a negative relationship with economic growth. It prevents innovative activity, weakens the performance of human capital and diverts resources from productive to unproductive activities. In addition to the above list, economic freedom and some of its subindices have their own significant impacts on economic growth and economic development as well. We can thus add them to good governance indices to complete our research package. Table 1 illustrates some empirical studies which have proven the significant relationship between economic development and institutional performance (World Bank Group 2017).

4   Introducing the Model and Analyzing the Results

As this study focuses on the relationship between institutions and economic development in Iran, we are using the following general model:

$$\text{Log}(\text{GDP}) = f\Big(\text{LOG}\big(\text{GDPPER}(-1)\big), \text{Log}(L), \text{Log}(K), \text{Log}(\text{Institopack})\Big)$$

Where the trend of GDP is used for indicating economic growth, instito-pack is a combination of institutional indices, including good governance and those for economic freedom. As above, good governance indices include voice and accountability, political stability, government efficiencies, regulatory quality, rule of law and control of corruption. In order to check the econometrical credibility of the model we use a KPSS test. KPPS is the abreviation of Kwiatkowski-Phillips-Schmidt-Shin, the sure name of four modelists who introduced an econometric test. We have used a GMM (generalized method of moments) estimator as well. Following Alesina et al. (1992) and Bond et al. (2001), we have used lagged per capita income (which is an efficient estimator for controlling the sustainability of economic growth). In the case of economic freedom, we follow Amartya Sen and other experts in this field. Nobel laureate Sen (2000) considers freedom to be a key element for democracy and the main determinant of economic development. Sen demonstrates the positive impact of freedom and democracy on development, even if it does not enhance economic growth directly. Tavares and Wacziarg (2001) also reveal the positive impact of democracy on economic growth via decreasing government expenditure on the one hand and reducing inequality on the other. The links between democracy and general development are, at the same time, debatable in some case studies (Hurlbut 2017).

Accordingly, we have estimated two categories of model. In the first category, we have used seven models for testing good governance in Iran as follows: Model (1) Voice and Accountability, Model (2) Political Stability and Absence of Violence/Terrorism, Model (3) Government Effectiveness, Model (4) Regulatory Quality, Model (5) Rule of Law, Model (6) Control of Corruption and Model (7): Good Governance. Table 2 indicates the results of the estimations of the above models. It shows the impact of good governance indices on economic growth in Iran for the period 1996–2016.

As we see, labor force (L) and physical capital (K) indicate positive and significant impacts on economic growth. Further, there is a positive relationship between per capita income and economic growth. The impacts of good governance indices on economic growth in Iran are significant. The same relationship in models (1), (4) and (6) is relevant but not not significant. Thus, the results clearly imply that improving in terms of good governance indices in Iran would enhance economic development in the country.

Table 2 The impact of good governance indices on economic growth in Iran

	Model (1)	Model (2)	Model (3)	Model (4)	Model (5)	Model (6)	Model (7)
C	0.24 (0.20)	0.51 (0.25)*	2.70 (2.31)**	0.82 (0.48)	−2.20 (−13.14)*	0.66 (0.47)	1.28 (1.33)
LOG(GDPPER(−1))	0.65 (9.36)*	0.29 (1.22)	0.65 (5.58)*	0.41 (1.95)***	0.28 (10.50)*	1.01 (0.22)	0.24 (1.94)***
LOG(L)	0.69 (8.00)*	0.87 (4.23)*	0.68 (3.92)*	0.74 (3.39)*	0.94 (48.70)*	0.99 (4.29)*	0.87 (6.01)*
LOG(K)	0.32 (7.37)*	0.29 (2.20)**	0.16 (2.12)***	0.31 (2.45)**	0.39 (18.12)*	0.22 (1.97)***	0.26 (4.45)*
LOG(VAR)	0.07 (2.09)***	–	–	–	–	–	–
LOG(PSR)	–	−0.05 (−1.46)	–	–	–	–	–
LOG(GER)	–	–	0.11 (2.24)**	–	–	–	–
LOG(RQR)	–	–	–	−0.02 (−0.71)	–	–	–
LOG(RLR)	–	–	–	–	0.07 (8.08)*	–	–
LOG(CCR)	–	–	–	–	–	−0.10 (−1.70)	–
LOG(GGR)	–	–	–	–	–	–	0.12 (3.74)*
R-squared	0.97	0.98	0.97	0.98	0.97	0.98	0.97
D–W	2.13	2.20	2.33	1.96	1.51	2.23	1.86
J statistic	12.81 (0.38)	12.94 (0.37)	11.51 (0.40)	10.96 (0.28)	12.01 (0.45)	6.82 (0.34)	5.59 (0.35)

The t statistics in parenthesis *, **, *** are significant at the level of 1%, 5% and 10% respectively

Table 3 The impact of economic freedom on economic growth in Iran

	Model (1)	Model (2)	Model (3)	Model (4)
C	3.30 (2.68)**	1.57 (4.54)*	3.18 (2.64)**	2.94 (8.92)*
LOG(GDPPER(−1))	0.67 (5.17)*	0.28 (6.74)*	0.61 (5.35)*	0.56 (7.76)*
LOG(L)	0.42 (3.24)**	0.86 (12.75)*	0.53 (4.67)*	0.5 (3.47)*
LOG(K)	0.26 (4.46)**	0.17 (5.14)*	0.26 (2.80)**	0.3 (4.41)*
LOG(GS)	0.18 (2.02)***	–	–	–
LOG(IF)	–	0.19 (8.41)*	–	–
LOG(TF)	–	–	0.004 (2.33)**	–
LOG(EF)	–	–	–	−0.01 (−0.13)
R-squared	0.96	0.97	0.96	0.94
D–W	2.04	1.89	1.90	1.91
J statistic	9.79 (0.55)	5.93 (0.88)	11.09 (0.27)	10.71 (0.47)

The *t* statistics in parenthesis *, **, *** are significant at the level of 1%, 5% and 10% respectively

Next, to test the impact of economic freedom and its sub-indices on economic development, we have estimated four further models. These are: Model (1) Government Spending, Model (2) Investment Freedom, Model (3): Trade Freedom, and Model (4) Economic Freedom. Table 3 shows the results of the estimation of the models in question.

As we see in Table 3, economic freedom and its sub-indices have a positive and significant relationship with economic development in Iran. The relationships in model (4) are relevant, yet not significant.

5   Concluding Remarks

1. One of our conjectures in this chapter concerns the huge developmental gap in Iran. We believe that shortcomings in the institutional environment and deficiencies in Iranian public governance are key factors in this regard. Consequently, we have tested the performance of an institutional package (a combination of good governance and freedom indices) for Iran.

2. The relationship between the voice and accountability index (a proxy for democracy) and economic growth in Iran (a proxy for development) is significantly positive.

3. The coefficient of corruption control for Iran is negative and significant. So, the greater the corruption, the less economic growth there will be. This is also consistent with the findings of a considerable number of empirical studies (Mauro 1995; Gagliadi 2017). The impact of

corruption on the Iranian economy was particularly insidious under the 2005–2012 administration. During this period, the massive scale of government corruption reduced economic growth to minus 7% (Presidential Report 2017; PRC 2016).

4. There is a negative relationship between political instability and economic growth in Iran; the higher the political instability, the lower the motivation for productive investment. International tension led to low productive investment and very low economic growth (−6.7%). The removal of international sanctions from 2016 onward caused relative improvement and higher economic growth in Iran (around 4%).

5. The relationship between economic growth and the rule of law has been demonstrated as positively significant. In periods when the Iranian legal system has worked irrationally, and economic contracts have not been enforced, economic growth declined. Consequently, the economic situation under the 1997–2004 and 2013–2017 administrations shows different results compared with that of the 2005–2012 administration (when Iran suffered from negative economic growth and development).

6. The coefficients of government effectiveness, regulation quality and general good governance in Iran are positive and significant. The more accountable the government is, the greater the level of productivity and economic growth there will be.

7. Estimation of democracy and economic freedom models in Iran indicate that, in relatively democratic periods (1997–2004 and 2013–2017), with relative improvement in political institutions, economic growth has shown a positive trend. Conversely, during periods of bad governance (2005–2012), there is a massive decline in economic growth and development.

References

Acemoglu, D. (2009). *Introduction to modern economic, growth*. Princeton: Princeton University Press.

Acemoglu, D., & Robinson, J. A. (2001). A theory of political transitions. *American Economic Review, 91*(4), 938–963.

Acemoglu, D., & Robinson, J. (2016). *Summary of why nations fail*. San Francisco, CA: Instraread Publishers.

Acemoglu, D., Johansson, S., & Robinson, J. A. (2004). *Institutions as the fundamental cause of long-run growth*. Department of Economics. Cambridge, MA: MIT.

Alesina, A., Ozler, S., Roubini, N., & Swagel, P. (1992). Political instability and economic growth. *Journal of Economic Growth, 1*(2), 189–212.

Barro, R. J. (1996). Determinants of economic growth: A cross-country empirical study. *Journal of Comparative Economics, 26*(4), 822–834.

Barro, R. J. (1999). Determinants of democracy. *Journal of Political Economy, 107*(6), 158–183.

Barro, R. J. (2000). *Rule of law, democracy, and economic performance, index of economic freedom*. Cambridge, MA: Harvard Publishers.

Bennedsen, M., Malchow-Moller, N., & Vinten, F. (2005). *Institutions and growth – A literature survey*. Report 2005–1. London: Center for Economic and Business Research) CEBR).

Bingham, T. (2011). *The rule of law*. London: Penguin Books.

Bond, S., Hoeffler, A., & Temple, J. (2001). *GMM estimation of empirical growth model*. CEPR discussion paper number 3048. London: Centre for Economic Policy Research.

Butkiewicz, L., & Yanikkaya, J. (2006). Institutional quality and economic growth: Maintenance of the rule of law or democratic institutions, or both? *Journal of Economic Modeling, 23*, 648–661.

Carnoy, M., & Shearer, D. (2017). *Economic democracy*. London: Routledge.

CBI. (2017). *The data center of central bank of Iran*. Tehran: CBI.

Chen, J. (2014). *A middle class without democracy*. Oxford: Oxford University Press.

Dadgar, Y. (2017). *Economic analysis*. Tehran (Persian): Gutenberg Press.

Das, A., & Paksha, B. P. (2011). Openness and growth in emerging Asian economies: Evidence from GMM estimations of a dynamic panel. *Economics Bulletin, 31*(3), 2219–2228.

Easterly, W., & Mirvat, S. (2002). *Global development network growth database*. Washington, DC: World Bank.

Fioretos, O. (2017). *International politics and institution in time*. Oxford: Oxford University Press.

Fosu, A. K. (2002). Political instability and economic growth. *American Journal of Economics and Sociology, 61*(1), 329–348.

Gagliadi, F. (2017). Institutions and economic change. *Journal of Comparative Economics, 45*, 213–225.

Glaeser, L. E., La Porta, R., Lopez-de-Silanes, F., & Schleifer, A. (2004). Do institutions cause growth? *Journal of Economic Growth, 9*, 271–303.

Hall, R. E., & Jones, C. I. (1999). Why do some countries produce much more. *Quarterly Journal of Economics, 114*, 83–115.

Hilhorst, D., & Weijs, B. (2017). *People, aid and institutions in socio economic recovery.* Abingdon: Routledge Publishing.

Hurlbut, B. (2017). *Experiments in democracy.* New York: Columbia University Press.

Index of Economic Freedom. (2017). The heritage foundation and Dow Jones & Company, Inc. *Wall Street Journal.*

Jalilian, H., Kirkpatrick, C., & Parker, D. (2006). The impact of regulation on economic growth in developing countries: A cross-country analysis. *World Development, 35*(1). World Bank Publishers.

Janine, A. (2000). Growth and institutions: A review of the evidence. *The World Bank Research Observer, 15*(1). World Bank Publishers.

Kaufman, D., Kraay, A., & Mastruzzi, M. (2006). *Governance matters V: Governance indicators for 1996–2005.* Washington, DC: World Bank.

Kim, B. (2017). *Unveiling the North Korean economy.* Cambridge: Cambridge University Press.

Knack, S., & Keefer, P. (1995). Institutions and economic performance: Cross-country tests using alternative institutional measures. *Economics and Politics, 7*(3), 207–227.

Laurent, B. (2017). *Democratic experiments.* Cambridge, MA: MIT Press.

Lessem, R. (2017). *Embodying integral development.* New York: Routledge Publishers.

Lipset, S. M. (1959). Some social requisites of democracy: Economic development and political legitimacy. *American Political Science Review, 53*, 69–105.

Marshal, M. (2016). Polity IV project.

Matsuo, H. (2006). *The rule of law and economic development: A cause or a result?* Nagoya: Nagoya University Press.

Mauro, P. (1995). Corruption and growth. *Quarterly Journal of Economics, 110*(3), 681–712.

Morishima, M. (1982). *Why has Japan 'succeeded'?* Cambridge: Cambridge University Press.

North, D. (1990). *Institutions institutional change and economic performance.* Cambridge: Cambridge University Press.

PRC. (2016). *Economic report, different years.* Tehran: Parliament Research Center.

Presidential Report. (2017). *Iranian economic performance.* Tehran: Tehran President Office.

Romer, P. M. (1990). Endogenous technological change. *Journal of Political Economy, 98*(5), 71–101.

Sariolghalam, M. (2010). *The evolution of state in Iran.* Kuwait City: Kuwait University Press.

Schwekendiek, D. J. (2016). *South Korea.* New Brunswick: Transaction Publishers.

Sen, A. (2000). *Development as freedom.* New York: Anchor Publishing Center.

Tavares, J., & Wacziarg, R. (2001). How democracy affects growth. *European Economic Review, 45*(8), 1341–1378.

TI. (2017). *Report of indices*. Berlin: Official Office of Transparency International.

World Bank. (2016). *The worldwide governance indicators*. Washington, DC: World Bank Publications.

World Bank. (2017). *World Development Indicators (WDI)*. Washington, DC: World Bank Publications.

World Bank Group. (2017). *World development report*. Washington, DC: World Bank Publications.

PART II

Theoretical Insights of Institutions

Critical Realism in the Analysis of National Innovation Systems

Emmanuel D. Adamides

1 INTRODUCTION

National Innovation Systems (NIS) are networks of institutions operating at the national level, which jointly contribute to the development and diffusion of innovations. As such, they are responsible for the creation, storage and transfer of knowledge, skills, and artefacts that define new technologies and innovative activities (Metcalfe 1995). They provide the framework within which governments form and implement policies to influence the innovation and technology production processes of a country. Having to deal with a "systemic" concept, the study of NIS focuses on the interrelations between institutions, rather than on the institutions themselves.

In general, the adoption of *systems approaches* to innovation, in which the NIS belongs to, is a result of the shift of interest from linear processes of innovation (basic research, followed by applied research, invention, commercialization, and diffusion) to *networked* and *open* ones involving a variety of actors embedded in re-enforcing and balancing *feedback loops*

E. D. Adamides (✉)
University of Patras, Patras, Greece
e-mail: adamides@upatras.gr

© The Author(s) 2018
S. Vliamos, M. S. Zouboulakis (eds.), *Institutionalist Perspectives on Development*, Palgrave Studies in Democracy, Innovation, and Entrepreneurship for Growth, https://doi.org/10.1007/978-3-319-98494-0_7

(Rothwell 1994; Chesbrough 2006; von Hippel 2006). They include essentially institutional-economics-based conceptualizations, such as Regional and Sectoral Innovation Systems (Edquist 1997), and sociological-institutions-based approaches, such as the Multi-Level Perspective (Geels 2010). Under the critical lens of the Science and Technology Studies (STS), NIS is considered as a socially-constructed "construct", developed to serve particular interests, mostly to defend state-driven policies to innovation against the neo-liberal/neo-classical view of *laissez-faire* market drivers (Sharif 2006). From the STS point of view, the interest is to investigate how NIS became "black-boxed" and to open the "black box".

In the conceptualisation and study of NIS, institutions and institutional arrangements are specific to a national economy/society. In this context, institutions are thought as routines/habits guiding everyday activity of individuals and organisations involved in the production, distribution and consumption of novel technologies, and innovative products and processes. Technological *trajectories* and *paradigms* that focus the innovative activities of scientists, engineers and technicians are also considered as institutions (Lundvall 2010). As *learning* is the most important process and knowledge the most important resource in modern economy, one of the most decisive factors for the performance of NIS is the strength and the quality of learning across the institutions and organisations that participate in a NIS. In fact, learning is an interactive socially embedded process that cannot be understood without taking into consideration its institutional and cultural context.

Consequently, one way to see how the institutional setup affects the rate and direction of (technological) innovation is to focus on the relationships and interactions of the actors participating in NIS (Lundvall 2010). Policies can facilitate the flow of qualitative information between actors and organizations, establishing appropriate mechanisms of communication (common language) and shortening the cultural distance between them. These policies will be based on a context-specific diagnosis of any inconsistencies/inefficiencies, as actor relationships differ from NIS to NIS, and the behaviours of agents that are the subjects, or the objects, of these policies are contingent to the rules and norms that reflect the specific (national) institutional setup.

In this paper, we focus on a particular relationship in the context of NIS: the relationship between universities and research centres (RC) on the one hand, and industry on the other, whose role over the last decades has been crucial in the development of novel technologies and innovations. Lately, the role of universities and public research institutes has changed, from independently setting problems and producing and stocking knowledge and expertise to be accessed and used by private and public organisations (users) at their will for (industrial) innovation (Mode 1 society), to working/interacting *with* users in setting and solving problems (Mode 2 society) (Gibbons 2000; Woolgar et al. 2009). Playing this role has not been always and everywhere successful, and the relationship between universities/RC and industry has not been unproblematic and up to the expectations. This has been attributed to asymmetries and policy failures (Komninos and Tsamis 2008; Chaminade et al. 2012) and to different organisational cultures and motivations (Perkmann et al. 2011). Here, our objective is to show that there are deeper the social context-specific structures and mechanisms that are responsible for the experienced failures of these relationships, which innovation policies should address explicitly.

This endeavour requires an appropriate methodological approach. Towards this end, in this paper, our analysis follows a critical realist perspective (Sayer 1992; Lawson 1997) and is based on Bourdieu's theory of the social structures of the economy (Bourdieu 2005a) that can explain the behaviour of economic agents on the basis of a generative structuralism which is compatible with critical realism (Vandenberghe 1999). We use the construct of *symbolic distance* (the discrepancy in symbolic capital) to argue that this is the enabler (causal power) of setting efficient university/RC-industry relationships, as far as learning and the production of innovation in the context of NIS is concerned. We substantiate our analytical approach by tracing the historical evolution of the social spaces (fields) of academic research and industrial production, and through the development of the corresponding social mechanisms, to explain the failure of university/RC-industry relationships in the Greek NIS. Following Lawson's (1997) rationale and taking into account speculation raised (Hodgson 2004), our objective is not to provide a thorough explanation of the phenomenon neither to develop theory, but rather to highlight methodological issues involved in this sort of analysis.

2   University-Industry Relations in the NIS Context

Universities have always been critical institutional actors in National Innovation Systems (Edquist 2005). Over the last years, shortages of government funding and increased competition made universities more "entrepreneurial" in seeking new sources of funding. Hence, at present, in general, in industrialized countries, university faculties are more inclined to participate in joint activities with society and business (Bergman 2010).

Although for some authors universities constitute infrastructural elements of NIS, and their contribution to innovation is through knowledge spillovers, rather than being part of the main chain of the production of knowledge, technology and value, their links with industry seem to constitute a systemic issue, and hence, weak links constitute a systemic problem (Chaminade et al. 2012). In the majority of industrialized countries, universities fulfil similar functions (education, research). However, their role in a specific NIS varies according to the structure of industry, the availability and type of other sources of innovation, as well as to the structure of other institutions (Mowery and Sampat 2005). Similarly, the links between universities and industry take many forms, ranging from research partnerships and provision of research services, through academic entrepreneurship and human resource mobility, to commercialization of the knowledge produced at universities and research centres (Perkmann and Walsh 2007; Perkmann et al. 2013). As knowledge creation and innovation are socially embedded processes (Brown and Duguid 1991), relationships/partnerships (academic engagement) are distinct from other mechanism based on "arms-length" transactional market links (Powell and Grodal 2005) and are the most important form of link. Such relationships are frequently based on (formal and informal) social relationships between individuals in organizations from both sides (Perkmann and Walsh 2007). Hence, individual agents' characteristics play an important role on the outcome of the university-industry relationships (Perkmann et al. 2013).

In general, university-industry relationships are problematic and have been speculated from different perspectives, in different contexts. For instance, it was found that, in the majority of cases, public research units and universities provide just ways of solving problems rather than suggesting new projects (Cohen et al. 2002). On the other hand, there is evidence that industrial partners are opportunists and not truly committed, and that relationships are broken as soon as public funds dry up (Feller et al. 2002; Bergman 2010). The issue of motivation and commitment in participation is very crucial and is a determinant of the sustainability and effectiveness of these relationships (Perkmann et al. 2011; Estrada et al. 2016). In academia, careers are based on the accumulation of reputation through academic publications and there are no actual incentives and motivations for working with industry, except for pure economic purposes if funds are not available otherwise. However, in addition to the misalignment of incentives, the most important obstacle in university-industry relationships is the difference in organizational and institutional culture (Cyert and Goodman 1997; Mowery and Sampat 2005). As a result, firms frequently assess their R&D issues as being irrelevant and of no interest to academia, and vice-versa (Arvanitis et al. 2008), a fact that indicates the existence of a long "cognitive and organizational distance" between these two institutions of NIS (Schartinger et al. 2001; Boschma 2005).

This difference can be attributed to different practices and asymmetries, as far as knowledge and information flows are concerned. Universities and research institutes seek the diffusion of their scientific achievements through publications and other means, whereas firms favour the protection of (proprietary) knowledge through patenting to achieve economic benefits (Welsh et al. 2008). As a result, it has been observed that the less "scientific" is a university/research organization the higher is the probability to cooperate with industry (Arvanitis et al. 2008; Sengupta and Ray 2017).

Overall, although associated with different contexts and NIS, the above observations show a trend attributing the problematic university/RC-industry relationships to cultural, organizational and motivational differences/discrepancies. Of interest is to explain the formation and persistence of these differences, despite deploying a diverse range of policy initiatives to attenuate them. Clearly, such a context-specific analysis should focus on a particular NIS, and in this paper we have chosen to examine the case of university/RC-industry relationships in the Greek NIS. Before, we outline our theoretical toolbox used in the process of analysis, namely critical realism and Bourdieu's theory of the social structure of the economy.

3 CRITICAL REALISM

Critical realism is a philosophy of science that was developed as a critique to naive empirical realism, and assumes a stratified (multi-level) socio-economic ontology (Bashkar 2007; Lawson 1997). Put in the NIS research context, it assumes that the behaviour/performance of a particular NIS is the emergent result of the behaviour of structures of organisations and institutions participating in it, which, in turn, is caused by the behaviour of individuals in organizational structures, which, again, is the emergent result of their personality characteristics influenced by the geo-historical context and positional identities of the individuals, and so on.

Critical realism accepts the relative independence of an ontological domain from the domain of observed events. That is, it accepts that there exists an independent world of (structured) reality (*the domain of the real*) containing generative structures/mechanisms (*of observed events*), which exist in activated or deactivated form, and are independent from the observer. *Mechanisms* create events which constitute the domain of the *actual*, which may also exist independent of the observer. What the observer/researcher experiences from the domain of the actual constitutes the *empirical* domain (Sayer 1992).

There are two fundamental questions that need to be answered when associating the ontological assumptions and epistemological directions of critical realism to the study of systems of organisations and institutions, such as NIS. First, what a philosophy of science (critical realism) has to offer to this domain of inquiry, and, second, what constitutes reality (the domain of the real) in the specific field of study. In answering the first question, the basic argument is that a direct reference to a philosophy of science plays a significant role on the way economics and management theories are created and tested (Lawson 1997; Miller and Tsang 2010), as well as on the shape and form of the subsequent knowledge generated. As systems of innovation are human-made constructs (Sharif 2006), the ability to formulate and resolve policy and performance issues depends on existing philosophies, worldviews and attitudes. After all, the maturity in a discipline can be judged by its practitioners' capacity for philosophical reflection on the fundamental assumptions about reality (ontology) and the process of learning about it (epistemology) (Solem 2003).

The second question concerns the ontological assumptions of the (institutional) approaches to national innovation systems. If NIS are intellectual constructs (Sharif 2006), and materiality and physical laws are absent in decision making, policy making and (inter)organisational behaviour, then, what does constitute reality in their study? In answering, Sayer (2004) indicates that "… there are practices, or constructions, which exist independently of those which (the researchers) can influence". These institutionalised and socially qualified practices that cannot be influenced, effectively, constitute the domain of the and they are referred to as socially real (Fleetwood 2005). This essentially implies a view of organisations, ensembles of organisations, and institutions as structures of positions-practices and relations between them, developed in time and place (Reed 2009). Hence, in a critical realist perspective, social phenomena are conceptualised ontologically, as being constituted by interlinked objects which are, or are part of, structures having innate causal powers (or tendencies) and liabilities, which are activated and mobilised under specific conditions.

This argument presupposes a routinization of social life and the existence of path dependency. This means that some habits and behaviours persist over time, against any "optimising" or "corrective" logic (Lawson 1997) and structures (ensembles of rules, relations and positions) are reproduced. As Lawson (1997) states "… social reality is conceived as intrinsically dynamic and complexly structured, consisting in human agency, structures and contexts of action, none of which is given or fixed, and where each presupposes each other without being reducible to, identifiable with, or explicable completely in terms of, any other." (p. 159).

The critical realist research methodology is driven by a *retroductive* inference procedure and includes a stage of *abduction*. Retroduction moves from the level of the phenomenon identified to a "deeper" level in order to explain the phenomenon and to highlight a causal mechanism responsible (Lawson 2003; Reed 2009). A hypothetical mechanism(s) (the product of abduction) is postulated, which, if it existed, would generate (would be responsible for) the observed phenomenon (events), or a phenomenon different from what was normally expected. Mechanisms are activated, or not, by *causal powers* and *liabilities*, respectively. Mechanisms are postulated and examined through methodological pluralism in research, i.e. a mixture of qualitative and/or quantitative methods (Mingers 2006) using primary and secondary sources of information.

The process of retroduction is facilitated by bringing into question the suitability and applicability of established social theories that form the basis for analytically structured narratives of causal sequences explaining (or not) the particular situation/phenomenon. In a critical realist perspective, an adequate understanding of a situation, as a result of underlying social mechanisms, necessitates, at least, knowledge of:

- how the supposed explanatory mechanism came about initially,
- how (by which processes) it persisted and was reproduced over time,
- which were the specific conditions that were responsible for the appearance and persistence of the situation.

The latter point corresponds to the description and explanation of the structure-position system (mechanism) underlying the situation. Below, after adopting a critical realist perspective, we apply the above inference procedure (as we are not dealing with a combination of known causes for which a *retrodictive* inference mode would be more appropriate Lawson 2003; Arvanitidis 2013) to explain the problematic university-industry relationships in the Greek NIS as result of deeper inconsistencies between the social spaces of university/research and industry. Such an explanation relies on Bourdieu's social practice theory that is briefly described in the following section.

4   THE SOCIAL STRUCTURES OF THE ECONOMY: BOURDIEU'S SOCIAL PRACTICE THEORY

In recent years, new institutional economic theory (North 1990) has been employed for the analysis of NIS and for finding differences among them, rooted in the social construction of institutions, influenced by cultural and historical processes (Scott 2001). Despite the advances made by institutional economics in building the theoretical basis of the institutional approach, institutional economics fall short when comes to explaining how beliefs and rules are (socially) constructed and influence individuals. For filling this gap on the micro-foundation of institutions, the torch of explanation was taken by "new social institutionalists", such as Bourdieu (Sieweke 2014) that explicitly consider cognitive and bodily (micro)processes in the creation of institutions.

Bourdieu can be considered as a post-structuralist social theorist, i.e. argued for a dialectic relationship between structure and agency, that provided a unified theory of social system reproduction and change. The key concepts of his theory are *capital, field, habitus* and *doxa*. Agents carry different forms of *capital* (economic, social, technical, organisational, etc.) and according to the capital they carry, take positions in specialized social spaces called *fields* (the field of research, education, religion, business, etc.—also fields of specific organisations). Capital is both a resource and stake. Fields are arranged in positions that can be analysed independent of the characteristics of their (current) occupants. The orthodox way of behaving in field is called doxa (a term with direct reference to institutional theory (Crawford and Ostrom 1995)). The agents' activity in fields is contingent to the capital they curry, their position in the field, as well as to their habitus. Habitus are dispositions resulting from the agents socialisation and activity in the specific field (internalisation of the structural elements of the field), as well as in other fields, currently and in the past.

Habitus is responsible for conscious and unconscious practices, including cooperation with (or avoidance of) specific individuals.

Capital can be *economic*, which refers to the financial resources that agents can mobilise, *bureaucratic*, associated with the possession of formal positions, *social* that values the involvement in networks of individuals, *technical* that refers to skills related to the development and use technologies, *organisational*, i.e. knowledge of procedures and rules and competency in their uses, and *informational* which is related to privileged access to information and knowledge (Bourdieu 1998). Actors possess combinations of these (and other) forms. All forms of capital are interrelated and contribute to *symbolic capital* according to the specific meaning given to it in each specific field, i.e. the combination of the forms of capital that counts more in the specific field, which provides status, power and recognition, and hence influences practice. The structure of the capital of a specific field is embedded in the practices of a field and the agents' habitus mediating their behaviour.

In institutional terms, the concept of habitus seeks to explain the relationship between the practices of agents (micro) and institutional objective structures (macro) (Bourdieu 2005b), being understood as a subjective system of internalized structures, schemes of perception, as well as actions that are common to a group. It is a mediational construct that attributes actions to subjective dispositions and to objective positions (in a field) (Vandenberghe 1999). As such, it provides the means to identify and describe underlying generative mechanisms in terms of a social space/field that produces specific observable effects/events only if the context is right (Bourdieu 1998) (causal power).

5   A Critical Realist Perspective
on the University-Industry Relations: The Case
of Greece

5.1   Industry and Innovation

In the neo-institutional "varieties of capitalism" school of political economy, Greece has been traditionally positioned in the "ambiguous position" (Hall and Soskice 2001) between liberal and coordinated market economies of "family-state capitalism" variety, or in the Mediterranean model along with other Southern European countries (Almond 2011). It is characterized by firms (large and SME) owned and managed by families or powerful individuals (Papadakis 2006) with an important role deserved for the state as producer, customer and regulator. This has been the result of the evolution of Greek economy since the end of WW II.

The end of the German occupation and the Civil War that followed left the Greek productive system in ruins. Since the early fifties, the restart of economic activity was largely based on foreign aid, agricultural production and foreign investments in industry to satisfy increasing domestic demand. Demand was triggered by money transfers from Greeks working abroad, as well as from tourism and international shipping (Vergopoulos 1987). This trend continued in the 60s and 70s, as the economic growth of the European South mirrored the economic wellbeing of the European North. In the context of this "imported" growth, Greek entrepreneurs and managers were focusing on the domestic market importing products or producing locally their substitutes. The only investments in manufacturing goods that could be exported were made by multinationals, or though foreign capital, mainly in five mature industries of limited innovation potential (refineries, products of petrol, chemical products, basic metals and shipbuilding).

In these conditions, enrichment and fortune-making in Greece was made possible without the necessary social, political and institutional modernization (Vergopoulos 1987). Inevitably, the oil crisis of the 70s that followed created severe problems in the foreign-technology- and energy-dependent industries and shifted business interest towards more traditional, light industries (clothes, textiles, shoes, beverages, non-metallic minerals, etc.) based on more traditional technologies. The crisis of Greek industry and management was further intensified in the 80s where extensive deindustrialization occurred.

Things started to change in the mid-nineties, where some attempts towards shareholder-owned public-traded firms and the related model of capitalism were made. These efforts were intensified after Greece joined the EMU, but in reality the underlying domestic business model and management practices remained intact, despite the dynamism that some Greek firms showed when they internationalised in Eastern Europe and the Balkans (Spanos et al. 2001). At the same time, as Greece's membership to the EMU eliminated market barriers, Greek industrial firms started to lose their domestic competiveness and market shares, mainly due to lack of innovativeness (Adamides et al. 2003). Subsequently, their products were displaced by foreign imports of technological superiority, for which the demand was financed by loans of low ECB interest rates (Mitsopoulos and Pealagidis 2009). This resulted in a new wave of de-industrialisation, and only the construction and agrifood sectors and a small number of high-technology firms showed dynamism (Voudouris et al. 2000). Nevertheless, despite their specialization and high technology basis, these sectors were mostly inwards looking and hence very vulnerable in the time of crisis that followed (Aghion and Roulet 2011).

An important characteristic of the Greek variety of capitalism has been the very large percentage of very small independent (family) firms. Small size and independence has had its costs: inability to take advantage of economies of scale, very weak innovation activity, difficulty of the state to collect taxes and check for undeclared work, and uncertain business continuity after the firm's founders/owners were withdrawn. Small size and environmental uncertainty resulted in short-termism and foreclosure, as well as unwillingness to cooperate in investing and managing common resources (Makridakis et al. 1997; Adamides et al. 2003; Adamides and Tsinopoulos 2015), while small business cooperation has concentrated on agreeing prices and exercising lobbying in governmental agencies.

In this environment, the dominant characteristics of modern Greek management culture have been high levels of collectivism, high power distance (level of acceptance of distribution of power within an organization) and a tendency to risk avoidance. In international and national studies (Hofstede 1997; Papalexandris 1999), Greece had the highest score in the uncertainty avoidance index. Both historical and geopolitical factors contribute to the insecurity and risk avoidance of Greek managers (Broome 1996). As a result, managers of Greek companies that have been operating in this relatively unstable environment have exhibited a reluctance to get involved in efforts towards innovation in products and process (Komninos and Tsamis 2008). Studies have shown that they tended to perceive anything new as rather threatening and that this induced resistance to change (Hofstede 1997).

Managers in secure jobs in large organizations were more likely to accept lower levels of uncertainty and to retain the ideas and practices that proved to be successful (Adamides et al. 2003). In other words, they were reluctant to initiate innovations in products and services that would result in organizational renewal and redistribution of power. This partly explains the fact that even in the first seven years of the 00s that the growth of the Greek economy was well above the rest of the EU countries the innovation activity of the Greek firms was reduced. The dominant form of technological modernization continued to be technology transfer in the form of imported machinery and equipment (Komninos and Tsamis 2008; Giannitsis et al. 2009).

5.2   *Research in Universities and Public Research Institutes*

Until the 70s, universities in Greece were straggling to satisfy the market demand for graduates, especially engineers and scientists. In the late 60s and 70s, new universities were established and the number of graduates was increasing. However, the expectations and orientation of teaching programmes and their graduates were towards satisfying the immediate demand of the domestic economy: to facilitate technology transfer from abroad, to operationally support the flourishing construction industry, and to cover the ever increasing demand for public and private education/ training at the primary and secondary level (Kintis 2001).

In the same period, the higher education system had a limited (insufficient) number of high rank faculty that held full power over research, teaching and staffing decisions. The rise of PASOK (Socialist Party) in government in 1981 was accompanied by a new legal framework for higher education. The initiatives provided to supporting staff (assistants) to complete PhD degrees locally or abroad, resulted in a massive "professorisation". However, old professors continue to exert power over the old staff through the supervision (and award) of PhDs, and through the promotion of new lower level professors to higher ranks.

At that time, Greece joined the EEC, and a new source of income was possible for the poorly-paid academic staff. As a new member with weak economy and an infant research and technology production system, Greece was in a favourable position for participating in EEC-sponsored research programmes. Hence, Greek universities and research institutes became preferred partners in European research and development consortia. Before that, government and industry support for research was very limited (and continued to be, lacking European funding by far). This access to EEC-based financial resources by high rank professors allowed them to continue exercising power over lower level ones, as well as researchers and graduate students. Given the backwardness of local economy, as far as demand for technology and innovation was concerned, research agendas and priorities were set by foreign partners and were out of pace with the needs of the local economic actors.

Regarding research funds distribution, in the early 80s research was undertaken mainly by the state research centres (approx 70%), 15% by private companies (mainly MNC), and only 14% by the universities. In the late 90s this changed to approx. 50% by the universities, 23% by research centres, and 28% by private companies. In 2013, research carried out in universities and research centres amounted to almost two thirds. An important initiative towards the (re)direction or research activity was the establishment of the General Secretariat of Research and Technology of the Ministry of Development in 1982 which contributed to the organization and management of the Greek Innovation System.

As research was driven by European competitive programmes, publishing in international scientific journals has been the main interest and priority of Greek academics. As a result, the performance of Greece, in metrics, such as the publications per researcher and citations per researcher, is well above more technologically advanced countries. A closer look at publications metrics, however, reveals a very low number of publications involving private (firms) and public institutions (DIW Econ 2016). EU institutions, multinational companies and foreign companies have benefited most from the results of these research programmes as research efforts in Greek universities and research centres continued to be out of pace with the demands of the domestic industry (Karra and Tolias 2012).

6 The Fields of Industry and Research in Greece as Underlying Causal Mechanisms: Homologies, Symbolic Distance and Idle Mechanisms

The previous two sections outlined the historical development of the social spaces (fields) of academia and industry in Greece by highlighting persisting trends in the behaviours of their principal agents. Structurally, "Bourdieu-wise", the current field of industry in Greece can be mapped along two dimensions: one, along the continuum national/domestic-international organisations, as far as range of activity is concerned, and the other along the dimension of ownership, i.e. public or private. This results in the formation of four quadrants: public international organizations (very few are present in Greece—can be limited to EU-related organizations), private international companies (MNC), and domestic public and private organizations. Each quadrant has distinct symbolic capital, as far as quantity and composition is concerned, and motivates actors accordingly.

For instance, EU-related organizations hold, and are principally interested in accumulating, organizational and economic capital to select, finance and support projects. Technical and informational capital are not of primary interest to them, as their main objective is to distribute economic resources. Economic capital is the basic asset for position taking (and a stake) for domestic and international companies, whereas obviously organizational capital is the main asset of national public organizations.

Domestic private organizations that are required to act as the locomotive of the Greek National Innovation System hold economic capital and are longing (especially, in the years of the economic crisis) to have fast access to economic capital as an input but also as an output of their operations. Accumulation of organizational capital has also been important to them, in order to be able to cope with the complexity and the bureaucracy of the business environment and the byzantine processes of the Greek State (despite late reforms). Social and informational capital have been of lower importance, while accumulation of technical/technological and information capital has been at odds with their interest of fast access to financial results and their short-termism in their strategic behaviour. As the development of technology, technological innovation and absorptive capacity require time, they have been more inclined to import and use ready-made technology.

Of course business strategies are the result of decisions made by individual managers who carry their habitus in the specific field(s) where decisions are made and actions are taken. Managers have a different culture from academics and a different agenda, as far as their positions and careers are concerned. Given the specific capital distribution in the fields of business their interest is to accumulate capital that contributes more to the symbolic capital of the field (economic and organizational capital).

Similarly, in the field of academic research, technology and innovation production, the activity of the main actors can be mapped in two dimensions. One dimension can be associated with the size of the technology and innovation producing organizations (research groups/laboratories/organisations), i.e. from small to large groups, whereas the other can be associated with their degree of specialization. There are groups that have a narrow specialization, as far as the object of their research is concerned, and groups that are involved in a wide range of projects for different technologies. Large groups have the resources to undertake a wide range of projects and hence they have, and are interested in accumulating, social capital for making contacts with a wide range of stakeholders in academic as well as in funding institutions. They also have, and seek, economic capital to be able to attract high-level collaborators for additional projects. Bureaucratic and organizational capital are also assets for them, as they are involved in different domains with diverse stakeholders.

On the opposite side, small specialized groups manage to survive due to their accumulation of specialized technical capital, as well as organizational capital to deal efficiently with project formation, funding and project management. Social and economic capital are always at stake. Technical capital is also the main asset for large specialized groups, who also have (and seek) informational capital (to be able to participate in decision-making in international scientific forums and steer research in directions favourable to them), as well as bureaucratic to take advantage of their size and position in the field. Small groups of limited specialization struggle to survive through forming and maintaining links with more powerful actors. They seek economic and technical capital to be able to keep their position.

Juxtaposing the two maps (industry and academia/research), one can clearly see the differences in symbolic capital across all quadrants. This signifies the absence of *homologies* (common ground and interest in the accumulation of the same type or capital) (Bourdieu 2005a) and a long *symbolic distance* (difference in the composition of symbolic capital) among them. As a consequence, actors of different habitus in different fields cannot be motivated by the cooperation/knowledge exchange mechanisms that remain inactive, as causal powers are suppressed. This can explain the poor university-industry relationships in the Greek National Innovation System which contribute negatively to its performance. In contrast, in other countries, e.g. Scandinavian countries, different historical developments resulted in fields of different structure and short symbolic distance (expressed in the importance given to industrial research) that enabled productive university-industry engagements (mechanisms), which, in turn, contributed to the performance of the corresponding National Innovation Systems.

7   CONCLUSIONS

In the context of National Innovation Systems, the relationships among institutional actors are of particular importance for the transfer of knowledge and the production of innovation. As over the last years, universities have started to play an economic, in addition to their academic role, the relationships between universities and industry have become even more important for the production of innovation. Nevertheless, at least in some NIS, this relationship remains problematic, as a result of the historical roles of these two institutions in the classic sequential model of production. This is mirrored in social structures that have been reproduced over the years and in the persisting distinct identities of the participating agents ("homo academicus" and "homo fabricus", respectively).

Through the adoption of a critical realist stance, in this paper, we have provided an approach for the analysis of university—industry relationships, exemplified in the realities of the Greek National Innovation System. We searched for deeper social structures and developed a structured description of them based on Bourdieu's social practice theory. In the same line, we showed how a historical analysis of the construction and reproduction of social spaces (academic and industrial production fields) could help in the identification of the underlying social mechanisms (symbolic distances) and the dispositions (habitus) of agents that participate in them and are responsible for their activation. A retroductive inference procedure based on the assessment of homologies between the two fields led to the acceptance of symbolic distance as the underlying reason for the observed performance of the relationships.

Clearly, the objective of the paper was to outline the process or analysis, rather than to demonstrate concrete results for the case, an enterprise that would require much more additional information, analysis and space. However, even at this level, it becomes apparent that adopting critical realism leads to being critical on "taken for granted" assumptions and related policies for fostering relationships in NIS, such as funding joint academia-industry projects. The underlying mechanism (discrepancies in symbolic capital) seems to suggest "deeper" interventions, such as providing entrepreneurship education at primary and secondary levels, or giving incentives for easy career moves between universities and industry and vice-versa. Nevertheless, as policies for NIS remain a complex issue, they are the subject of different research efforts and related publications.

REFERENCES

Adamides, E. D., & Tsinopoulos, C. D. (2015). Survival in economic crisis through forward integration: The role of resilience capabilities. In R. Bhamra (Ed.), *Organisational resilience: Concepts, integration and practice* (pp. 103–124). London: CRC Press – Taylor & Francis Group.

Adamides, E. D., Stamboulis, Y., & Kanellopoulos, V. (2003). Economic integration and strategic change: The role of managers' mental models. *Strategic Change Journal, 12*(2), 69–82.

Aghion, P., & Roulet, A. (2011). *Repenser l'État. Pour une social-démocratie de l'innovation.* Paris: Éditions du Seuil.

Almond, P. (2011). Nations, regions and international HRM. In T. Edwards & C. Rees (Eds.), *International human resource management* (pp. 50–66). New York: FT/Prentice Hall.

Arvanitidis, P. A. (2013). Critical realism: The philosophical underlabourer of heterodox economics. *Bulletin Political Economy, 7*(2), 199–221.

Arvanitis, S., Kubil, U., & Woerter, M. (2008). University-industry knowledge transfer in Switzerland: What university scientists think about co-operation with private enterprises. *Research Policy, 37,* 1865–1883.

Bashkar, R. (2007). *A realist theory of science.* London: Verso Books.

Bergman, E. M. (2010). Knowledge links between European universities and firms: A review. *Papers in Regional Science, 89*(2), 311–333.

Boschma, R. A. (2005). Proximity and innovation: A critical assessment. *Regional Studies, 39,* 1865–1883.

Bourdieu, P. (1998). *Practical reason.* Cambridge: Polity Press.

Bourdieu, P. (2005a). *The social structures of the economy.* Cambridge: Polity Press.

Bourdieu, P. (2005b). Principles of economic anthropology. In N. J. Smelser & R. Swedberg (Eds.), *The handbook of economic sociology* (pp. 49–74). Princeton: Princeton University Press.

Broome, B. (1996). *Exploring the Greek mosaic: A guide to intercultural communication in Greece.* New York: Intercultural Press.

Brown, J. S., & Duguid, P. (1991). Organizational learning and communities-of-practice: Towards a unified view of working, learning and innovation. *Organization Science, 2,* 40–57.

Chaminade, C., Intarakumnerd, P., & Sapprasert, K. (2012). Measuring systemic problems in national innovation systems: An application to Thailand. *Research Policy, 41,* 1476–1488.

Chesbrough, H. (2006). *Open innovation: The new imperative for creating and profiting from technology.* Cambridge, MA: Harvard Business School Publishing.

Cohen, W. M., Nelson, R. R., & Walsh, J. P. (2002). Links and impacts: The influence of public research on industrial R&D. *Management Science, 48*(1), 1–23.

Crawford, S. E. S., & Ostrom, E. (1995). A grammar of institutions. *American Political Science Review, 89*(3), 582–600.

Cyert, R. M., & Goodman, P. S. (1997). Creating effective university-industry alliance: An organizational learning perspective. *Organizational Dynamics, 25,* 45–57.

DIW Econ. (2016). *The impact of research on Greek economic growth.* Athens: Dianeosis Research and Policy Institute.

Edquist, C. (Ed.). (1997). *Systems of innovation: Technologies, institutions and organizations.* London: Routledge.

Edquist, C. (2005). Systems of innovation: Perspectives and challenges. In J. Fagerberg, D. C. Mowery, & R. R. Nelson (Eds.), *Oxford handbook of innovation* (pp. 181–208). Oxford: Oxford University Press.

Estrada, I., Faems, D., Martin Cruz, N., et al. (2016). The role of interpartner dissimilarities in industry-university alliances: Insights from a comparative case study. *Research Policy, 45*(10), 2008–2002.

Feller, I., Ailes, C. P., & Roessner, J. D. (2002). Impacts of research universities on technological innovation in industry: Evidence from engineering research centers. *Research Policy, 31*, 457–474.

Fleetwood, S. (2005). Ontology in organization and management studies: A critical realist perspective. *Organization, 12*(2), 197–222.

Geels, F. W. (2010). Ontologies, socio-technical transitions (to sustainability), and the multi-level perspective. *Research Policy, 39*(4), 495–510.

Giannitsis, T., Zografakis, S., Kastelli, I., et al. (2009). *Competitiveness and technology in Greece.* Athens: Papazisis Publishers (in Greek).

Gibbons, M. (2000). Mode 2 society and the emergence of context sensitive science. *Science and Public Policy, 27*(3), 159–163.

Hall, P. A., & Soskice, D. (2001). An introduction to varieties of capitalism. In P. A. Hall & D. Soskice (Eds.), *Varieties of capitalism: The institutional foundations of comparative advantage* (pp. 1–68). Oxford: Oxford University Press.

Hodgson, G. M. (2004). Some claims made for critical realism in economics: Two case studies. *Journal of Economic Methodology, 11*(1), 53–75.

Hofstede, G. (1997). *Culture and organization: Software for the mind.* London: McGraw-Hill International.

Karra, S. C., and Y. A. Tolias. 2012. Greek universities and knowledge transfer performance: Assessment, implications and prospects. Paper presented at the 2th International Conference of the Economic Society of Thessaloniki, Thessaloniki, 11–12 October 2012.

Kintis, A. A. (2001). *Greek universities in the beginning of the new century.* Athens: Gutenberg (in Greek).

Komninos, N., & Tsamis, A. (2008). The system of innovation in Greece: Structural asymmetries and policy failures. *International Journal of Innovation and Regional Development, 1*(1), 1–23.

Lawson, T. (1997). *Economics and reality.* London: Routledge.

Lawson, T. (2003). *Reorienting economics.* London: Routledge.

Lundvall, B.-Ä. (2010). Introduction. In B.-Ä. Lundvall (Ed.), *National systems of innovation: Towards a theory of innovation and interactive learning* (pp. 1–19). London: Anthem Press.

Makridakis, S., Caloghirou, Y., & Papagiannakis, L. (1997). The dualism of Greek firms and management: Present state and future implications. *European Management Journal, 15*(4), 381–402.

Metcalfe, S. (1995). The economic foundations of technology policy: Equilibrium and evolutionary perspectives. In P. Stoneman (Ed.), *Handbook of the economics of innovation and technological change* (pp. 409–512). Oxford: Blackwell Publishers.

Miller, K. D., & Tsang, E. W. K. (2010). Testing management theories: Critical realist philosophy and research methods. *Strategic Management Journal, 32,* 139–158.

Mingers, J. (2006). *Realising systems thinking: Knowledge and action in management science.* New York: Springer.

Mitsopoulos, M., & Pelagidis, T. (2009). Vikings in Greece: Kleptocratic interest groups in a closed, rent-seeking economy. *Cato Journal, 29*(3), 399–416.

Mowery, D. C., & Sampat, B. N. (2005). Universities in national innovation systems. In J. Fagerberg, D. C. Mowery, & R. R. Nelson (Eds.), *Oxford handbook of innovation* (pp. 209–239). Oxford: Oxford University Press.

North, D. C. (1990). *Institutions, institutional change and economic performance.* Cambridge: Cambridge University Press.

Papadakis, V. M. (2006). Do CEOs shape the process of making strategic decisions? Evidence from Greece. *Management Decision, 44*(3), 367–394.

Papalexandris, N. 1999. *Greece: From ancient myths to modern realities.* Globe Anthology.

Perkmann, M., & Walsh, K. (2007). University-industry relations and open innovation: Towards a research agenda. *International Journal of Management Reviews, 9*(4), 259–280.

Perkmann, M., Neely, A., & Walsh, K. (2011). How should firms evaluate success in university-industry alliances? A performance measurement system. *R&D Management, 41*(2), 202–2016.

Perkmann, M., Tartari, V., McKelvey, M., et al. (2013). Academic engagement and commercialisation: A review of the literature on university–industry relations. *Research Policy, 42,* 423–442.

Powell, W. W., & Grodal, S. (2005). Networks of innovators. In J. Fagerberg, D. C. Mowery, & R. R. Nelson (Eds.), *Oxford handbook of innovation* (pp. 56–85). Oxford: Oxford University Press.

Reed, M. I. (2009). Critical realism in critical management studies. In M. Alvesson, T. Bridgman, & H. Willmott (Eds.), *The Oxford handbook of critical management studies* (pp. 52–75). Oxford: Oxford University Press.

Rothwell, R. (1994). Towards the fifth-generation innovation process. *International Marketing Review, 11*(1), 7–31.

Sayer, A. (1992). *Method in social science: A realistic approach.* London: Routledge.

Sayer, A. (2004). Foreword: Why critical realism? In S. Fleetwood & S. Ackroyd (Eds.), *Critical realist applications in organisation and management studies* (pp. 6–20). London: Routledge.

Schartinger, D., Schibany, A., & Gassler, H. (2001). Interactive relations between universities and firms: Empirical evidence for Austria. *Journal of Technology Transfer, 26*, 255–268.

Scott, W. R. (2001). *Institutions and organizations* (2nd ed.). Thousand Oaks, CA: Sage Publications.

Sengupta, A., & Ray, A. S. (2017). University research and knowledge transfer: A dynamic view of ambidexterity in British universities. *Research Policy, 46*(5), 881–897.

Sharif, N. (2006). Emergence and development of the national innovation systems concept. *Research Policy, 35*(5), 745–766.

Sieweke, J. (2014). Pierre Bourdieu in management and organization studies – A citation context analysis and discussion of contributions. *Scandinavian Journal of Management, 30*(4), 532–543.

Solem, O. (2003). Epistemology and logistics: A critical overview. *Systemic Practice and Action Research, 16*(6), 437–454.

Spanos, Y., Prastacos, G., & Papadakis, V. (2001). Greek firms and EMU: Contrasting SME and large-sized enterprises. *European Management Journal, 19*(6), 638–648.

Vandenberghe, F. (1999). "The real is relational": An epistemological analysis of Pierre Bourdieu's generative structuralism. *Sociological Theory, 17*(1), 32–67.

Vergopoulos, K. (1987). Economic crisis and modernization in Greece. *International Journal of Political Economy, 17*(4), 106–140.

Von Hippel, E. (2006). *Democratizing innovation*. Cambridge, MA: MIT Press.

Voudouris, I., Lioukas, S., Makridakis, S., & Spanos, Y. (2000). Greek hidden champions: Lessons from small, little-known firms in Greece. *European Management Journal, 18*(6), 663–674.

Welsh, R., Glenna, L., Lacy, W., et al. (2008). Close enough but not too far: Assessing the effects of university-industry research relationships and the rise of academic capitalism. *Research Policy, 37*, 1854–1864.

Woolgar, S., Coopmans, C., & Neyland, D. (2009). Does STS mean business? *Organization, 16*(1), 5–30.

From Commons Dilemmas to Social Solutions: A Common Pool Resource Experiment in Greece

Paschalis Arvanitidis and Fotini Nasioka

1 INTRODUCTION

The common pool resources (CPR) is a special category of goods with two main attributes: non-excludability, meaning that it is too difficult (i.e. too expensive) to exclude someone from using them, and rivalry, meaning that consumption by someone reduces availability to others (Ostrom 1990, 2003). These characteristics make possible overuse of the resource giving rise to conflicts of interest (Ghosh 2007); a situation in which users have to choose between overexploiting the common good to maximise their short-term personal returns, and refraining from doing so for the shake of the long-term, common benefit and the sustainability of the resource (Ostrom 2010a). A term which is commonly used to refer to

P. Arvanitidis (✉) • F. Nasioka
University of Thessaly, Thessaly, Greece
e-mail: parvanit@uth.gr; fotnasio@uth.gr

© The Author(s) 2018
S. Vliamos, M. S. Zouboulakis (eds.), *Institutionalist Perspectives on Development*, Palgrave Studies in Democracy, Innovation, and Entrepreneurship for Growth,
https://doi.org/10.1007/978-3-319-98494-0_8

125

such a situation is 'social dilemma' or 'social trap' in CPR (Kollock 1998; Ostrom 1998, 2010b; Van Lange et al. 2013).

Over the years, many scholars (e.g. Kollock 1998; Lichbach 1996; Vatn 2007) have discussed such social dilemmas arising in public goods and environmental resources, whereas others (e.g. Davis and Holt 1993; Isaac and Walker 1988; Isaac et al. 1994) have conducted experiments to explore precisely how individuals behave in such situations. In turn, Ostrom (2009, 2010a), among others, has used experiments and games to shed light on social dilemmas individuals face in CPR and to offer insights for dealing with them. In such games, conventional game theory proclaims that rational individuals have actually no choice but to maximize their personal returns, reaching appropriation levels at a Nash equilibrium that is above the social optimum (Cárdenas and Ostrom 2006; Ostrom 1998, 2010a). As such, the resource is overused and overexploited and so gradually depleted and led to degradation and destruction. This, rational choice models assert, is inevitable even in the case that some individuals decide to cooperate, opting for a sustainable use of the resource (Ostrom 2009). Others, theory predicts, will free-ride on the contributions of the cooperators leading eventually to 'the tragedy of the commons' (Hardin 1968). Therefore, what is required is an external mediation, where power to enforce the sustainable use of the resource is assigned either to a central authority or to a third party (Ostrom 1989).

However, extensive field and laboratory research has established that users enjoying good communication and feedback about the effect of their actions on a CPR would craft institutions that enable them to overcome commons dilemmas and to sustainably manage the resource (Carpenter 2000; Mason and Phillips 1997; Ostrom 2009). Key factors that increase cooperation in such situations is the existence of trust and reciprocity among involved parties, enable them to build a reputation for being trustworthy, as well as previous experience and engagement in collective action (Berg et al. 1995; Chaudhuri et al. 2002; Ortmann et al. 2000; Ostrom 1998, 2011; Putnam 1993). This is also the case in CPR dilemma experiments conducted in repeated games. Studies (e.g. Ahn et al. 2011; Cárdenas and Ostrom 2006; Ostrom and Walker 1991; Ostrom et al. 1994) have found that the possibility of encountering the same individuals in subsequent rounds is likely to increase cooperative behaviour, even under the condition of anonymity. This is because interaction with the same people allows participants to acquire information, to credibly signal their intentions to others (including readiness to punish defectors) and to build reputation and trust, all of which are crucial for reciprocal behaviour and the emergence of cooperative equilibria (Cárdenas and Ostrom 2006).

In addition, experimental findings on social dilemmas have revealed that face-to-face communication is not simply a 'cheap talk' (i.e. non-binding costless communication), but has an important effect in fostering cooperation among participants (Ahn et al. 2011; Cárdenas and Ostrom 2006; Kollock 1998; Ostrom 1998; Ostrom et al. 1992; Sally 1995). Face-to-face communication allows players to effectively exchange powerful signals, embodied even in body language, facial expressions and eye movements, which are beyond conscious manipulation and cannot be mimicked be free riders (Ahn et al. 2004; Poteete et al. 2010). These allow individuals to build trust amongst them, to mould a group identity and to establish informal arrangements and norms that make cooperation among players credible (Ahn et al. 2011; Janssen et al. 2011; Kollock 1998; Ostrom 1998; Ostrom and Nagendra 2007). As such, Sally (1995) concludes that face-to-face communication in repeated experiments significantly raises the cooperation rate by 40 percentage points, on average, as compared to no communication among subjects. However, as stakes increase or as the game closes to an end, the temptation to cheat on prior agreements increase and communication becomes less efficacious (Ostrom 1998).

Changing the rules of the game by using scarce resources to punish those who do not cooperate or keep agreements is not regarded as a viable option in CPR experiments. This is because participants face a kind of a second-order social dilemma (of equal or greater difficulty) in any effort to use costly sanctions to punish defectors (Heckathorn 1989; Oliver 1980), a situation which conventional rational choice theory predicts that would lead to failure. Yet, empirical evidences in many field settings and laboratory experiments reveal that participants do exactly this, that is, they make agreements and use monitoring mechanisms and graduated sanctions to enforce compliance (Fehr and Gächter 2000; Ostrom 1990, 1998; Ostrom et al. 1992; Sefton et al. 2007; Yamagishi 1986). Interestingly, scholars found that not only subjects are willing to pay a fee in order to fine noncooperators, but also that when sanctioning is combined with face-to-face communication outcomes improve substantially and defections are reduced (Ostrom et al. 1992).

Aiming to contribute to the above literature, the current paper uses an experimental setting to explore the ability of small groups of individuals by communicating with each other to cooperate and to form institutions that overcome commons dilemmas. For this purpose, three experiment sessions were undertaken with 77 final-year undergraduate students of Economics studying at the University of Thessaly in Greece. The game was played in eight rounds, where every two the rules were slightly changed. The study recorded the decisions of the subjects in each round examining whether, under different communication conditions, they would refrain from personal maximisation towards the sustainable use of the CPR. The purpose and design of the game was primarily pedagogical. However, from the beginning one of the goals was to conduct the sessions in such a manner that the results could be used for research purposes. To the best of our knowledge this is the first time that such a CPR dilemma experiment is reported using Greek subjects. Following this short introduction, the rest of the text is structured as follows. The next section outlines, respectively, the design of the game and the results of the experiment, whereas the final section concludes highlighting the key findings emerged.

2   THE GAME

Aiming to shed some preliminary light on how Greeks would behave in simple social dilemma situations we conducted a typical laboratory CPR experiment similar to that of Ahn et al. (2011) (for a more detailed discussion on such experiments see Anderies et al. 2011). However, in an attempt to explore further the role that sanctions play in enhancing cooperation and collective action, we extended the original game by allowing subjects to punish noncooperators (or individuals who do not keep agreements) at a cost to themselves.

Following many other experiment studies in public goods and CPR (inter alia: Carpenter 2000; Fischer et al. 2004; Isaac and Walker 1988; Isaac et al. 1994; Mason and Phillips 1997; Ostrom and Walker 1991; Ostrom et al. 1992) we used university students as subjects. These were final year undergraduates, studying at the Department of Economics at the University of Thessaly, Greece. Carrying out the recommendations of Anderies et al. (2011), data on the participants were collected through a questionnaire that was filled in by the subjects at the end of the experiment. The questionnaire recorded basic sociodemographic characteristics along with views, attitudes and aspects of their behaviour that the relevant literature (e.g. Anderies et al. 2011; Kollock 1998; Ostrom 1998) acknowledges as significant for facilitating cooperation in CPR dilemmas. All subjects were Greek nationals; their gender composition was 57.9%

male and 42.1% female and their average age was somewhat above 21 years, with the oldest student being 40 years old. Participants had met before in classes and in other occasions, and so they knew each other to an extent. Therefore, they had a history of trust, reciprocity and reputation that was not unknown to subjects at the time of the experiment. The experiment was conducted in three sessions; one took place in 2015 (S2015) and the other two in 2016 (S2016a and S2016b).

2.1   Design

The experiment was explained as a game of harvesting a renewable CPR. In particular, participants were asked to imagine themselves as fishermen, fishing for fish in a local lake. The game was played for 8 rounds keeping a fixed match protocol in which each student was assigned randomly to a group of seven. The group composition was initially (up to round 5) unknown to participants. In rounds 1 and 2 subjects were sitting in the same seminar room but they made their decisions in private, having no discussion at all. In rounds 3 and 4, subjects were allowed to communicate as a large group for ten minutes. The communication in these rounds was among all participants of the current session, but subjects did not know the exact composition of their groups. In round 5 and onwards subjects were informed of their fellow group mates, and groups were instructed to move to separate rooms where members could communicate in private, again for ten minutes. As in previous studies using face-to-face communication, subjects were explicitly told that they could not threaten others or make offers of side payments. Finally, in rounds 7 and 8, being informed of the total (group) as well as the individual (each members') harvesting levels in their group, subjects were given the opportunity to punish (at a cost) any group member they reckoned it did not comply with the strategy (rule) of the group.

In each round participants made their decisions in private, marking on a paper form (given to them) the units of the resource willing to extract. These papers were collected by the experimenters (in each round), who calculated the total harvesting level and average cost of the group. The papers were, then, given back to subjects who, on the basis of the reported group aggregate and their own harvesting level, were asked to calculate their individual earnings according to a payoff function.[1] This payoff

---

[1] Note, that during the first six rounds, subjects did not know the individual decisions of the others in the group; they were informed only of the total aggregate extraction of their group.

function was the same as that used in Ahn et al. (2011), replicating Walker et al. (2000), in which the marginal cost of appropriation from the CPR increases with the aggregate level of harvesting. Specifically, the per-round pay-off function for player i was:

$$\pi_i = \left[0.761x_i - 0.007x_i^2\right] - \left[x_i\left(\frac{0.01(X+1)}{2}\right)\right],$$

where x_i denotes the harvesting units of individual i and X denotes total number of units extracted by the group (of seven people). According to the payoff function, and as is typical in CPR experiment settings, increasing harvesting units yields higher individual earnings while aggregate extraction reduces them.

Walker et al. (2000) provided the one-shot game Nash equilibrium and social optimum of this setting. If the sum of units extracted by the six other members of a group is Y, then the payer i's best respond function is $32.5–0.208Y$. Assuming the monetary payoff function as the utility function of the game, the unique symmetric Nash equilibrium of the one-shot game involves each individual in a group harvesting 14 units. This outcome gives to each player a per-round monetary payoff of €2.35. In turn, the socially optimal outcome involves each subject harvesting 9 units with a corresponding per-person payoff of €3.40. However, if all team members decide to harvest 9 units, a player maximise her monetary payoff by extracting 20 units.

The game and the cost and benefit functions were explained orally to the subjects and handed out to them in a form of written instructions. This included a table showing the gross benefits of each harvesting unit from 1 to 60 (provided in Appendix). The benefits were the same to all participants (for the same extraction units) but the average costs were increasing as the total appropriation units were accumulating. Subjects undertook a number of handwritten exercises to ensure that they understood the game.

2.2   Results

This section discusses the results of the game. Following Ahn et al. (2011) the presentation focuses on individual decisions, organized around experiment sessions, instead of seven-person groups. This allows certain comparisons to be made between our Greek subjects and those participated in Ahn's et al. experiment sessions (coming from 41 countries). Harvesting levels and earnings at the Nash equilibrium and the social optimum are used as behavioural benchmarks.

Table 1 displays summary information on the harvesting levels aggregating across the three sessions, whereas Table 2 provides information for each individual session, i.e. S2015, S2016a and S2016b. As becomes evident from Table 1, in round 1 the individual harvesting averaged at 17.92 units, well above the social optimum of 9, as well as above the Nash equilibrium prediction of 14. As the game progressed and experience accumulated, the average extraction level fell from 17.92 units in round 1, to 14.82 units in round 2, and to 14.78 in round 3, in which large-group communication was allowed. Both figures are very close to the Nash equilibrium. The average extraction level rose somewhat in round 4 (as some participants attempted to capitalise the information obtained through large-group communication for their own benefit) and fell immediately after small-group

Table 1 Summary of harvesting levels

	Round	N	Mean	Standard deviation	Median	Percentiles			Min	Max
						25	50	75		
No communication	1	77	17.92	14.35	15	8.0	15.0	23	1	54
No communication	2	77	14.82	12.33	11	8.0	11.0	17.5	1	60
Large-group communication	3	77	14.78	10.60	12	8.0	12.0	17.5	2	54
Large-group communication	4	77	15.90	9.53	13	10.0	13.0	20.0	2	54
Small-group communication	5	77	11.10	3.49	10	9.0	10.0	12.0	5	26
Small-group communication	6	77	10.73	3.69	9	9.0	9.0	12.0	8	30
Small-group communication & sanctioning	7	77	11.07	2.70	10	9.0	10.0	13.0	5	20
Small-group communication & sanctioning	8	77	10.17	2.02	9	9.0	9.0	10.0	6	17

Note: Nash equilibrium = 14; Social optimum = 9

Source: Own construction

Table 2 Average level of extraction by session

	Round	S2015	S2016a	S2016b	All sessions
No communication	1	18.18	15.64	20.62	17.92
No communication	2	12.04	12.68	21.24	14.82
Large-group communication	3	15.39	13.04	16.43	14.78
Large-group communication	4	15.89	15.25	16.76	15.90
Small-group communication	5	10.82	11.29	11.24	11.10
Small-group communication	6	9.75	9.79	13.29	10.73
Small-group communication & sanctioning	7	10.93	11.71	10.38	11.07
Small-group communication & sanctioning	8	9.61	10.39	10.62	10.17

Note: Nash equilibrium = 14; Social optimum = 9

Source: Own construction

communication was allowed, from 15.90 in round 4 to just above 11 in round 5. Introduction of sanctioning (along with face-to-face communication in small groups) further improved outcomes bringing the mean harvesting level in round 8 down to slightly over 10 units. As can be noticed, the average extraction levels in rounds 5 to 8 are very close to the social optimum of 9 units. As regards the dispersion of the decisions, we observe that, as communication was improving and players gained more experience in rounds, the standard deviation decreased sharply, from 14.4 units in round 1, to 3.69 units in round 6. Similarly, when sanctioning was combined with face-to-face communication standard deviation dropped further, to just above 2 in round 8, indicating reduction of non-cooperation or defection among the players. Interestingly, similar findings are reported in Ahn et al. (2011), as well as elsewhere in the literature (e.g. Ostrom et al. 1992).

As regards the variation in the levels of appropriation, information is also provided by the minimum and maximum values (Table 1). Interestingly, similar to Ahn et al. (2011), we see that at the beginning of the game in rounds 1 and 2, there were subjects who extracted 54 or even 60 units. These were no single cases; in fact, there were five participants who decided to harvest 54 units in round 1, one of whom continued with the same strategy in round 2. In rounds 3 and 4, average extraction levels dropped, but again one player persisted in extracting the high amount of 54 units. Obviously, harvesting a very high (or a very low) amount of CPR units suggests confusion or misunderstanding over the payoff properties of the game; a situation which was improved substantially as the game progressed. Indeed, the subjects who extracted a very high number of resource units in rounds 1 and 2 immediately reduced their harvesting close to the social optimum in the rounds that followed.

Now let us move to the results of each session, described in Table 2. We observe that in round 1 average harvesting levels in all sessions lay well above the Nash equilibrium prediction, ranging from 18.18 units (in S2015) to 20.62 (in S2016b). In round 2, where still no communication was allowed among participants, appropriation was reduced but remained high and close to the Nash equilibrium benchmark, showing a trend that is consistent with the pattern found in Ahn et al. (2011) as well as in other experiments (e.g. Herr et al. 1997). In particular, the average extraction volumes in sessions S2015 and S2016a fell below the Nash equilibrium prediction, but stayed closer to it rather than getting near to the social optimum benchmark.

In rounds 3 and 4, where open discussion among all participants was allowed, decisions on levels of appropriation in all three sessions converged closer to the Nash equilibrium benchmark. In particular, in round 3, S2015 and S2016a, which in the previous round exhibited an average extraction level below the Nash equilibrium, raised their harvesting level to get closer to it, whereas S2016b (which in round 2 had an extraction level above the Nash equilibrium) lowered it. This stands in contrast to the findings of Ahn et al. (2011). We argue that possible explanations of this behaviour should be sought in relation to the profile of the players. Their cultural/national background or rather the fact that they are all well trained economists should play a role, since the strategy the subjects seem to follow was to use the information and knowledge gained from the group discussions in order to maximise their personal utility. This behaviour is also apparent in round 4.

The picture changed when small group face-to-face communication was at play (rounds 5 and 6). Knowing personally the others in the group and having private discussions with each other led players to reduce their harvesting units to levels that lie closer to the social optimum, in all sessions. Similar findings are reported in Ahn et al. (2011), who argue that small groups and face-to-face contact among members enhance cooperation and make easier optimal decisions to be reached. This trend repeated even when sanctioning was also allowed, reaching harvesting levels in round 8 which were the closest possible to the social optimum benchmark

(9.61 units in S2015, 10.39 in S2016a and 10.62 in S2016b). Interestingly, in round 7, when sanctioning was introduced, participants increased their harvesting as compared to this of the previous round (in S2015 and S2016a). We argue that the fact that many students not only knew each other in their group prior to the game, but some were also friends, led them to believe that no fine will be imposed on them by their group mates, and as such they could not resist the temptation to take advantage of others' cooperativeness by increasing somewhat their harvesting levels. This was also verified at the private discussions the experimenters had with the subjects right at the end of the game and afterwards.

Further conclusions on the behaviour of the subjects can be drawn from the average returns, presented in Tables 3, 4, and 5. Table 3 summarizes the results related to absolute earnings per round. As can be seen, due to the large harvesting levels both in rounds 1 and 2 (without communication) and 3 and 4 (large-group communication), the average payoffs to individuals were either negative or very low and variation was high. In particular, in round 1 the mean payoff was negative ($-€2.14$) and standard deviation the

Table 3 Average earnings (in €)

	Round	N	Mean	Standard deviation	Median	Percentiles		
						25	50	75
No communication	1	77	−2.14	6.54	0.05	−2.13	0.05	0.92
No communication	2	77	0.09	5.29	1.69	−0.31	1.69	3.00
Large-group communication	3	77	0.87	3.82	1.76	0.83	1.76	2.51
Large-group communication	4	77	0.55	2.74	1.21	0.34	1.21	1.92
Small-group communication	5	77	2.93	0.68	3.22	2.57	3.22	3.40
Small-group communication	6	77	2.96	1.03	3.12	2.91	3.12	3.40
Small-group communication & sanctioning	7	77	3.25	0.77	3.40	2.98	3.40	3.40
Small-group communication & sanctioning	8	77	3.23	0.36	3.40	3.31	3.40	3.40

Note: Nash equilibrium earnings = 2.35; Social optimum earnings = 3.40

Source: Own construction

Table 4 Average earnings (in €) and as a percentage of benchmarks

	Round	N	Mean	Percentage earnings of Nash	Percentage earnings of optimum
No communication	1	77	−2.14	−91.06	−62.94
No communication	2	77	0.09	3.83	2.65
Large-group communication	3	77	0.87	37.02	25.59
Large-group communication	4	77	0.55	23.40	16.18
Small-group communication	5	77	2.93	124.68	86.18
Small-group communication	6	77	2.96	125.96	87.06
Small-group communication & sanctioning	7	77	3.25	138.30	95.59
Small-group communication & sanctioning	8	77	3.23	137.45	95.00

Note: Nash equilibrium earnings = 2.35; Social optimum earnings = 3.40

Source: Own construction

Table 5 Average earnings by session (in €)

	Round	S2015	S2016a	S2016b	All sessions
No communication	1	−2.06	−0.96	−3.83	−2.14
No communication	2	1.92	2.10	−5.04	0.09
Large-group communication	3	0.53	2.26	−0.53	0.87
Large-group communication	4	0.53	0.94	0.04	0.55
Small-group communication	5	3.16	2.80	2.78	2.93
Small-group communication	6	3.21	3.34	2.11	2.96
Small-group communication & sanctioning	7	3.67	2.83	3.25	3.25
Small-group communication & sanctioning	8	3.32	3.18	3.18	3.23

Note: Nash equilibrium earnings = 2.35; Social optimum earnings = 3.40

Source: Own construction

highest (€6.54), owing to the costly externality created by some players who opted for a very high level of resource appropriation. The average earnings in rounds 2 to 4 were higher (and standard deviation dropped) but again below the Nash equilibrium prediction of €2.35 (and, of course, much below the social optimum). In turn, rounds 5 to 8 showed increasing average earnings (and low variation), getting much closer to the social optimum benchmark and above this predicted by the Nash equilibrium.

Table 4 summarizes the results related to absolute earnings and earnings relative (as percentage) to the two theoretical benchmarks. As becomes evident, in rounds 1 and 2 (without communication) the average payoffs to individuals were negative or very low due to the large average level of extraction. In rounds 3 and 4 average earnings improve, but not enough in order to get closer to the theoretical benchmarks. This, again, was a result of the decision of some participants to harvest a high volume of resource units, increasing substantially the social costs. Only in round 5 and onwards (where face-to-face communication was made possible) the average earnings were multiplied, getting very close to those at the social optimum (ranging from 86.18% in round 5, to 95.00% in round 8), and above those at the Nash equilibrium (ranging from 124.68% in round 5, to 137.45% in round 8). These results are similar to those of Ahn et al. (2011), verifying that personal discussions and agreements among participants in small groups improve outcomes to a great degree.

Finally, Table 5 provides the average earnings at a session level. We observe that the average earnings in the first two rounds (no-communication) showed substantial variability, with a high of €2.10 (round 2 of S2016a) and a low of −€5.04 (round 2 of S2016b). The highest average is still closer to that predicted by the Nash equilibrium than it is to the social optimum. Of the 6 reported averages in these rounds, only 2 were positive. Low average earnings were evident in the next 2 rounds, in which large-group communication was allowed, but negative earnings were apparent only once (round 3 of S2016b). As the game progressed all sessions improved the average earnings, getting closer to these prescribed by the social optimum. Similar results are also reported in Ahn et al. (2011). As was expected, the imposition of fines at a cost to participants (in rounds 7 and 8) reduced the average returns (round 8 in S2015, round 7 in S2016a, and round 8 in S2016b) as compared to those gained at the previous state (since sanctioning costs were subtracted from earnings); a finding that has been reported by others as well (e.g. Ostrom et al. 1992).

3   Conclusions

The current study employed an experimental setting to explore the ability of small groups of individuals by communicating with each other to cooperate and to fashion institutions that overcome CPR dilemmas. For this purpose, three experiment sessions were undertaken with final year undergraduates in Economics studying at the University of Thessaly in Greece. The game was played in eight rounds, where every two the rules and communication conditions were changed. The study recorded the decisions of the subjects in each round (in terms of appropriation levels and payoffs), examining whether, under different conditions, they would refrain from personal maximisation towards the sustainable use of the resource. To the best of our knowledge this is the first time that such a CPR experiment is reported using Greek subjects. A number of points that have emerged are highlighted next. These are important not only for our scientific understanding but also for the design of institutions to facilitate individuals' achieving higher levels of productive outcomes in CPR dilemmas.

First, in cases of both no communication among subjects and communication in one large group, outcomes were suboptimal, that is, closer to the Nash equilibrium benchmark rather than to the social optimum. In contrast, when small-group, face-to-face, communication was allowed decisions converged to achieve social optimal (or near optimal) outcomes. This suggests that both direct, personal contact among individuals and association in small groups are important factors in achieving and maintaining a cooperative outcome that enable sustainable use of CPR. Similar findings are reported by Ahn et al. (2011) and Herr et al. (1997), amongst others.

Second, our research indicated that individuals (if given the possibility of sanctioning each other) are willing to assume material costs in order to enforce agreed rules and to punish violations of social norms in general. This mechanism (and especially the threat of sanctioning) deters noncooperation and aligns individuals' behaviour along collective interests, as other scholars have also pointed out (inter alia: Anderies et al. 2011; Cárdenas and Ostrom 2006; Fehr and Gächter 2000; Ostrom 1998; Stout 2006). Moreover, our experiment also revealed that the number of actual punishment events was quite small, enabling us to conjecture that in small groups of known individuals, costly punishment can be employed but remains rather low.

Third, related studies (e.g. Ahn et al. 2011; Ostrom 1998) have reported that in finitely repeated CPR experiments subjects appear to be learning how to cooperate as the game progresses, but cooperation rates drop in the last round (whenever this occurs) and participants revert to maximising behaviour. This does not seem to be the case in our experiment. Instead, we observed instances of personal maximisation in progressive rounds of the game (when communication as a large group was allowed) and high degrees of cooperation and rule compliance in the last round. We assert that possible explanations of this should be sought in the profile of the subjects. The fact that they are all final year undergraduates in Economics should play a role in the strategy they followed in early stages of the game to capitalise the information provided for their own benefit, attempting to maximise their individual utility. In turn, in the last round it seems that personal acquaintance and friendly relations among participants (prior the experiment and onwards), in addition to the threat of sanctioning, forged a group identity and a reputation for being trustworthy that remained in force to sustain cooperative behaviour despite the increased temptation to cheat and to maximize personal returns.

Fourth, the differences between outcomes in successive rounds with no rule change (e.g. between rounds 3 and 4, 5 and 6, etc.) were relatively small, suggesting that single repetition of a round without variation in the conditions might not have a significant effect in altering the results of the game. This also corroborates the finding that direct contact in small groups is a powerful condition for efficient communication and increased cooperation towards the sustainable management of CPR.

Finally, although norms are developed in a social milieu and can vary noticeably across cultures (or given settings) we found no particular differences in behaviour between our Greek subjects and those of other countries, reported in Ahn et al. (2011). This certifies the generalization of the discussed behavioural traits, affirming that individuals in commons dilemmas are inclined, under certain conditions, to articulate cooperation-facilitating institutions that help avoid social dilemmas as much as possible.

APPENDIX

Table 6 Benefits per harvesting unit (in €)

Harvesting units	Benefits	Harvesting units	Benefits	Harvesting units	Benefits	Harvesting units	Benefits	Harvesting units	Benefits
1	0.75	13	8.71	25	14.65	37	18.57	49	20.48
2	1.49	14	9.28	26	15.05	38	18.81	50	20.55
3	2.22	15	9.84	27	15.44	39	19.03	51	20.60
4	2.93	16	10.38	28	15.82	40	19.24	52	20.64
5	3.63	17	10.91	29	16.18	41	19.43	53	20.67
6	4.31	18	11.43	30	16.53	42	19.61	54	20.68
7	4.98	19	11.93	31	16.86	43	19.78	55	20.68
8	5.64	20	12.42	32	17.18	44	19.93	56	20.66
9	6.28	21	12.89	33	17.49	45	20.07	57	20.63
10	6.91	22	13.35	34	17.78	46	20.19	58	20.59
11	7.52	23	13.80	35	18.06	47	20.30	59	20.53
12	8.12	24	14.23	36	18.32	48	20.40	60	20.46

Source: Adapted from Ahn et al. (2011, 1587)

REFERENCES

Ahn, T. K., Janssen, M. A., & Ostrom, E. (2004). Signals, symbols and human cooperation. In R. W. Sussman & A. R. Chapman (Eds.), *Origins and nature of sociality* (pp. 122–139). New York: De Gruyter.

Ahn, T. K., Ostrom, E., & Walker, J. (2011). Reprint of: A common-pool resource experiment with postgraduate subjects from 41 countries. *Ecological Economics, 70*(9), 1580–1589.

Anderies, J. M., Janssen, M. A., Bousquet, F., Cardenas, J. C., Castillo, D., Lopez, M. C., Tobias, R., Vollan, B., & Wutich, A. (2011). The challenge of understanding decisions in experimental studies of common pool resource governance. *Ecological Economics, 70*(9), 1571–1579.

Berg, J., Dickhaut, J., & McCabe, K. (1995). Trust, reciprocity, and social history. *Games and Economic Behavior, 10*(1), 122–142.

Cárdenas, J.-C., & Ostrom, E. (2006). How norms help reduce the Tragedy of the Commons: A multi-layer framework for analyzing field experiments. In J. N. Drobak (Ed.), *Norms and the law* (pp. 105–136). New York: Cambridge University Press.

Carpenter, J. P. (2000). Negotiation in the Commons: Incorporating field and experimental evidence into a Theory of Local Collective Action. *Journal of Institutional and Theoretical Economics, 156*(4), 661–683.

Chaudhuri, A., Sopher, B., & Strand, P. (2002). Cooperation in social dilemmas, trust and reciprocity. *Journal of Economic Psychology, 23*(2), 231–249.

Davis, D. D., & Holt, C. A. (1993). *Experimental economics.* Princeton NJ: Princeton University Press.

Fehr, E., & Gächter, S. (2000). Fairness and retaliation: The economics of reciprocity. *Journal of Economic Perspectives, 14*(3), 159–181.

Fischer, M. E., Irlenbusch, B., & Sadrieh, A. (2004). An intergenerational common pool resource experiment. *Journal of Environmental Economics and Management, 48*(2), 811–836.

Ghosh, S. (2007). How to build a commons: Is intellectual property constrictive, facilitating, or irrelevant? In C. Hess & E. Ostrom (Eds.), *Understanding knowledge as a commons, from theory to practice* (pp. 209–246). Cambridge, MA: MIT Press.

Hardin, G. (1968). The tragedy of the commons. *Science, 162,* 1243–1248.

Heckathorn, D. D. (1989). Collective action and the second-order free-rider problem. *Rationality and Society, 1*(1), 78–100.

Herr, A., Gardner, R., & Walker, J. M. (1997). An experimental study of time-independent and time-dependent externalities in the commons. *Games and Economic Behavior, 19*(1), 77–96.

Isaac, R. M., & Walker, J. M. (1988). Group size effects in public goods provision: The voluntary contributions mechanism. *The Quarterly Journal of Economics, 103*(1), 179–199.

Isaac, R. M., Walker, J. M., & Williams, A. W. (1994). Group size and the voluntary provision of public goods: Experimental evidence utilizing large groups. *Journal of Public Economics, 54*(1), 1–36.

Janssen, M. A., Bousquet, F., & Ostrom, E. (2011). A multimethod approach to study the governance of social-ecological systems. *Natures Sciences Sociétés, 19*(4), 382–394.

Kollock, P. (1998). Social dilemmas: The anatomy of cooperation. *Annual Review of Sociology, 24*(1), 183–214.

Lichbach, M. I. (1996). *The cooperator's dilemma*. Ann Arbor: University of Michigan Press.

Mason, C. F., & Phillips, O. R. (1997). Mitigating the tragedy of the commons through cooperation: An experimental evaluation. *Journal of Environmental Economics and Management, 34*(2), 148–172.

Oliver, P. (1980). Rewards and punishments as incentives for collective action: Theoretical investigations. *American Journal of Sociology, 85*(6), 1356–1375.

Ortmann, A., Fitzgerald, J., & Boeing, C. (2000). Trust, reciprocity, and social history: A re-examination. *Experimental Economics, 3*(1), 81–100.

Ostrom, E. (1989). Microconstitutional Change in multiconstitutional political systems. *Rationality and Society, 1*(1), 11–50.

Ostrom, E. (1990). *Governing the commons: The evolution of institutions for collective action*. Cambridge, MA: Cambridge University Press.

Ostrom, E. (1998). A behavioral approach to the rational choice theory of collective action: Presidential Address, American Political Science Association, 1997. *American Political Science Review, 92*(1), 1–22.

Ostrom, E. (2003). How types of goods and property rights jointly affect collective action. *Journal of Theoretical Politics, 15*(3), 239–270.

Ostrom, E. (2009). Building trust to solve commons dilemmas: Taking small steps to test an evolving theory of collective action. In A. S. Levin (Ed.), *Games, groups, and the global good* (pp. 207–228). Berlin: Springer.

Ostrom, E. (2010a). Analyzing collective action. *Agricultural Economists, 41*(s1), 155–166.

Ostrom, E. (2010b). A Multi-scale approach to coping with climate change and other collective action problems. *Solutions, 1*(2), 27–36.

Ostrom, E. (2011). Reflections on "Some Unsettled Problems of Irrigation". *American Economic Review, 101*(1), 49–63.

Ostrom, E., & Nagendra, H. (2007). Tenure alone is not sufficient: Monitoring is essential. *Environmental Economics and Policy Studies, 8*(3), 175–199.

Ostrom, E., & Walker, J. (1991). Communication in a commons: Cooperation without external enforcement. In T. R. Palfrey (Ed.), *Laboratory research in political economy* (pp. 287–322). Ann Arbor: University of Michigan Press.

Ostrom, E., Walker, J., & Gardner, R. (1992). Covenants with and without a sword: Self-Governance is possible. *American Political Science Review, 86*(2), 404–417.

Ostrom, E., Gardner, R., & Walker, J. (1994). *Rules, games, and common-pool resources*. Ann Arbor: University of Michigan Press.

Poteete, A., Janssen, M., & Ostrom, E. (2010). *Working together: Collective action, the commons, and multiple methods in practice*. Princeton, NJ: Princeton University Press.

Putnam, R. D. (1993). *Making democracy work: Civic traditions in modern Italy*. Princeton, NJ: Princeton University Press.

Sally, D. (1995). Conservation and cooperation in social dilemmas. A meta-analysis of experiments from 1958 to 1992. *Rationality and Society, 7*(1), 13–34.

Sefton, M., Shupp, R., & Walker, J. M. (2007). The effect of rewards and sanctions in provision of public goods. *Economic Inquiry, 45*(4), 671–690.

Stout, L. A. (2006). Social norms and other-regarding preferences. In J. N. Drobak (Ed.), *Norms and the law* (pp. 105–136). New York: Cambridge University Press.

Van Lange, P. A., Joireman, J., Parks, C. D., & Van Dijk, E. (2013). The psychology of social dilemmas: A review. *Organizational Behavior and Human Decision Processes, 120*(2), 125–141.

Vatn, A. (2007). *Institutions and the environment*. Cheltenham: Edward Elgar.

Walker, J. M., Gardner, R., Herr, A., & Ostrom, E. (2000). Collective choice in the commons: Experimental results on proposed allocation rules and votes. *The Economic Journal, 110*(460), 212–234.

Yamagishi, T. (1986). The provision of a sanctioning system as a public good. *Journal of Personality and Social Psychology, 51*(1), 110–116.

Public Goods, Club Goods and Specialization in Evolving Collaborative Entities

Vasilis Zervos

1   Introduction

Research partnerships generally exhibit a collaborative behavior of the agents involved. Although the term partnership is wide reaching, in recent economics literature it is frequently confined to specific modes like strategic research partnerships or public-private-partnerships, while military alliances, or research organizations may be considered also a form of partnership. Research organizations of a public nature that produce scientific results are frequently associated with outputs of a public goods nature as they become openly available to the global scientific community and are subject to non-rivalry and non-excludability.

Space-based organizations like NASA and ESA have explicit open data policies and availability, partly also because of the international character of 'benefit to mankind' of outer space exploration. Although excludability can be enforced (at a cost), its lack of enforcement results in the public good

V. Zervos (✉)
Department of Economics, University of Strasbourg (BETA),
Strasbourg, France

International Space University (ISU), Strasbourg, France

© The Author(s) 2018   143
S. Vliamos, M. S. Zouboulakis (eds.), *Institutionalist Perspectives on Development*, Palgrave Studies in Democracy, Innovation, and Entrepreneurship for Growth,
https://doi.org/10.1007/978-3-319-98494-0_9

nature of scientific data being by convention, rather than by nature. Besides scientific data whereby public goods and services exist by convention, particularly in collaborative programs, similar experiences and practices are found in other areas of economic activity, such as defense alliances whereby data and information (like other goods and services) are provided by convention openly to the alliance members.

While the case of outputs is characterized frequently by such sharing behavior, the inputs allocation and the inter-alliance, or collaboration specialization impacts upon industrial performance. The input costs, distribution and specialization towards a joint public-nature good are frequently following an equal return approach, whereby partners provide resources developed indigenously. The scientific and common-good rational of the scientific program selection and associated benefits along with the indigenously industrial specialized production contributed seemingly provide significant benefits for the partners to engage in such endeavors on a regular basis.

The situation is slightly different though when the 'common target' which is of a public good nature (within the partners, or internationally) evolves into a collaborative good which is of a commercial nature. This may clearly impact upon long-term competitiveness and relative positions of partner sectors and economies. Thus, the institutional arrangements of such an evolution, as well as the public good conventional character also need to be examined within a dynamic framework.

To begin with, this chapter looks at the output implications of the options of public good versus market provision of candidate public goods by convention. Those are the demand and cost conditions that result in higher output equilibrium under a pure public good versus a private market provision for goods and services.

Beyond that, the specialization, cross-product and market dynamics are also examined within a partial-industrial sector framework. This framework is characterized by multiple market failures like the presence of economies of scale and scope, but also significant spinoffs and externalities. Companies and public sectors are interacting in a strategic format with specialization in collaborations being of critical importance for relative performance and competitiveness of agents in a static analytical framework. As collaborative institutions evolve so do the dynamics of this static analysis.

The rest of the chapter is structured as follows, the economics of specialization are next examined along with the allocative implications for public goods by convention. This is followed by an illustrative model of comparison between the cases of provision of goods under a public good regime, or under a market-based environment by two countries that place indigenous demand in their industries that compete simultaneously in commercial markets for goods linked through economies of scale and scope. The analysis concludes with a discussion on the results of the model and its implications for further research.

2   ECONOMIC APPROACHES AND SPECIALIZATION

Since Plato, trading and specialization was seen as a means to achieving efficiency in the provision of basic goods and services for the individual through collective effort. These basic goods and services were referred to, in order of importance, as survival (security), nutrition and clothing. This collective arrangement was perceived as leading from 'xenoikia' to a 'polis' framework whereby autonomy was exchanged for specialization and trade.

Clearly, the gains of specialization result in a better overall production efficiency for these goods. This then brings forth the next logical point, namely the distribution of this overall efficient production to the specialized individuals. Plato thus, as a second step, proceeds to focus more extensively into the justice and organization of the society (polis).

By analogy, Adam Smith's emphasized specialization as a means of achieving efficiency in production, which when extrapolated led to the global trade concept of welfare improvements of trading partners. An important point to note is that specialization does not necessarily follow from a 'natural' allocation, but may be owing to 'community/social' factors: '*As Smith famously wrote in the Wealth of Nations, the differences between a philosopher and a street porter may be small prior to their individual commitment to their respective profession (WN I.ii.4, pp. 28–29)*' (Meoqui 2014: 6).

Taken a step further, the sources of comparative advantage that determine trade patterns and national specialization were seen as irrelevant to their impact by Adam Smith: "*Whether the advantages which one country has over another, be natural or acquired, is in this respect of no consequence. As long as the one country has those advantages, and the other wants them, it will always be more advantageous for the latter, rather to buy of the former than to make. It is an acquired advantage only, which one artificer has over his neighbor, who exercises another trade; and yet they both found it more advantageous to buy of one another, than to make what does not belong to their particular trades*" (Smith 1976: 458).

Natural endowments are clearly an important source of specialization selection, be it in the case of Plato's citizen, or Smith's trading nation. However, artificial advantages may find their roots in strategic choices, rather than random, or cultural processes. In that respect, Plato devotes an extensive discussion on the specialization dynamics and choices within a society that is otherwise comprised of equally empowered individuals.[1] The criticality of the specialization distribution process, especially with regards to the artificial advantages obtained is crucial, as it determines the systemic stability and sets the background for resource allocation across citizens, or nations that specialize. The dynamics of this process are perhaps even more important than the static implications. In that sense, factors affecting the specificity of long-term cost advantages, such as technological orientation, education and economies of learning are critical, as well as demand attitudes and cultures further determine comparative advantage patterns and relevant institutional structures through time.

There are thus two implications emerging from the discussion on specialization so far. The first relates to the impact of specialization through economies of scale and scope to the comparative advantage and efficiency enhancement in a static sense as we compare the autonomous state with the state of exchanges (be it across individuals, or nations), while the second relates to the impact of specialization to long-term patterns associated with the comparative advantage as efficiency is enhanced further (and so is specialization) through economies of learning, cultural and education adaptation and related institutional patterns. Both of these interrelate to the all-crucial distribution/allocation of benefits that is central to the long-term sustainability.

Specialization however carries certain dangers, especially as long-term institutional adaptation results in enhancing comparative advantages at the expense of autonomy.[2] Even though such 'lock-in' effects are extensively examined in contracting and transaction cost literature (Williamson 1989; Laffont and Tirole 1993), specialization challenges are also extensively examined within the international trade literature. One example is the case of the famous Dutch-disease approach, whereby extreme specialization,

---

[1] A. Smith focuses in his examples mostly on the natural endowments as a source of specialization, though seemingly not distinguishing them from artificial advantages in terms of their importance.

[2] This is seen as a key reason why Plato devotes much of his attention to the 'just' political arrangements once individuals move from 'xenoika' towards a social partnership development (polis).

even in the absence of limited considerations for the own-economic security from global demand shocks for the leading exporting sector (or other shocks) can lead to allocative challenges and pauperization.

Moreover, following an extension of the Balassa-Samuelson framework, where a competitive tradable sector affects the relative wages of the non-tradable sector, tradable-sector specialization and development of artificial advantages can have multiplier effects across the economy. This is not only in the presence of global supply chains, but also in the case where the specialization follows a collaborative negotiated and agreed approach across partners, as is the case of alliances (NATO), or joint organizations like the European Space Agency (ESA).

Zervos (2011) shows how in strategic industries where economies of scale and scope co-exist with a tradable and governmental non-tradable sectors (defense), the non-tradable sectors are not only interconnected, but can also have an unexpected impact upon the performance of the tradable sector by perverse incentives. That means that the economy with the cost advantage in the non-tradable sector may not see this advantage extended into the tradables sector, since rent-seeking behaviors prevail. This leads to an introverted focus of firms to their domestic lucrative market, rather than the more competitive global one, even though the country enjoys a theoretical cost advantage should its industry decided to capture the later market.

3   SPECIALIZATION IN COLLABORATION: FROM PRODUCTION TO ALLOCATIVE EFFICIENCY

From the previous discussion, it then follows that societal, or inter-alliance specialization is of significant and accumulated consequences, as is—by analogy—the distribution of tasks under Plato's polis.[3] The mechanism for introducing sustainability into the economic-wide system coincides with a 'fairness' mechanism, as discussed in Plato through education and an elaborate social structure. Adam Smith considers that rich individuals through the invisible hand mechanism will diffuse their wealth to the less fortunate by increased consumption, while in the case where the system is comprised

---

[3] This is clearly assuming that the differences in rewards to economic agents stem from specialization and not from effort differences, even though in the long-run these may be related (e.g. higher rewarding specialized sectors clearly are expected to result in more effort and motivation).

of trading nations as economic agents, the classical approach calls for mobilization of the exchange rate mechanism and resource flows (capital/labour) that equilibrate the system in the long-run (Smith 2006). So, for example, long-run trade surpluses and deficits are unsustainable without adjustments in the foreign direct investment flows (from the surplus area to the deficit area), or labour migration, or exchange rate adjustments, or all of the above. Such balancing mechanisms across 'winners and losers', both internally and externally would be compatible with the Kaldor-Hicks compensating mechanism.[4]

The compensating principle is critical for the stability of the firm, partnership, or alliance. The advocated invisible hand that transfers wealth from the rich to the poor at the national economy level can be extended to global trade partnerships, whereby development approaches and FDI literature call for synergies across trade and investment that have mutually beneficial impact. In that sense, countries with trade surpluses (by analogy to capital abundance) are envisaged as increasing their FDI towards the countries with deficits enhancing productivity and 'supply-side' economic performance, in parallel to exchange rate fluctuations. FDI patterns develop and lead overall economic development for both countries as natural resource-seeking FDI transforms into higher value-adding types (market-seeking/strategic asset-seeking FDI, see Dunning 1992). The invisible hand premise seems to point out how the transfer of wealth is beneficial for the sustainability of the relevant economic system, by creating virtuous cycles either within societies, or across them.

The analysis so far has not considered the challenges associated with extreme cases of asymmetrical economic agents in terms of their contribution and ownership. It is however conceivable that specialization may result in different long-run dynamics owing, for example to different economies of scale and scope characteristics in association with relative market sizes. In the presence of pure public goods, e.g. in alliances like NATO, or in the case of a research organization (like ESA), such specialization-distribution effects may be less important in view of the equal-access to the public good benefits.[5] In such case, a country that provides contributions

---

[4] Arguably this is a more realistic mechanism offering a high level of flexibility compared to the pareto principle. Furthermore, the compensating mechanism may offer the option of overall improvements across the whole set of agents.

[5] A possible alternative term to use here would be to introduce the term 'pure' to club goods, allowing for non-rivalry and non-excludability within the club, as opposed to situations where there exist discretion leading to partial access. In this case we could refer to 'pure

in economic sectors that enjoy limited economies of scale/scope and therefore economic gains besides access to the pure public good may nonetheless choose to contribute owing to the significant benefits arising from access to this pure public good.

Public goods within an alliance, or a research organization are complex goods and services. For example 'security' within NATO would refer to more than a single technological asset (intercontinental ballistic missiles— ICBMs), but would require a network comprised of supportive nodes (including assets like global positioning systems—GPS, intelligence, logistical support, tactical weapons, etc.). Thus, the main provider is seen more as an integrator and less as a vertical integrated entity. There are clear resemblances with supply chains and production technologies where 'subcontractors' or lower tier suppliers exist and contribute at different levels. The distribution of contributions in the presence of economies of scale and scope is of paramount importance for the allocative efficiency.

The one-producer mode that arises in the presence of economies of scale/scope for a pure public good within an alliance is also known as 'best shot case':

> The best-shot case poses serious problems. In the case of a single superpower, that country will naturally be the low-cost provider and is likely to end up being the single provider. The equilibrium outcome is likely to be the most inefficient of all three cases. This result occurs because the low-cost provider still equates marginal private cost with marginal private benefit, but other providers drop out and produce nothing. Thus, in the cases of providing security guarantees, GPS systems, or combating international security threats, the United States is clearly the dominant provider, with more than half of defense and intelligence spending. It is likely to remain the sole provider of the public good (if this term is aptly applied here) as long as it remains so dominant. (Nordhaus 2005: 12)

The long-term dynamics of the 'hegemonic' benevolent dictator become obvious in the case of pure public good within an alliance, or a global system: '*Alas, it is but a small step from the benevolent actor to the nationalistic actor, one who acts unilaterally and concentrates on the benefits to the dominant country, perhaps with a bow to the interests of friends and coalitions of the coerced*' (Ibid.: 13).

club goods' as the sharing of benefits would be equal across all members, while maintaining the non-excludability and non-rivalry characteristics within the club (see McNutt 1999 for a discussion on club goods). Hence, the terms 'public' is defined within the context of the alliance, or system, or collaborative organization/partnership (like ESA).

The issue of control is therefore of paramount importance, as moral hazard situations may develop whereby within a collaborative entity specialization privileges may lead to unforeseen at the initial time of the entity's formation allocative outcomes. This may be become somewhat clearer by a simple example, by looking at the services provided in a military camp. The watchmen that stay awake to guard provide a pure public good to the camp as there is no rivalry, or excludability to their services. However, the bakers that bake the bread the next morning provide a good that is far more subject to rivalry and excludability. The benefits from this security-related service differ though also in terms of their unintended/ external impact. Assuming the baker's service is subject to economies of scale and scope, one can see how the watchmen may enjoy far less 'side' economic benefits (spinoffs) from their collaborative specialization as opposed to the bakers. Besides the economic benefits, access to bread may therefore through time become more restrictive for colleagues, as discretion in excludability is applicable.

The public goods economic literature recognizes four classifications of goods in the rivalry-excludability domain, namely club goods, pure public goods, private goods and contestable goods. However, it is not always clear whether the boundaries and characterization is based on convention, or technical characteristics. For example, in the absence of rivalry, excludability would be seen as violating the assumption that one's utility is independent of each other, for otherwise there would be no reason why an extra cost associated with excludability application (however small) would be applied to a non-rivalrous good. The goods, or services that are offered within a collaborative entity as a club good, deserve therefore special attention as to their implications for their relevant economic positions, but also the discretion employed in defining the 'club' by the providing agent(s).

In the presence of discretion there are therefore three different attitudes (demand relationships) one agent may experience over goods and services compared to others: rivalry, indifference, sharing.

A simple illustrative model follows later in this paper demonstrating the equilibrium outcomes for multi-product industries that compete in commercial/private goods markets, while at the same time serving pure public goods markets. The comparison focuses on the outcome of this structure with one where the pure public goods market is instead a normal goods market, or even rivalrous. The model expands the analysis of Fig. 1, whereby there are conditions under which the quantities produced (for a price range) are higher under a pure public good versus a private good

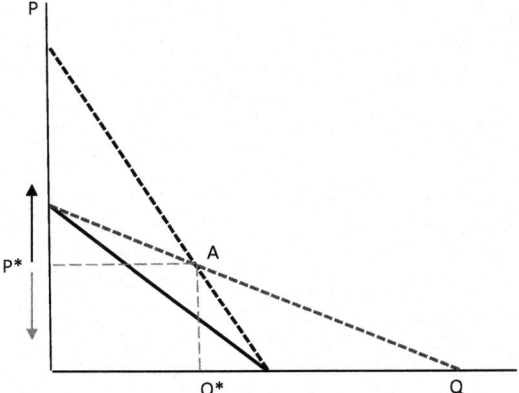

Fig. 1 Compares the vertical additive case of demand curves (public good—*green line*) with the horizontal additive case (private goods—*blue line*). In the case where the public good is by convention these two cases represent real alternatives. Hence at prices below Q* horizontal additions lead to higher overall levels of output demanded (*blue arrow*) than prices above Q* (*green arrow*), when compared to vertical summation. The cost schedules are not necessarily different as a later example illustrates. Point A corresponds to (P*, Q*), while a sequence of expanded additive points would be connected by a line of the form P = *b**Q, assuming the demand equation is P = *a−b**Q

added-demand schedule.[6] Though this seems less important for the case whereby the goods are natural public and private goods, in the case where this is by convention can have implications for efficiency.

4   Government-Industry Interactions
in Strategic Sectors

Sectors subject to economies of scale and scope are long considered as strategic on the grounds that they exhibit significant industrial consolidation, frequently resulting in national champions that may collaborate in

---

[6] Though the quantities under the public good and the private good additive cases can be compared more meaningfully compared to relative prices and profits. Prices may be comparable, though under a public good case one would expect significant externalities and shadow price effects when compared to the private good additive case. In this case, a comparison of the profits seems less meaningful.

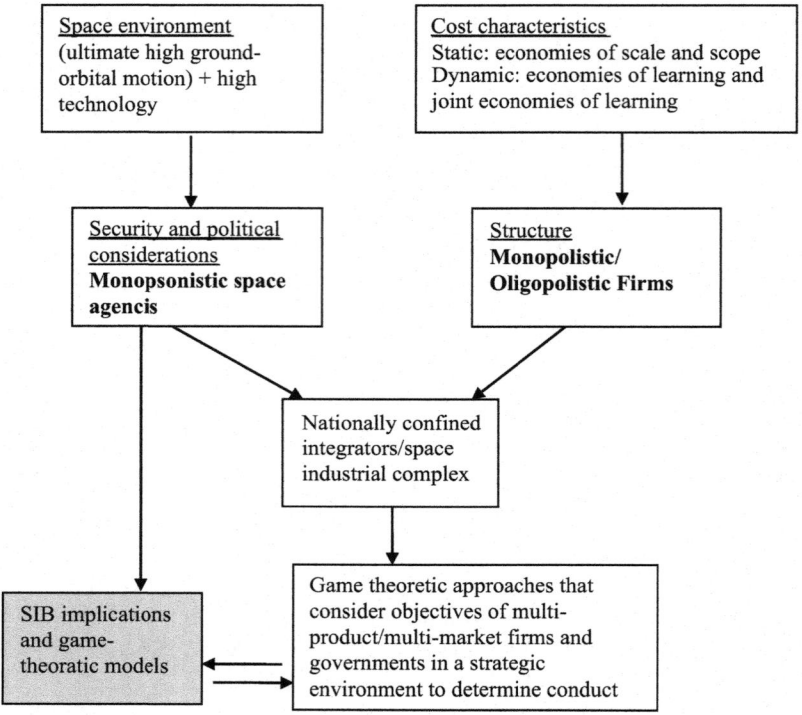

Fig. 2   The space industrial complex analytical framework

multi-national institutional markets either at the industry, or at the government level, while at the same time compete in commercial markets. Figure 2 captures such a framework for the space sector (not unlike the wider aerospace and defense sectors) and the resulting formation of institutional-industrial complexes.

In its simple form, such a framework is depicted by a structure whereby a national industrial champion exists (largely owing to the economies of scale and scope cost characteristics) that must also provide a level of national security in autonomous provision of security-sensitive goods. Such national champions face domestic monopolistic markets, while compete in commercial markets of an international nature.

The nationally-confined and security-sensitive goods and services may be of an autonomous nature, or of a collaborative nature whereby each nation (and its domestic industry) specializes in its contributions. The presence of such collaborative schemes is justified on grounds of avoidance of duplication, but also on security-enhancements of collaborations for the participating countries (France—Germany in the WWII aftermath). Although institutional environment is in reality more complicated (Appendix 1, Fig. 4), the basic elements of industrial and governmental interactions in space and defense-related strategic industries as depicted in Fig. 2 are quite plausible owing to the cost characteristics and the collaborative programs and institutions that enhance jointly evolving capabilities and applications.[7]

5   AN ILLUSTRATIVE MODEL

Assume an alliance in space (or defense) programs whereby two countries join forces and demand a product such as navigation and positioning services as a single entity. This then results in them developing a pure public good approach within the partnership where the service is shared freely and both of them are subject to the same level of production and consumption. In addition, the cost characteristics for their respective industries are subject to economies of scale and scope.

Thus there are two firms, each producing one good for the join space market and another for the commercial market where they compete.

Rivalry results in a race environment whereby the demand for a certain security-related good is a positive function of the rival's consumption. Indifference would result in a demand function that would be quite similar in nature to the standard demand function of different economic agents whose demand is not linked to the other's (co-users, or joint consumption), while in the case of a pure public good approach, there would be discretion employed in not excluding the other agent in the case of absence of rivalry in the use of relevant goods/data. We are primarily concerned with the cases of public good (by convention) as it comperes to the private goods that would exist within a standard trading model. The case of rivalry is clearly also a relevant case, but one reserved for situations examining an arms race, or equivalent framework and will be presented only for purposes of completeness.

---

[7] The issue of governance of such systems that evolve from research and development collaborations into full-blown merged entities (Arianespace, Airbus) and programs with operational characteristics (like EC Galileo) arises for Europe specifically in view of dual-usability and the complex institutional environment of Appendix 1.

For purposes of simplicity of the model, it is assumed that there is symmetry in demand and cost characteristics for the two parties and the respective industries. In addition, it is assumed that the cost characteristics are subject to economies of scale and scope for the relevant range of production.[8] Based on the above, the TC function is of the following form:

$$C_i = F - (q_i q_{di}) + (q_i^2 + q_{di}^2), \quad \text{for } i, j = 1, 2 \tag{1}$$

where F = fixed costs (including R&D).

The inverse demand function of the commercial market is assumed to be of the following form:

$$p = a - b(q_1 + q_2) \tag{2}$$

where p = price of the private commercial good.

q_1 = the quantity of the private commercial good supplied by agent 1.
q_2 = the respective quantity supplied by agent 2.
a = the vertical intercept.
b = the slope of the demand line.
(a and b are assumed greater than zero)

In the joint good (by convention) market, the inverse demand schedule is added vertically for the pure public good case, while horizontally for the private collaborative good one as follows:

- Private good case: Adding the two demand curves for the public sectors results in a joint demand line, where the slope coefficient is $\left(\dfrac{b}{2}\right)$:

$$p_d = a - \frac{b(q_{di} + q_{dj})}{2}, \quad \text{for } i, j = 1, 2 \tag{3}$$

where p = price of the government good

[8] There are also certain desired theoretical properties for such a cost function: a TC function must be non-negative, non-decreasing, concave and linearly homogenous in input prices (Baumol et al. 1982). The cost function employed is presumed to be a function only of output quantities and not input prices. This method of formulating cost functions makes the analysis less complicated, without much loss in generality when the main concern is to examine the impact of output changes (Baumol et al. 1982: 453).

q_{di} = the quantity of the government good supplied by its respective industry.
a = the vertical intercept.
b = the slope of the demand line.
(a and b are assumed greater than zero).

- Public good case: adding the two demand curves in the case of a pure public good results in a joint demand schedule with the slope coefficient being equal to $2b$:

$$p_d = 2\left(a - b\left(q_{di} + q_{dj}\right)\right), \quad \text{for } i, j = 1, 2 \tag{4}$$

Firms are assumed to compete 'a la Cournot' and maximize profits subject to cost constraints. The equilibrium results are a function of demand coefficients (a, b) for the case of pure public good and competitive collaboration. Table 1 summarizes the output, prices equilibrium results.

As Table 1 shows for the comparison of equilibrium outputs for Cases 1 and 2, there is a value of 'b' for which the respective outputs are equalized. For values of b below this critical value, the equilibrium outputs under Case 1 are higher compared to the relevant values under Case 2.

This is shown in Fig. 3, whose vertical axis is the difference between outputs under Case 1 and Case 2.[9] What we see is that equilibrium outputs are higher under private market provision compared to a (conventional) public good provision as demand becomes more elastic.

The model can be further used to illustrate how changing the magnitude of the economies of scale and scope for one of the industries (nosymmetry) will result in a favorable outcome for the industry that exhibits relatively stronger scale effects. This, impacts upon inter-collaboration specialization selection and outcomes.

The implications of specialization distribution within a collaborative entity are thus apparently important and become increasingly so, when the nature of the collaboration entity and its primary objectives shift. In the case of the space sector, the transformation of an otherwise research collaboration organization into a value-adding and competitiveness-enhancing entity, where the institutional roles evolve needs thus to be examined in this

---

[9] The vertical axis measures the difference: q_i (Case 1)–q_i (Case 2) which is the same as q_{di} (Case 1)–q_{di} (Case 2), for i = 1, 2.

Table 1   Equilibrium results under alternative government-market structures

Cases	Variable	Firm i (i = US, Europe)	Notes
Case 1 Competitive collaboration	q_i	$q_i = \dfrac{a(b+2)}{3b^2+6b+2}$	For $b = 0.4$, same to Case 2
	q_{di}	$q_{di} = 2\dfrac{a(b+1)}{3b^2+6b+2}$	For $b = 0.4$, same to Case 2
	p	$p_i = \dfrac{a(b^2+2b+2)}{3b^2+6b+2}$	
	p_d	$p_{di} = \dfrac{a(b^2+4b+2)}{3b^2+6b+2}$	
Case 2 Pure public good	q_i	$q_i = 2/3\dfrac{a(3b+2)}{6b^2+6b+1}$	For $b = 0.4$, same to Case 1
	q_{di}	$q_{di} = 1/3\dfrac{a(6b+5)}{6b^2+6b+1}$	For $b = 0.4$ same to Case 1
	p	$p_i = a - 4/3\dfrac{ba(3b+2)}{6b^2+6b+2}$	
	p_d	$p_{di} = 2a - 4/3\dfrac{ba(6b+5)}{6b^2+6b+1}$	

new context with regards to benefit allocation and the Kaldor-Hicks principle discussed earlier. Security considerations add another dimension to the institutional challenge as relevant benefits may not be equally enjoyed (as pure public goods) across all areas, especially as the issue of governance of developed capabilities comes into question for mature systems entering operational phases. The intra-trade and export-performance of the various European countries with regards to the A&D sector is quite different for each one, as is its respective evolution through time.[10]

[10] Appendix 2 shows the export performance of selected economies with regards to the A&D industry through time. Even in the absence of the all-important intra-European trade patterns, the export-leading activity of economies like France is obvious while the rising character of German industry and the mixed results of the UK as the leading European A&D nations are observed. Finally, the cases of countries like Greece that has experienced a significant income shock in recent years (post-2009) is visible in the narrowing of initial significant trade deficits that are quite sharp, especially in the A&D sector.

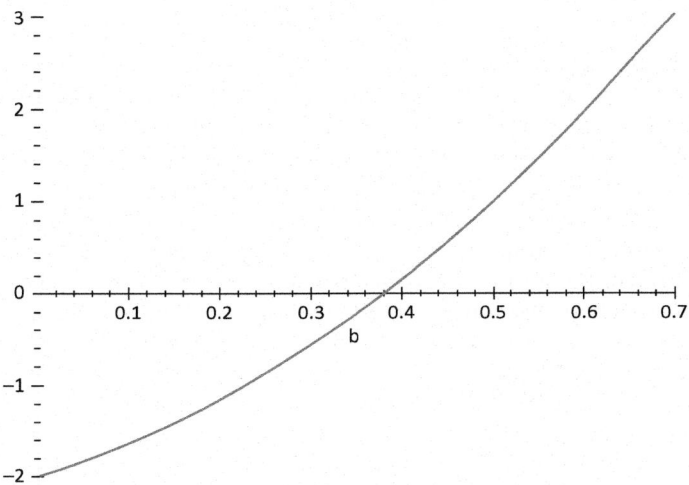

Fig. 3 Equilibrium output difference under Case 1 and under Case 2. Notes: The vertical axis measures the difference: q_i (Case 1)–q_i (Case 2) which is the same as q_{di} (Case 1)–q_{di} (Case 2), for $i = 1, 2$. The difference is a well-behaved relationship that is determined by the market characteristics (value of 'b') as shown, but also by the cost-specific relationship (magnitude of economies of scale/scope)

In conclusion, by examining a multi-firm and multi-country framework, open procurement policies are desirable in the absence of conflict between nations and can lead to advancements in commercialization and a more globalized space industry. The political elements are crucial in this process and extend beyond the space sector. The use of dual-use applications and partnerships can facilitate this process and nullify critical conflict potentials, thus avoiding the transformation of outer space from 'ultimate high ground' to 'ultimate battlefield'. A prerequisite for a virtuous arrangement within alliances and relevant types of collaboration is clearly the matching of the evolution of the institutional landscape and allocative mechanisms to the evolution of the collaboration following its success from a 'public good' to a commercial-enhancement entity. Finally, the demand/user characteristics in combination with the cost characteristics may indicate that a competitive collaboration, rather than a 'public good' collaboration result in an optimized level of output.

6   CONCLUSIONS

Specialization in collaborative entities is a historically efficient economic mechanism for achievement of common objectives. The success of such partnerships though may lead to evolutionary challenges for the allocation of benefits as they transform into commercialization-enhancing institutions. The unintended impact of specialization through externalities, presence of economies of scale and scope puts under scrutiny simple models of collaboration-contributions and the resulting allocative efficiency in the absence of compensating mechanisms from winners to losers. This paper analyzed this framework using as a benchmark the aerospace sector, with specific focus in the European collaborative experience in space. A simple illustrative model shows that economies of scale and scope in areas of inter-partnership contributions involving governments and the provision of public goods can impact upon the respective relative national industrial performance in competitive commercial markets. Moreover, provision under a pure public good mode of collaborative government goods and services may not lead to higher equilibrium quantities, compared to a private-mode of market structure. Further research towards identifying compensating mechanisms in the presence of multiple market failures and a variety of institutional modes of partnerships is required for policymakers to ensure better stability and sustainability through development-enhancing compensations.

APPENDIX 1

The non-simple political, security and defense and space-related framework at the European level is illustrated in the different partnership compositions of collaborative institutions. The dynamic nature of the memberships and political landscape has to be considered when examining this membership mapping (UK's expected withdrawal from the EU, while seemingly reinforcing of its interest in the space domain and ESA) (Fig. 4).

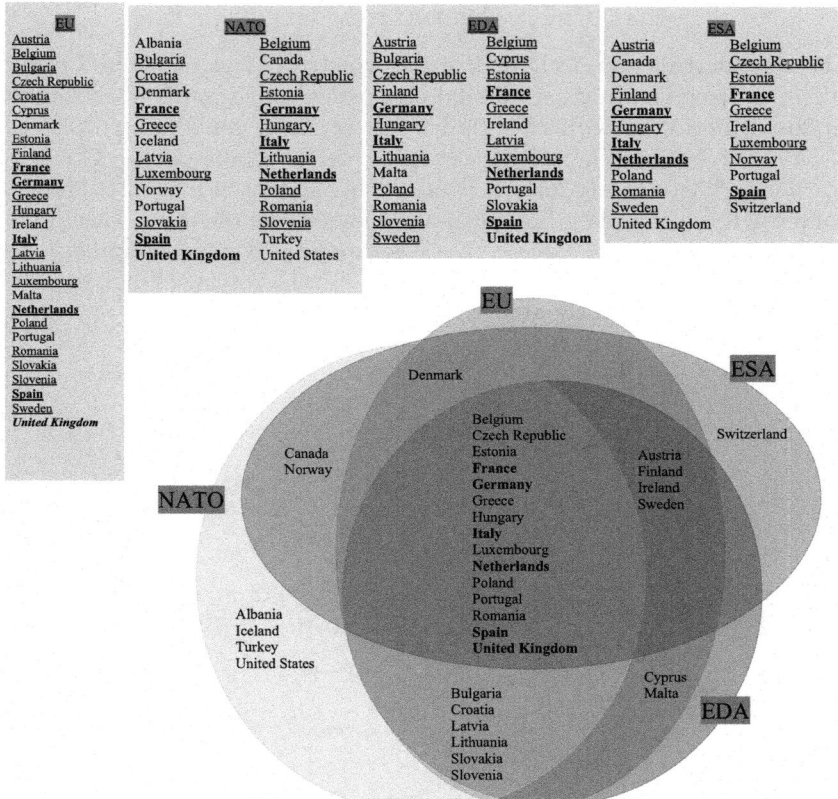

Fig. 4 European and North Atlantic space and security alliances. Source: Updated, based on Zervos 2015. Notes: The countries in *bold* are members of OCCAR. In addition, The Western European Union (WEU) is comprised of the following members: Belgium, France, Germany, Greece, Italy, Luxembourg, Netherlands, Portugal, Spain, United Kingdom. Finally, the underlying countries are members of PESCO. United Kingdom is in italics under the EU, as it is engaged in departing negotiations

APPENDIX 2

The overall trade and A&D trade data presented in Figs. 5, 6 and 7 reveal the export performance of selected economies with regards to the A&D industry through time. Even in the absence of the all-important intra-European trade patterns, the export-leading activity of economies like France is obvious while the rising character of German industry and the mixed results of the UK as the leading European A&D nations are observed. Finally, the cases of countries like Greece that has experienced a significant income shock in recent years (post-2009) is visible in the narrowing of initial significant trade deficits that are quite sharp, especially in the A&D sector.

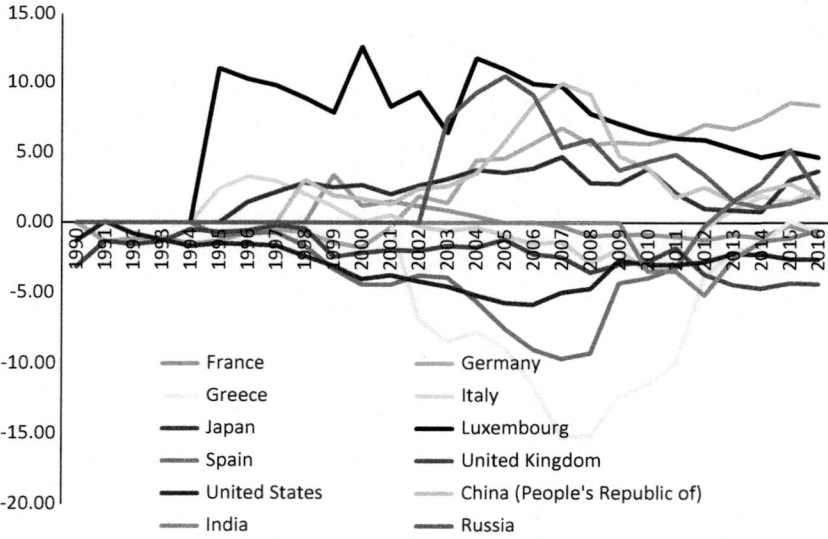

Fig. 5 Trade balance of manufactured goods for selected economies (% of GDP). Data Source: OECD

Fig. 7 Exports of aerospace manufactured goods for selected economies (% of total exports). Data Source: OECD. Notes: The data is (annual) time series. The variables are as follows: %FR refers to French data, %DE refers to German data, %GR refers to Greek data, %IT refers to Italian data, %JP refers to Japanese data, %ES refers to Spanish data, %UK refers to UK data, %US refers to US data, %PRC refers to Chinese data, %IN refers to Indian data, %RU to Russian data and %LUX to Luxembourg data

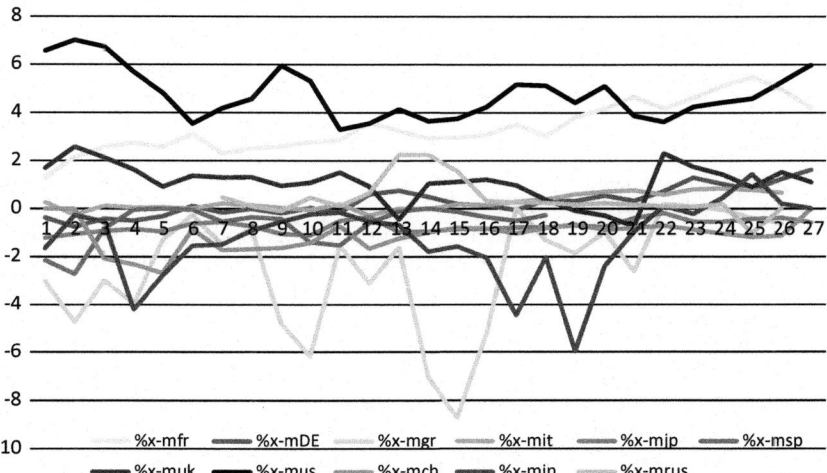

Fig. 6 Trade balance (*X–M*) of manufactured aerospace goods for selected economies (% of total exports). Data Source: OECD. Notes: The data is (annual) time series, where 1 = 1990 ... 27 = 2016. The variables are as follows: %x-mfr refers to French data, %x-mDE refers to German data, %x-mgr refers to Greek data, %x-mit refers to Italian data, %x-mjp refers to Japanese data, %x-msp refers to Spanish data, %x-muk refers to UK data, %x-mus refers to US data, %x-mch refers to Chinese data, %x-min to Indian data and %x-mrus to Russian data

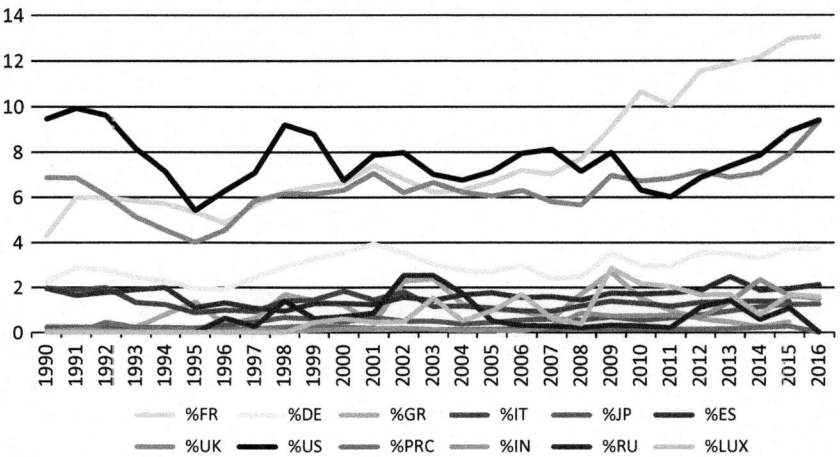

Fig. 7 (continued)

REFERENCES

Baumol, W. J., Panzar, C. J., & Willig, D. R. (1982). *Contestable markets and the theory of industry structure.* New York: Harcourt Brace Jovanovich.

Dunning, J. (1992). *Multinational enterprises and the global economy.* Wokingham: Addison-Wesley.

Laffont, J. J., & Tirole, J. (1993). *Theory of incentives in procurement and regulation.* Cambridge, MA: MIT Press.

McNutt, P. (1999). Public goods and club goods. In B. Bouckaert & G. De Geest (Eds.), *Encyclopedia of law and economics, Vol. I. The history and methodology of law and economics* (pp. 927–951). Cheltenham: Edward Elgar.

Meoqui, J. M. (2014). Reconciling Ricardo's comparative advantage with Smith's productivity theory. *Economic Thought, 3*(2), 21–37. Retrieved May 12, 2017, from https://www.academia.edu/1950826/Reconciling_Ricardo_s_Comparative_Advantage_with_Smith_s_Productivity_Theory.

Nordhaus, W. D. (2005). Paul Samuelson and global public goods. Unpublished commemorative essay for Paul Samuelson, Yale University, May 5. Retrieved May 12, 2017, from http://www.econ.yale.edu/~nordhaus/homepage/PASandGPG.pdf.

Smith, A. (1976). In R. H. Campbell & A. Skinner (Eds.), *An inquiry into the nature and causes of the wealth of nations.* Indianapolis: Liberty Classics.

Smith, A. (2006). *Theory of moral sentiments.* Dover Philosophical Classics (reprint from Sixth Edition, 1790, A. Millar. Original printed in 1759).

Williamson, O. E. (1989). Transaction cost economics. In R. Schmalensee & R. Willig (Eds.), *Handbook of industrial organization* (pp. 135–182). Amsterdam: North Holland.

Zervos, V. (2011). Conflict in space. In L. Braddon & K. Hartley (Eds.), *Handbook of the economics of conflict.* Cheltenham: Edward Elgar Publishers.

Zervos, V. (2015). European policies and the space industry value chain. Conference Paper, 19th Annual International Conference on Economics and Security, Grenoble, France.

PART III

International Organizations and Development

The International Financial System and the Role of Central Banks in the Great 2007–9 Recession and the 'Monetary Peace'

Spyros Vliamos and Konstantinos Gravas

1 Introduction

The emergence of central banks in economic history as institutions serving the public interest is a phenomenon of the twentieth century.[1] '*As had been famously recommended by Bagehot (1873 [1897]), the source of the classic dictum that central banks should address panics by lending freely at a penalty rate*', their major role was the lending of last resort in times of crisis.[2] For this purpose, it was necessary for them to cooperate with the

[1] See Psalidopoulos (2014, p. 5).
[2] See Bernanke (2013, p. 4).

S. Vliamos (✉)
Neapolis University Pafos, Pafos, Cyprus
e-mail: s.vliamos@nup.ac.cy

K. Gravas
University of Athens, Athens, Greece
e-mail: k_gravas1@yahoo.gr

© The Author(s) 2018
S. Vliamos, M. S. Zouboulakis (eds.), *Institutionalist Perspectives on Development*, Palgrave Studies in Democracy, Innovation, and Entrepreneurship for Growth, https://doi.org/10.1007/978-3-319-98494-0_10

State. This relationship has become more relaxed over time and their relative independence vis-à-vis the State became, until nowadays, institutionally established.[3]

The evolution of central banks as independent financial institutions, played an important role in the modern design of monetary policy[4] particularly in response to the '*Great Recession*' of 2008–9 after the bankruptcy of Lehman Brothers in the US and the perceived risk of the '*direct collapse of the global financial system*'.[5] Today not only is the number of central banks around the globe approximately ten times larger compared with what existed at the beginning of the twentieth century, but since the 1990s the central banks of thirty-four countries have amended their statutes in order to strengthen the institutional functioning of the financial system.[6] As a consequence, the scientific interest in the operation and the initiatives of central banks intensified from that decade, when the history of central banking institutions became a distinct and specialized subject of economic history with the aim of drawing conclusions from the past and defining the desired steps for the future, particularly with regard to their institutional role in the contemporary international economic system.[7]

[3] See Psalidopoulos (2014, p. 5); Pollard (2003, p. 24).

[4] For an excellent overview of the idea of independence of C.B. ('The Case for Central Bank Independence') see Bernanke (2010a, pp. 2–7); Mishkin (2007, pp. 37–42) summarizes '*seven basic principles that can serve as useful guides for central banks to help them achieve successful outcomes in their conduct of monetary policy.*' These are: price stability, fiscal policy in line with monetary policy, avoiding the problem of time inconsistency between short and long period, forward-looking monetary policy in advance of long lags from actions to their intended effects, accountability as a basic principle of democracy, monitoring of fluctuations in production and prices, prevention and maintaining of financial instability.

[5] See Bernanke (2009): '*This strong and unprecedented international policy response ... averted the imminent collapse of the global financial system ...*'; Greenspan (2013, p. 149) characterizes the financial crisis '*in the immediate aftermath of the Lehman bankruptcy*' as '*a once-in-a-century-event*' and '*once-in-a-lifetime-event*'.

[6] See Touffut (2008, p. 1). However, the number of central banks has increased not only because of changes in the international financial and monetary system. Geopolitical developments also played an important role. According to Pollard (2003, p. 11), at the time of the creation of the Federal Reserve of the United States of America (US Fed) in 1913, there were only twenty central banks in the world. Due to two important geopolitical factors, firstly, decolonization which took place in the period after the second world war, and secondly, the collapse and disintegration of the Soviet Union in the early 1990s that led to the establishment of separate former Soviet republics, the number of central banks around the globe reached 172 by the year 1997. One year later, in 1998, the European Central Bank (ECB) was founded as the institutional independent monetary authority for the entire Eurozone.

[7] See Psalidopoulos (2014, p. 6).

The purpose of this article is the study of *'monetary peace'* as an important treaty that defines the *political economy of the recent economic crisis* through the institutional role and the coordinated action of the two leading central banks worldwide.[8] We define *monetary peace* as the coordinated action and international cooperation among USA, Germany (within the Eurozone) and China, to maintain the status quo of the US dollar as a *global reserve currency* in order to preserve the global monetary regime.[9] The authors of this chapter believe that the effective functioning of the real world depends on the existence of adequate institutional infrastructure. As Sohmen puts it, *'many economists express their theories in a weird way: they first view a theory and then ask for the institutional conditions which would render the theory feasible'*.[10] We have followed exactly the reverse procedure: we first describe the institutional preconditions for the implementation and consolidation of 'monetary peace' and then we formulate our theory. This view is supported by both Eichengreen (2014, p. 154), *'... the economic historian's approach differs in that it pays more attention to context, to politics and to institutions when evaluating both the formulation and effects of monetary policy'*, and Greenspan (2013, p. 54), *'Every policy initiative reflects both a forecast of the future and a paradigm of the way an economy works.'*

In this study, therefore, we approach the evolution of central banks as powerful institutions in the international economic system under the new ideological structure (paradigm) of 'monetary peace' to tackle the 'Great Recession'. For this to be achieved, we follow the *'case study method'*. In Bernanke and Mishkin's (1992, p. 185) words '[Case studies do two things]... *First, they can help establish the historical and institutional context, an essential first step in good applied work. Second, historical analysis of actual policy experiences is a natural way to find substantive hypotheses that subsequent work can model and test formally.'*

Within this epistemological framework, the questions which will be addressed are:

---

[8] According to Boulding (1972), 'the *uncertainty principle in quantum mechanics (Heisenberg's Uncertainty Principle) can be generalized and transferred also in the social space. This means that the neoclassical hypothesis for an economic world that is independent (not affected) by the science is completely non-existent. In truth the economic (social) science does not explore just the knowledge of the object, but it also manufactures it.'* (Karantonis 2006, p. 191).

[9] For an introduction in *Monetary Peace*, see our recent paper Vliamos and Gravas (2016).

[10] See Karantonis (2006, p. 119).

- What was the role of Central Banks initially?
- How was this role influenced by economic and financial circumstances of the time?
- What is the role of central banks today in ensuring monetary peace after the 'Great Recession' of 2007–9?

The structure of the article is as follows: Section 2 discusses the role of Central Banks as institutions for the stability of the international monetary system. Section 3 outlines the actions of the Central Banks after the 'Great Recession' of 2007–9. Finally, Sect. 4 provides a summary and states the conclusions.

2   CENTRAL BANKS AS STABILITY FACTORS OF THE INTERNATIONAL FINANCIAL SYSTEM

Experience has shown that, in order to avoid inherent methodological and research shortcomings when recording the history of Central Banks, one has to bear in mind the following:

First, studies[11] based solely on the reports of Governors and the decisions of the General Councils do not identify the activities of Central Banks both, as lenders of last resort, and as regulatory and supervisory authorities. Instead, studies based on the institutional framework of rules and regulations—in particular the international coordination of actions—are an important field of information.

Second, central bankers' personalities play an important role. Their ideas and principles form the framework within which they exercise their function. El-Erian (2014) stresses that '*Central bankers, a group of largely independent technocrats, wield more power over the fates of politicians, investors and regular folk than ever before. In the absence of government action, they are bearing most of the burden of supporting economic recoveries in the U.S. and Europe. With their bond purchases and other unconventional policies, they have become a major force holding up financial markets around the world.*'

---

[11] Psalidopoulos (2014, pp. 6–9) summarizes the relevant discussion about the question '*How to Write a History of a Bank*' based on an academic conference with the participation of the most respective economic and central bank historians who shared their arguments on methodological and research issues.

Third, since actions of central banking institutions do not unfold in a vacuum but at specific times loaded with particular economic and political circumstances and issues, a holistic approach of the historic route of central banks requires knowledge of both national and global economic environments. Actions at national level interact with international events and developments. Changes of this international context lead to changes of aims and objectives of the intervention of these banking institutions.[12]

The institutional arrangements in the evolution of central banks over the course of time watched the progress of globalization and the evolution of macroeconomic phenomena. *'The pattern is that each crisis leads to a new set of regulations. The banking crisis of 1907 led to establishment of the Federal Reserve. [...] The 2008 banking crisis led to Dodd-Frank,[13] which further limited the lending activities of banks'* (Kindleberger and Aliber 2015, pp. 239–240). As *'the political economy recognizes the fact that the performance of the economy depends ... largely upon the institutional mechanisms that society chooses to use',*[14] the gradual strengthening of the role of CBs as sovereign institutions in the international financial system should be seen as a reflection of changes in the (international) monetary system.

As these institutional arrangements gradually turned into practice, central banks *'became the repository for most banks in the banking system'.* They also *'allowed them to become the lender of last resort in the face of a financial crisis'*, in other words, becoming *'willing to provide emergency cash to their correspondents in times of financial distress.'*[15]

In the post-2008 era, independent central banks in advanced economies proceeded in an unprecedented relaxation of monetary policy in order to prevent a repeat of the episode of the *Great Depression* of the 1930s. Both the Federal Reserve of the United States (*Fed*) and the

---

[12] Ibid.

[13] The *Dodd-Frank Wall Street Reform and Consumer Protection Act* is 'an act to promote the financial stability of the United States by improving accountability and transparency in the financial system, to end "too big to fail", to protect the American taxpayer by ending bailouts, to protect consumers from abusive financial services practices, and for other purposes.' (Congress, Public Law 111–203); *'The Federal Reserve's post-crisis efforts to strengthen its regulation and supervision of large banks have focused on promoting the safety and soundness of these firms and on limiting the adverse effects that their distress or failure could have on the financial system and the broader economy. This orientation is consistent with section 165 of the Dodd-Frank Wall Street Reform and Consumer Protection Act (Dodd-Frank Act), which directs the Board to impose enhanced prudential standards on large banking organizations "in order to prevent or mitigate risks to financial stability"'* (Yellen 2016).

[14] See Vliamos (1992, p.5).

[15] See Bordo (2007, p. 1).

European Central Bank (*ECB*) which, according to Buiter, have already been '*the only two truly systemically important central banks*'[16] even before the global financial crisis, exceeded their differences relating to monetary objectives dictated by their statutes and worked in *coordination* based on the institutional and operational independence from respective governments.[17]

In practice, all actions of major central banks (mainly through the cooperation between the Fed and the ECB), which followed the outbreak of the 2008 crisis, aimed at keeping '*monetary peace*' in order to support the current monetary regime with the dominant status of the dollar as a global reserve currency.[18] For this to succeed, cooperation in the conduct of monetary policy is a necessary condition which was realized through the mutually beneficial moratoria (economic cooperation) between the three dominant Global Powers of our times: a. the United States, in America, b. Germany, in Europe (within the Eurozone), and c. China, in Asia. In light of this coordinated action, we recall that '*The problem is a general one in politics and business and centers on who should look out for the public interest.*'[19]

---

[16] See Buiter (2007, p. 3).

[17] In this context, 'transparency ...' (with the meaning of 'information disclosure') which is '...the most dramatic difference between central banking today and central banking in earlier historical periods' (Dincer and Eichengreen 2008, p. 1), led to the strengthening of the institutional role of central banks as a crucial factor preserving financial stability within the International Financial System. '*Transparency is seen as a key element of accountability in an era of central bank independence*' (Dincer and Eichengreen 2013, p. 2); For an excellent focus on the '*world's two most prominent central banks—the Federal Reserve System and the European Central Bank*', see Pollard (2003) and especially for the differences between their respective statutes, monetary goals and tools, see ibid., pp. 19–21.

[18] See Vliamos and Gravas (2016, pp. 90 & 101). The crisis began in the United States and threatened the dominant status of the dollar as a global reserve currency. USA, China and Germany had a shared interest to preserve this currency regime. Firstly, the interest of the US to preserve greenback's '*exorbitant privilege*' was obvious. Secondly, for China, dollar stability has been vital regarding foreign exchange reserves and SAFE investments in US treasuries; a possible massive selling of both dollars and treasuries to hedge against the exchange rate risk would only accelerate the collapse of the global reserve currency. Thirdly, Germany shared the same interest to prevent the risk of a dollar collapse, because exports would have been significantly hit in case of an (abruptly) overvalued euro as a shadow Deutsche Mark; therefore, Germany cooperated with '*Chimerica*', a neologism put by Ferguson (2008) to describe the close relationship between China and [the United States of] America.

[19] See Kindleberger and Aliber (2015, p. 102).

However, current developments are hardly windfall effects. The role of Central Banks now is based on the internationalization of financial affairs and the *mentalité* developed then. Therefore current developments have evolved over time, starting from the 'first globalization' era. The so-called *'first age of globalization'* today from (roughly) 1870 until the start of WWI in 1914,[20] is regarded as crucial, both for the evolution of the role of central banks and for international currency and trade relations. The growth of global trade created favorable conditions for the expansion of lending. The development of international capital markets has contributed to better functioning of borrowing between debtors and creditors, who through the grid of trade were also producers of products and customers respectively. The monetary regime assisted the proper functioning of the system. This regime existed throughout the period of early globalization, with the system of fixed exchange rates between currencies to prevent adverse effects on international trade by sudden changes in the exchange rate or monetary crises.[21] As Eichengreen (1992, p. 3) argues in his famous *Golden Fetters*, *'The gold standard had been a remarkably efficient mechanism for organizing financial affairs.'*

The stability of the monetary regime, namely the prewar gold standard, during this first globalization period was not coincidental; it was instead the result of two different factors: *credibility* and *cooperation*.[22] Specifically concerning the period between 1880 and 1913, Eichengreen (1992, p. 5) notes that *'it was exclusively in this period that the political and economic elements necessary to establish the credibility of the system and facilitate international cooperation were all present at the same time.'* Kindleberger (1986) argues that the stability of the prewar gold standard resulted from effective management by its leading member, Great Britain, and her agent, the Bank of England, which stabilised the monetary system by acting as an *international lender of last resort.*[23]

---

[20] See Psalidopoulos (2014, p. 11); According to Borio and Toniolo (2006, p. 5), *'With the Reichsbank's commitment to convert its notes into gold in 1876, the yellow metal became the unchallenged monetary standard of the developed "core" of the world economy. For the following 40-odd years, until the outbreak of World War I in 1914, the "classical gold standard" provided the background for a relatively efficient and stable system of international payments, in an epoch of rapidly expanding commodity trade, record-high labour migration, and free and growing capital mobility, often called the "first globalisation".'*

[21] See Eichengreen and Bordo (2002, pp. 3–4).

[22] See Eichengreen (1992, p. 5).

[23] Ibid., p. 4.

The preservation of financial stability was also the primary goal of the *'Great Experiment'*, as the founding of the Fed is characterized in academic literature.[24] Over time, *'the stability need—i.e. the need of a public institution to establish "public" confidence in a currency that has no intrinsic value—remains an uncontested argument in favour of the central bank solution.'*[25] As Akerlof and Schiller (2009, pp. 204–6) put it in terms of *Animal Spirits*, the lack of *trust* that is created in the system, a lack of *confidence* to banks as well as among banks themselves, exacerbates or even multiplies *panic*, thus creating an atmosphere of defeatism. *'After another particularly bad panic and ensuing recession in 1907, bankers and the Congress decided it was time to reconsider a centralized national bank'.*[26] Therefore, *'a collective body was, first and foremost, needed in order to treat and prevent with combined strength a prospective crisis—instead of every single bank or local association of banks struggling to meet its needs.'*[27]

3   CENTRAL BANKS ACTIONS AFTER THE 'GREAT RECESSION' OF 2007–9 AND 'MONETARY PEACE'

Therefore, today the prevailing view about central banks is that they are institutions charged with the conduct of monetary policy and protect the banking system in general and the currency in particular, i.e. institutions serving the public interest.[28] Goodfriend (2014) argues that *'Monetary policy is suitable for delegation to an independent central bank because monetary policy is about managing aggregate bank reserves, currency, interest on reserves and the general level of interest rates for the whole economy.'* and also that *'Central bank initiatives must be regarded as legitimate by the legislature and the public, otherwise such initiatives will lack credibility essential for their effectiveness.'*[29]

In the historical evolution of central banking, *'a key force has been central bank independence'*. The original central banks, which were private

---

[24] See Bernanke (2013, pp. 3–4).

[25] See Padoa-Schioppa (2003, p. 272).

[26] See Federal Reserve Bank of Minneapolis. 'A History of Central Banking in the United States', available at: https://www.minneapolisfed.org/community/student-resources/central-bank-history/history-of-central-banking.

[27] See Akerlof and Schiller (2009, p. 206).

[28] See Psalidopoulos (2014, p. 58).

[29] See Goodfriend (2014, pp. 113 & 118).

and independent, '*depended on the government to maintain their charters but were otherwise free to choose their own tools and policies.*'[30] In the United States, today, '*Fed independence is … the institutional foundation for effective monetary policy*'.[31] In the Eurozone since 1999, the European Central Bank is the independent monetary authority in accordance with the Treaties of the European Union that constitute primary legislation. The ECB is a (supranational) institution of the EU, responsible for monetary policy decision-making in the euro area.[32] The main objective of the Eurosystem, which is constituted by the European Central Bank and the national central banks in the Eurozone, is to maintain *price stability*,[33] thus safeguarding the value of the euro.[34]

The authors of this article believe that the lessons of the interwar period and the evolution of economic thought parallel with the globalization of the economy have prevented a recurrence of such a '*period of unease of the central banks*' (Psalidopoulos 2011, p. 44). Friedman and Schwartz[35] studied the American economic history using empirical data, developing the monetarist counter-revolution against the Keynesian view of the Great Depression in the realm of economic theory. As the latency of the Fed in the United States is attributed to reluctance or inability to '*exercise of national economic policy, as Friedman and Schwartz would have wished*' (Psalidopoulos 2011, p. 44), monetary peace today requires monetary policy cooperation and coordination at an international, not national, level.

3.1   *The Cooperation of Central Banks*

As early as 1921, the Governor of the Bank of England Montagu Collet Norman issued a 'manifesto' with the four principles of good operation of Central Banks:

[30] See Bordo (2007, p. 3).

[31] See Goodfriend (2014, p. 119).

[32] For a historical review of the political and economic developments that led to the Maastricht Treaty and the birth of the European System of Central Banks and the Euro, see Issing (2008, pp. 22–26).

[33] For the definition of 'price stability', see ECB (2003, pp. 11–13); ECB (2011, p. 64).

[34] See the ECB's official website, https://www.ecb.europa.eu/ecb/html/index.en.html; For the ECB's monetary policy strategy (general principles and key elements), see ECB (2011, pp. 62–64).

[35] Friedman, M., & Schwartz, A. (1963). *A Monetary History of the United States, 1867–1960*.

    a. independence from national governments,
    b. separation from commercial banks,
    c. banking supervision and
    d. (international) cooperation.[36]

The inclusion of 'international cooperation' of Central Banks as a basic principle of their institutional operation, demonstrates the important role it has always had for the functioning of the international monetary system. This, of course, does not mean that throughout the period since the adoption of the gold standard in 1876, until today, the form and the eagerness of central banks to cooperate remains the same. While economic historians disagree on the extent of central bank emergency cooperation during the classical gold standard and on its usefulness for the viability of the system, they do agree that whatever cooperation did occur was carried out on a strict bilateral basis and was undoubtedly less intense than in the years following 1914.[37] Moreover, in the academic literature, views differ as to whether at certain times there is cooperation (*monetary peace*) or controversy (*currency war*).[38]

There is also a different approach among researchers on whether the result is positive or negative in relation to the scope of international cooperation. Rogoff refers to Taylor's review for the coordination of monetary policy at an international level (*International policy coordination*) considers that '*in normal times, when economies are not over borrowed and international credit markets are fully operational, international coordination of monetary policy may be considered to be a secondary problem*' (Taylor 2013, p. 29). Still, Borio and Toniolo (2006, p. 18) studying the financial cooperation of central banks indicate that 'not *all episodes of financial instability could act as a trigger for cooperation*' and that 'as *long as such instability remained a domestic affair, there was no need [for cooperation]*'. But 'in *an increasingly globalised economy, in which financial markets knew no borders, instability could not entirely be contained within national boundaries.*'

---

[36] See Borio & Toniolo (2006, p. 8).

[37] See Borio and Toniolo (2006, pp. 6 and 25–26).

[38] Eichengreen (2013a) discusses the issue of 'Currency war or international policy coordination?'; See also other works of Eichengreen, Eichengreen & Sachs, Reinhart & Rogoff, Taylor; See references in Vliamos and Gravas (2016); Interestingly, in a recent blog-post, Bernanke (2016) finds '*little support for the claims that the Fed's monetary policies of recent years has engaged in currency wars*'.

Therefore, a counter argument to support the need for monetary policy cooperation could be developed as follows. Once the financial crisis broke out in 2008, the global economy was in a status of, on the one hand, over-leverage of both the public and the private sector due to a loose monetary policy in a low interest-rate environment, and on the other hand, complete financial market liberalization in a relatively weak supervisory and regulatory environment. The globalization of the economy changed the 'domestic' problem into an international one very quickly. Even six years after the onset of the financial crisis, Lo and Rogoff (2015)[39] observed that '*recent years have seen a sharp increase in public debt, private domestic credit, and external debt, all as a percentage of GDP*'.[40] Therefore in the context of this study we consider that, since the recent episode of financial instability was global, international cooperation and coordination of monetary policy held by the major central banks (especially the Fed and the ECB) is a primary need. Let alone when it comes to '*a once-in-a-century-event*' (Greenspan 2013, p. 149).

The thesis of these authors indicates that the institutional evolution of central banks may gradually, in the medium-to-long-term either lead to a *multipolar* monetary system,[41] or approach, in a next phase longer-term, a model of a *world currency*[42]; both provided that the perceptions of policy makers coexist in the direction of cooperation (*monetary peace*) rather than conflict (*currency war*).[43]

The need for policy coordination at an international level arises from the recognition of the risk of a mutually destructive outcome in the case of unilateral policy options. King (2015b) reports historical examples of policy coordination, first, in the 1980s with the *Plaza* (in September 1985)[44] and the *Louvre* (in February 1987)[45] *Accords*, and second, in 2009

---

[39] They examine the average statistics across twenty-two advanced countries.

[40] See Lo and Rogoff (2015, p. 9).

[41] For an excellent analysis, see the chapter 'Monopoly No More' in Eichengreen (2011, pp. 121–153).

[42] See Mundell (2012).

[43] Bernanke (2016) separates Fed's monetary policy to tackle the *Great Recession*, from the classic interpretation of '*currency wars*'.

[44] The Plaza Accord '*was probably the most dramatic policy initiative in the dollar foreign exchange market since Richard Nixon originally floated the currency in 1973. [...] US officials and their counterparts among the Group of Five largest industrialized countries [G-5] agreed to act to bring down the value of the dollar. Public statements from the officials were backed up by foreign exchange intervention, selling dollars in exchange for other currencies in the foreign exchange market. The Plaza is justly celebrated as a high-water mark of international policy coordination*' (Frankel 2015).

[45] See Eichengreen (2008, p. 147).

with the meeting of G-20 countries in London. In this context he under-lines that '*Today's outbreak of deflationary currency wars threatens some-thing similar*' and he wonders '*How should the world break away from this cycle of deflationary devaluations?*'[46]

We believe that international cooperation is most likely in the following circumstances. (Eichengreen 2013b, pp. 43–44). First, when '*cooperation is institutionalized*[47]' in the sense that '*procedures and precedents create presumptions about the appropriate conduct of policy and reduce the transac-tions costs of reaching an agreement.*' Second, when there is an existing '*policy regime*' *(a set of policies and behaviors)* as '*an incentive for policymak-ers [central banks] to cooperate in its preservation*'. In this sense, '*much successful international cooperation is therefore of the regime—preserving type.*'[48]

This study, as it will be shown further on,[49] supports that:

a. The institutional and operational independence of the central banks (Fed, ECB) implies de jure but also de facto institutionalized coop-eration in the fields of monetary policy and the safeguarding of financial stability.
b. The existing 'policy regime' should support *monetary peace*, which serves the mutually beneficial economic cooperation framework between the United States, Germany and China. The preservation of this regime leads to international cooperation between Fed and ECB, which reinforces their role as institutions within the interna-tional financial system.

By the 1880s there had been an established international monetary regime to preserve. The leading central banks provided emergency assistance to the system with the goal of preserving this regime. A typical example back in 1890 was the preservation of the sterling exchange rate and, therefore, the protection of the sovereign status of the British currency in the inter-

---

[46] See also King (2015a).

[47] '*One definition of an institution is a set of durable rules and understandings shaping expec-tations, interests, and behaviors—rules and understandings that can range from informal norms to formal obligations for what constitutes acceptable behavior and that are sometimes embodied in an organization, sometimes not*' (Eichengreen 2013b, p. 44).

[48] Ibid.

[49] In the following analysis we draw heavily on facts and arguments presented in Eichengreen (2013b, pp. 52–71).

national monetary system during the Baring crisis. More than a hundred years later, during the great financial crisis of 2008, the leading central banks provided analogous emergency assistance; the dollar and euro swap lines extended by the Fed and the ECB, with the goal of protecting a fragile banking and financial system.

International cooperation at the level of central banks also observed in two consecutive episodes in economic history, both related to the normal economic cycle: ascendant, overheating, boom (bubble), bust (burst of the bubble). In particular, it is interesting that the first episode happened to prevent the adverse effects of a financial '*boom*' in the United States which drew gold from the London market in the early twentieth century, while in contrast, the second episode refers to concerted central banks actions aiming to halt the banking crisis which occurred when the bubble created during this boom finally burst ('*bust*'). In the first case, there has been cooperation between the Bank of England and the Bank of France as both central banks '*were in contact with one another*'.[50] They cooperated in the sense that sterling support movements by the latter (Bank of France) were made in light of the mutual interest of both central banks. In the second case, the Bank of France and the German Central Bank (Reichsbank) protected the gold standard and British sterling's status in the international monetary system, as the Bank of England found itself in the eye of the storm because of the banking crisis on the other side of the Atlantic.

The reconstructing of the monetary system after World War I, founded, in a sense, the need for even greater international cooperation among sovereign institutional actors. The International Conference in Genoa, in 1922, resulted in '*an agreement under which central banks could supplement their gold holdings with reserves of convertible foreign exchange.*'[51] The aim of the systematic application of this alternative rule, i.e. restoration of the prewar status of the gold standard, was to avoid a deflationary spiral due to a mismatch between global gold production, on the one hand, and the significant rise in prices due to the War, on the other. However, it is not controversial that the agreed in Genoa connection of monetary policies in different countries, had planted the seeds of instability in the monetary system of the interwar period, which was just one factor that made the international cooperation among the central banks of these countries necessary.

[50] Ibid., p. 53.
[51] Ibid., p. 54.

The above has been questioned by academic writers such as Rogoff, Meltzer and Buiter, among others. Their position strongly opposes the thesis that international cooperation is beneficial. Rogoff (1985) demonstrates that increased international monetary cooperation may actually be counterproductive. Meltzer (2003) invokes the case of '*moral hazard*' during England's rehabilitation phase in the gold standard during the 1920s: the deviation from normal Fed monetary policy within the gold standard in order to support the Bank of England in the context of international cooperation, has led to an extremely loose monetary policy that fueled the rampant credit expansion and the credit bubble that popped abruptly at the end of the 1920s.[52] Buiter (2007), finally, states that '*coordination could make sense if monetary policy were an effective instrument for fine-tuning the business cycle*', however, '*in a world with unrestricted international mobility of financial capital ... the lingering belief in the effectiveness of monetary policy as a cyclical stabilization instrument is evidence of the 'fine tuning illusion' or 'fine tuning fallacy' at work.*'[53]

Nevertheless, the monetary crisis of 1992–93 with the speculative attack on the British pound and the instability of the Exchange Rate Mechanism (ERM) highlighted the need for further institutional collaboration of monetary policy, as '*it was necessary to create a European central bank and a single European currency, as foreseen in the Delors Report in 1989 and endorsed in the Maastricht Treaty of 1992.*'[54] We consider the creation of the ECB, which is '*the monetary pillar of the Economic and Monetary Union*',[55] as a case of monetary policy coordination and a decisive step towards *monetary peace* within the European continent.

However, to make this cooperation effective, there must be a '*collective interest*'.[56] An additional strong indication for the existence of monetary

---

[52] Ibid., p. 55.

[53] See Buiter (2007, p. 1).

[54] See Eichengreen (2013b, pp. 70–71).

[55] See Issing (2011, p. 748).

[56] Interestingly, Eichengreen (2013b, p. 61) refers to the Gold Pool arrangement at the beginning of the 1960s, '*through which the European members committed to reimbursing the reserve-currency country, the United States, for a portion of its gold losses*'. Although this ad hoc rather than fully institutionalized arrangement '*did not resolve the fundamental contradictions of the gold-dollar system, it bought time to seek a permanent solution.*' As Eichengreen states, '*the contrast with the early 1930s is apparent. On both occasions there was an established international monetary and financial system in whose preservation the leading countries had a shared interest. But, in contrast with the high tensions of the 1930s, the principals this time were allies in the Cold War*'.

policy coordination between these two central banks of the leading economic powers came in January 2012, when under Bernanke the Fed formally adopted an explicit 2 percent inflation objective,[57] which is the same numerical inflation target according to the Statute of the ECB.[58]

The coordination of ECB's monetary policy with the non-conventional measures taken by the US Fed was a milestone for the capital markets at the height of the Eurozone debt crisis by mid-2012. In Mario Draghi's own words, *'within our mandate, the ECB is ready to do whatever it takes to preserve the euro.'* (ECB 2012a). In September 2012 the Governing Council of the ECB decided on the modalities for undertaking Outright Monetary Transactions (OMTs)[59] in secondary markets for sovereign bonds in the euro area, effectively committing itself to providing unlimited liquidity in the Government bond market of the Eurozone. This fact certainly constituted a *'regime change'* in the Eurozone and contributed to a significant decline in interest rate spreads between North and South bond yields.[60] *Monetary peace* was secured even using the loosest definition of non-(monetary) war.

3.2   IMF and Monetary Peace

Following the 2001 Argentine crisis, the International Monetary Fund (IMF) has modified the institutional framework with regards to exceptional access arrangements for a member country to borrow from the IMF. The lending framework that was in force since 2002 and was still valid with minor modifications and revisions up to 2009, provided that in exceptional circumstances, a member country could be granted a loan in

---

[57] See Federal Open Market Committee (2012, pp. 7–8).

[58] Particularly because this happened one year after the replacement of Jean-Claude Trichet, head of the ECB in 2011, by current ECB chairman Mario Draghi who is considered to belong to the same school of economic thought with both former Fed president Bernanke and his successor Janet Yellen.

[59] See ECB (2012b, pp. 7–9); Greenspan (2013, p. 222) characterizes ECB's OMT program as *'the ultimate weapon in the fight to preserve the euro'*.

[60] See De Grauwe (2013, p. 520); For the pressure on the central bank to support government bond prices, see also Eichengreen et al. (2011, p. 24); From an alternative point of view, Kindleberger and Aliber (2015, p. 229) argue that *'in effect, the ECB has moved beyond the role of a lender of last resort and become an informal deposit insurance agency.'* In this sense, one can assume that the ECB functioned as a hybrid of both the Fed and the FDIC (Federal Deposit Insurance Corporation).

excess of its quota. For this to be held the member's public debt had to be sustainable in the medium term.[61]

Bypassing this specific criterion of the lending institutional framework under extraordinary conditions, the IMF decided in May 2010 to grant Greece a three-year loan of EUR 30 billion (SDR 26.4 billion or 3,212 percent of quota).[62] To justify this exception, the IMF has invoked the 'systemic' risk of spreading of the Greek crisis across Eurozone, since Greece was a member of a monetary union that constitutes the second largest global economic bloc, thus requiring more flexibility in lending by the Fund in exceptional circumstances.[63] As the world economy went through its worst crisis in several decades, the IMF reformed its functions to facilitate the needs of its Member States.[64]

However, the authors of this study argue that the main reason for the participation of the IMF and the exception to the Greek program in 2010 has been to serve the objective of *monetary peace*. As the European Monetary Union still lacks an institution comparable to the IMF, the euro area made use of the expertise and assistance of IMF's fiscal adjustment programmes for the economies of southern Europe.[65] As Schadler (2016, p. 6) puts it, '*the case for IMF involvement stemmed in large part from a conviction that the IMF was the best-equipped institution for the technical rigors of negotiating and monitoring the program.*'

3.3   The Fourth Era of Central Banks

Academic literature after the 2007–9 financial crisis, questions if there is a new era in the role of central banks. Goodhart ([2010] 2011) mentions that central banks bear the following four main objectives over time:

1. price stability, financial stability,
2. support of financial needs of the State in times of war,
3. limitation of State power in normal periods (peace) from the misuse of monetary policy for political benefits.

[61] See Schadler (2016, p. 3).
[62] See IMF (2010b); Xafa (2014, p. 14).
[63] See Xafa (2014, p. 14); '*The Greek case is quite unique in the sovereign debt Literature … The debt sustainability criterion was waived based on the systemic concerns arising from spillover risks if the program was not approved.*' (Ibid., p. 12 & 14).
[64] See IMF (2010a).
[65] See Vliamos & Gravas (2016, pp. 100–101).

Furthermore, he characterizes the period from 1980 to 2007 as a '*triumph of markets*'.[66] This period coincides with the third phase as described by Reinhart and Rogoff (2013). In their words, '... *from 1979, beginning with an aggressive inflation stabilization plan until the crisis of 2007, the third phase, (an independent) Fed was guided by a mandate of price stability and macroeconomic stabilization.*' (p. 49).

These authors consider, in Goodhart's words, that we have already entered '*a fourth epoch, in the aftermath of the financial crisis of 2007–9*'.[67] In our view though, not only will the institutional dependence of Central Banks not be harmed as Goodhart (2010, 2011, p. 15) speculates,[68] but on the contrary, they will remain powerful independent institutions within the international financial system. The fourth era that we already live in, after 2010, is the epoch of *monetary peace*.

4   Conclusions

It is claimed that '*in the level of macroeconomics, overall, confidence comes and passes ... It is not simply a rational prediction. It is the first and most important of our animal spirits.*' (Akerlof and Schiller 2009, pp. 60–63).

Similarly this chapter claims that self-preservation forces of the international system were developed to address the severe risks coming from the *Great 2007–9 Recession*. Central Banks as independent monetary authorities rushed to cooperate in order to preserve the global monetary regime that existed before the great financial crisis. In the words of Eichengreen (2013b, p. 44), first, '*history suggests that international policy coordination is more likely when it is institutionalized*', and second, 'a condition that favors cooperation is when there already exists a set of policies and behaviors as a "*policy regime*" that must be preserved.'

---

[66] See Goodhart (2010, pp. 5–6).

[67] Ibid., p. 15.

[68] Commenting on Goodhart (2010), Stanley Fisher stresses the benefits of having an independent central bank which can take an apolitical view of what is good for the economy longer term. '*One interpretation is that even an independent central bank needs to get used to the idea of working cooperatively with the government in those areas that are of mutual concern, while jealously guarding its independent right to make key decisions according to the authority granted it under the law. If not, the benefits of having a central bank that can take a longer term and apolitical view of what is good for the economy and take actions in support of that view will be lost – and that would be a costly mistake*' (p. 19).

If indeed *'social peace (consistency) is included in the value of social secur-ing in both theory and practice of economic policy'* (Karantonis 2006, p. 248), then monetary policy of central banks which either serves exclu-sively the objective of price stability (ECB) or the dual objective of price stability and full employment in the economy (Fed), aims to safeguard social peace. In the words of Bernanke (1995, p. 1), if we really accept that, *'understanding the Great Depression is the Holy Grail of macroeconom-ics'*, as *'... the experience of the 1930s continues to influence macroeconomists' beliefs, policy recommendations, and research agendas..'*, then, it is not too much to say that the study of the recent period of the Great Recession starting in 2007 is an equally *'... fascinating intellectual challenge'*.

As the lessons of the Great Depression were learned for tackling the Great Recession after 2007–9, *monetary peace*, i.e., the coordinated action by central banks among U.S., Germany (Eurozone) and China, in order to maintain the status quo of the US dollar as a global reserve currency—[69] healed two fundamental mistakes made after the Great Crash of Wall Street in 1929 which led to the global economic crisis in the early 1930s. First, the contraction of the money supply, which deep-ened the financial crisis turning it from a recession to depression, under the assumption that the crisis was rather isolated in a domestic sphere, mainly in the USA,[70] and second, the misplaced return to the 'gold stan-dard', reconstructed amid a different political and economic context to link currencies with gold as in the pre-war era, under the alternative assumption that the crisis was in the international sphere, hardly isolated in the American economy.[71]

Regarding the former, Friedman and Schwartz (1963, 2012) have shown that monetary policy exercised by the Federal Reserve in 1929 restricted the money supply to the domestic economy, thus worsening the recession and the financial crisis, and causing the Great Depression. On the contrary, in 2008, the successive *'Quantitative Easing'* Programs (*QE1, 2, 3*),[72] which were adopted by the Fed after the outbreak of the crisis with the collapse of Lehman Brothers, aimed exactly in this direc-

[69] See Vliamos and Gravas (2016).

[70] The classic interpretation of this view is Friedman and Schwartz (1963) and, particularly for the Great Depression period, Friedman and Schwartz (2012).

[71] The most influential expression of this view is Kindleberger (2013).

[72] See Bernanke (2015, pp. 417–421), where the former Fed chairman refers to the 'US Treasury Large-Scale Asset Purchase Program' which, in his view, defers in many respects from the classic term 'quantitative easing' known from Japan experience.

tion: the provision of liquidity to the financial system to direct monetary injections in overleveraged balance sheets of the banking sector. At the same time, the Federal Reserve quickly lowered short term interest rates near the zero lower bound (ZLB).[73]

Regarding the latter—the interwar return to the 'gold standard'—, international monetary relations under the regime which existed in the period prior to World War I, were more vulnerable and less effective in the interwar period that followed. Kindleberger (2013) argues that imbalances of the interwar period in the international monetary system have destabilized the global economy. The basic imbalance was created by the time lag between the decline of Britain's hegemony—and consequently of the sterling currency's status—after WWI, and the emergence of the United States as the dominant economic power—and hence the dollar as the global reserve currency—in the period after World War II.[74] The time gap concerning the transitional period until the new equilibrium in international monetary arrangements, destabilized the global economy as the political and economic landscape had changed.

Mutatis mutandis after the global financial crisis of 2008, *monetary peace* addressed the need to prevent a U.S. currency collapse as long as the Eurozone—and hence the euro—lacked the institutional conditions for approaching the status of an optimum currency area.[75] Following the outbreak of this crisis, senior officials representing supranational organizations and institutions such as the European Union and the International Monetary Fund underlined the risk of a catastrophic monetary war. In the event of the euro's failure and the demise of the Eurozone, '*Europe today would be in the throes of monetary war. France against Germany, Germany against Italy, Italy against Portugal and Spain, and so on and so forth.*', [candidate for] President of the European Commission, Jean-Claude Juncker, stated in his Opening statement in the European Parliament plenary session (July 2014), stressing that '*Thanks to the discipline and the ambitions of the euro, we have a monetary order which protects us. The euro protects Europe.*'[76]

---

[73] For a detailed review of academic literature, see the paragraph 'Monetary peace: the interest rate conundrum' in Vliamos and Gravas (2016).
[74] For the international role of the dollar, see also Krugman (1984).
[75] See Mundell (1961).
[76] See European Commission (2014).

Yet, monetary peace for the sake of the international financial and monetary system came at a cost of an undeclared 'economic war' in the Eurozone between North and South, which had collateral damage and casualties. The wounds are still great and many: unemployment (particularly youth), enlarged social inequality, inadequate demand for investments and asymmetry between North-South in the absence of the necessary surplus recycling mechanism. The authors of this chapter believe that the euro was always, first and foremost, a political project, not just a financial one. In the case of France a great battle was won, but not yet the war. Stratfor's Friedman predicted a war in our century by arguing that there had never been a century without a systemic war and giving the historical examples of the Napoleonic Wars of the 19th and the two World Wars of the twentieth century.[77] We would urge European leaders to end this economic war while still protecting monetary peace. At the Bretton Woods conference, Keynes suggested a 'surplus recycling mechanism'. While we are not quite sure if his ideas are more needed today than in 1944, we are certainly convinced that *in the long run we will all be dead.*

According to ECB's president Mario Draghi, the year 2016 *'ended with the [euro area] economy on its firmest footing since the crisis'*,[78] while Fed chairman Janet Yellen stated in a recent speech that *'… the considerable progress the economy has made toward the attainment of the two objectives that the Congress has assigned to the Federal Reserve—maximum employment and price stability.'*[79] The *'unusual uncertainty of the economic outlook'* described by Bernanke (2010b) in the Humphrey-Hawkins testimony,[80] has nowadays been reduced as the institutional arrangements during the Great Recession shaped the scope of policy action and the successful implementation of *monetary peace.* Of course, the question put forward by Minsky (1982), *'Can this [crisis] happen again?'* requires an answer that will ultimately be given by real life. After all, *'money [as it has evolved over time] is a social institution.'*[81] In the words of Mervyn King

---

[77] See http://www.businessinsider.com/stratfor-george-friedman-predictions-for-the-future-2016-2.

[78] See ECB (2017).

[79] See Yellen (2017).

[80] *'…even as the Federal Reserve continues prudent planning for the ultimate withdrawal of extraordinary monetary policy accommodation, we also recognize that the economic outlook remains unusually uncertain.'*

[81] See Bank of England (2014, p. 4); For an excellent discussion of the ascent of money as a social institution, see King (2006).

(2006, p. 2), a market economy requires social institutions which represent collective agreements about how to constrain our actions. '*For example, a market economy cannot flourish in a world of anarchy in which we suspect that everyone else will cheat.*' Since the Central Banks' collective agreements prevented the collapse of the International Financial System in the Great 2007–9 Recession and established '*Monetary Peace*', they can be viewed as social institutions as well.

References

Akerlof, G., & Schiller, R. (2009). *Animal spirits: How human psychology drives the economy, and why it matters for global capitalism* (E. Kotsifou, Trans.). Princeton and Oxford: Princeton University Press.

Bagehot, W. (1873 [1897]). *Lombard street: A description of the money market.* New York: Charles Scribner's Sons.

Bank of England. (2014). Money in the modern economy. *Quarterly Bulletin*, Q1. Retrieved from http://www.bankofengland.co.uk/publications/Documents/quarterlybulletin/2014/qb14q1prereleasemoneycreation.pdf.

Bernanke, B. (1995). The macroeconomics of the Great Depression: A comparative approach. *Journal of Money, Credit and Banking, 27*(1), 1–28 https://doi.org/10.2307/2077848.

Bernanke, B. (2009). Reflections on a year of crisis, Speech at the Federal Reserve Bank of Kansas City's Annual Economic Symposium, Jackson Hole, Wyoming. Retrieved from https://www.federalreserve.gov/newsevents/speech/bernanke20090821a.htm.

Bernanke, B. (2010a). Central bank independence, transparency, and accountability. Speech at the Institute of Monetary and Economic Studies International Conference, Bank of Japan, Tokyo, Japan, 26 May. Retrieved from https://www.federalreserve.gov/newsevents/speech/bernanke20100525a.htm.

Bernanke, B. (2010b). Semiannual monetary policy report to the Congress. testimony before the Committee on Banking, Housing, and Urban Affairs, U.S. Senate, Washington, D.C., July 21. Retrieved from https://www.federalreserve.gov/newsevents/testimony/bernanke20100721a.htm.

Bernanke, B. (2013). A Century of US central banking: Goals, frameworks, accountability. *Journal of Economic Perspectives, 27*(4), 3–16 https://doi.org/10.1257/jep.27.4.3.

Bernanke, B. (2015). *The courage to act: A memoir on a crisis and its aftermath.* New York: W. W. Norton.

Bernanke, B. (2016). What did you do in the currency war, Daddy?, Brookings. Retrieved from http://www.brookings.edu/blogs/ben-bernanke/posts/2016/01/05-currency-war-daddy.

Bernanke, B., & Mishkin, F. (1992). Central bank behavior and the strategy of monetary policy: Observations from six industrialized countries. *NBER Macroeconomics Annual, 7*, 183–228.

Bordo, M. (2007). A brief history of central banks. Federal Reserve Bank of Cleveland Research (December). Retrieved from https://www.clevelandfed.org/en/newsroom-and-events/publications/economic-commentary/economic-commentary-archives/2007-economic-commentaries/ec-20071201-a-brief-history-of-central-banks.aspx.

Borio, C., & Toniolo, G. (2006). One hundred and thirty years of central bank cooperation: A BIS Perspective (February). BIS Working Paper No. 197. Available at SSRN: https://ssrn.com/abstract=891902 or https://doi.org/10.2139/ssrn.891902.

Boulding, K. (1972). Toward the development of a cultural economics. *Social Science Quarterly, 53*(2), 267–284.

Buiter, W. (2007). *Central Banks as economic institutions.* Cournot Centre for Economic Studies. Retrieved from http://willembuiter.com/cournot.pdf

De Grauwe, P. (2013). The European Central Bank as lender of last resort in the government bond markets. *CESifo Economic Studies 2013, 59*(3), 520–535. https://doi.org/10.1093/cesifo/ift012.

Dincer, N., & Eichengreen, B. (2008). *Central bank transparency: Where, why, and with what effects? in Touffut, J. (ed) Central banks as economic institutions* (1st ed.). Cheltenham, UK: Edward Elgar Retrieved from http://www.nber.org/papers/w13003.pdf.

Dincer, N., & Eichengreen, B. (2013). Central bank transparency and independence: Updates and new measures. *SSRN Electronic Journal.* https://doi.org/10.2139/ssrn.2579544

Eichengreen, B. (1992). *Golden fetters: The Gold Standard and the Great Depression, 1919–1939.* New York: Oxford University Press.

Eichengreen, B. (2008). *Globalizing capital: A history of the international monetary system.* Princeton: Princeton University Press.

Eichengreen, B. (2011). *Exorbitant privilege.* Oxford: Oxford University Press.

Eichengreen, B. (2013a). Currency war or international policy coordination? *Journal of Policy Modeling, 35*(3), 425–433.

Eichengreen, B. (2013b). International policy coordination: The Long View. In R. Feenstra & A. Taylor. (2014). *Globalization in an age of crisis: Multilateral economic cooperation in the twenty-first century.* National Bureau of Economic Research. Chicago: University of Chicago Press, pp. 43–82.

Eichengreen, B. (2014). Methodology of economic history as an approach to assessing monetary policy. *Journal of Economic Dynamics and Control, 49*, 154–155.

Eichengreen, B., & Bordo, M. (2002). Crises now and then: What lessons from the last era of financial globalization. doi:https://doi.org/10.3386/w8716.

Eichengreen, B., El-Erian, M., Fraga, A., Ito, T., Pisani-Ferry, J., Prasad, E., et al. (2011). *Rethinking central banking*. Washington, DC: Brookings Institution.

El-Erian, M. (2014). Why you should care about Jackson Hole. *Bloomberg View*, 19 August. Retrieved from https://www.bloomberg.com/view/articles/2014-08-19/why-you-should-care-about-jackson-hole.

European Central Bank. (2003). *Background studies for the ECB's evaluation of its monetary policy strategy* (Otmar Issing, Ed.). Frankfurt: European Central Bank, pp. 10–13.

European Central Bank. (2011). *The Monetary policy of the ECB*. Frankfurt: European Central Bank.

European Central Bank. (2012a). Verbatim of the remarks made by Mario Draghi, Speech by Mario Draghi, President of the European Central Bank at the Global Investment Conference in London, 26 July 2012. Retrieved from https://www.ecb.europa.eu/press/key/date/2012/html/sp120726.en.html

European Central Bank. (2012b). *Monthly Bulletin*, October. Retrieved from https://www.ecb.europa.eu/pub/pdf/mobu/mb201210en.pdf.

European Central Bank. (2017). Annual Report 2016. Retrieved from https://www.ecb.europa.eu/pub/pdf/annrep/ar2016en.pdf?f7090bb266c06d6c8857f41220370bfb.

European Commission. (2014). A new start for Europe. Opening statement in the European Parliament plenary session. Retrieved from http://europa.eu/rapid/press-release_SPEECH-14-567_en.htm.

Federal Open Market Committee. (2012). Minutes of the FOMC Meeting, January 24. Retrieved from https://www.federalreserve.gov/monetarypolicy/files/fomcminutes20120125.pdf.

Ferguson, N. (2008). *The ascent of money: A financial history of the world*. New York: Penguin.

Frankel, J. (2015). The Plaza Accord, 30 years later (No. w21813). National Bureau of Economic Research. Retrieved from https://sites.hks.harvard.edu/fs/jfrankel/PlazaAccord-PIIE2016.pdf.

Friedman, M., & Schwartz, A. (1963). *A monetary history of the United States, 1867–1960*. Princeton: Princeton University Press.

Friedman, M., & Schwartz, A. (2012). *The great contraction, 1929–1933*. Princeton: Princeton University Press.

Goodfriend, M. (2014). Lessons from a century of FED policy: Why monetary and credit policies need rules and boundaries. *Journal of Economic Dynamics and Control, 49*, 112–120.

Goodhart, C. (2010). The changing role of central banks. *BIS Working Papers, 326*(November). Retrieved from http://www.bis.org/publ/work326.htm.

Goodhart, C. (2011). The changing role of central banks. *Financial History Review, 18*(2), 135–154. https://doi.org/10.1017/S0968565011000096.

Greenspan, A. (2013). *The map and the territory: Risk, human nature, and the future of forecasting*. New York: Penguin Books.

IMF. (2010a, April). The IMF is changing – facing the crisis. Retrieved from http://www.imf.org/external/lang/Greek/np/exr/facts/changingg.htm.

IMF. (2010b, May). Greece: Staff report on request for stand-by arrangement. Retrieved from https://www.imf.org/external/pubs/ft/scr/2010/cr10110.pdf.

Issing, O. (2008). *The birth of the euro*. Cambridge: Cambridge University Press.

Issing, O. (2011). The crisis of European Monetary Union â lessons to be drawn. *Journal of Policy Modeling, 33*(5), 737–749.

Karantonis, E. (2006). *Theory of economic policy*. Athens: Typothito.

Kindleberger, C. (1986 [2013]). *The world in depression, 1929–1939* (1st ed.). Berkeley: University of California Press.

Kindleberger, C., & Aliber, R. (2005 [2015]). *Manias, panics, and crashes*. London: Palgrave Macmillan.

King, M. (2006). Trusting in money: From Kirkcaldy to the MPC. Speech at The Adam Smith Lecture. Bank of England. Retrieved from http://www.bankofengland.co.uk/archive/Documents/historicpubs/speeches/2006/speech288.pdf.

King, S. (2015a). Deflation poses central banks with an existential problem. *Financial Times*, March 5. Retrieved from https://www.ft.com/content/115e2c52-0940-31d2-9eed-156379abe486.

King, S. (2015b). Deflation is a global problem and needs collective action. *Financial Times*, April 1. Retrieved from https://www.ft.com/content/3f32ab43-cd32-31ec-b4ec-abd53ddaf1b3.

Krugman, P. (1984). The international role of the dollar: theory and prospect. In *Exchange rate theory and practice*. Chicago: University of Chicago Press, pp. 261–278.

Lo, S., & Rogoff, K. (2015). Secular stagnation, debt overhang and other rationales for sluggish growth, six years on, BIS Working Paper No. 482. Retrieved from http://ssrn.com/abstract=2552574.

Meltzer, A. (2003). *A history of the Federal Reserve, Volume 1, 1913–1949*. Chicago: University of Chicago Press.

Minsky, H. (1982). Can "it" happen again? A reprise. Hyman P. Minsky Archive. Paper 155. Retrieved from http://digitalcommons.bard.edu/hm_archive/155.

Mishkin, F. (2007). *Monetary policy strategy*. Cambridge: The MIT Press.

Mundell, R. (1961). A theory of optimum currency areas. *American Economic Review, 51*, 657–665.

Mundell, R. (2012). The case for a world currency. *Journal of Policy Modeling, 34*(4), 568–578.

Padoa-Schioppa, T. (2003). Central banks and financial stability: Exploring a land in between. In European Central Bank (2003). *The transformation of the European financial system* (V. Gaspar, P. Hartmann, & O. Sleijpen, Eds.). Retrieved from http://central.banktunnel.eu/pub/pdf/other/transformatio-neuropeanfinancialsystemen.pdf#page=270.

Pollard P (2003, January/February). A look inside two central banks: The European Central Bank and the Federal Reserve. Federal Reserve Bank of St. Louis Review pp. 11-30. Retrieved from https://research.stlouisfed.org/publications/review/2003/01/01/a-look-inside-two-central-banks-the-european-central-bank-and-the-federal-reserve/.

Psalidopoulos, M. (2011, July). *Monetary management and economic crisis. The policy of the Bank of Greece, 1929–1941*. Bank of Greece.

Psalidopoulos, M. (2014). *History of the Bank of Greece 1928–2008*. Centre for Culture, Research and Documentation. Bank of Greece.

Reinhart, C. M., & Rogoff, K. S. (2013). Shifting mandates: The Federal Reserve's first centennial. *The American Economic Review, 103*(3), 48–54. https://doi.org/10.1257/aer.103.3.48.

Rogoff, K. S. (1985). Can international monetary policy cooperation be counter-productive? *Journal of International Economics, 18*(3–4), 199–217.

Schadler, S. (2016). Living with rules: The IMF's exceptional access framework and the 2010 Stand-by Arrangement with Greece. Independent Evaluation Office of the International Monetary Fund. Retrieved from http://www.ieo-imf.org/ieo/files/completedevaluations/EAC__BP_16-02_08__Living_with_Rules_-_The_IMF_s_Exceptional_Framework_and_the_2010_SBA_with_Greece.PDF.

Taylor, J. (2013). *International monetary policy coordination: Past, present and future (December)*. BIS Working Paper No. 437. Available at SSRN: https://ssrn.com/abstract=2384452.

Touffut, J. (2008). *Central banks as economic institutions* (1st ed.). Cheltenham: Edward Elgar.

Vliamos, S. (1992). *Economic theorising and policy making*. International Economic Conflict Discussion Paper No. 56. Economic Research Center, Nagoya University. Retrieved from https://hephaestus.nup.ac.cy/handle/11728/6631.

Vliamos, S., & Gravas, K. (2016). Monetary war and peace. *Foreign Affairs The Hellenic Edition, 42*, 86–105 Retrieved from https://hephaestus.nup.ac.cy/handle/11728/8850?show=full.

Xafa, M. (2014). *Sovereign debt crisis management: Lessons from the 2012 Greek debt restructuring*. CIGI Paper No. 33, June. Retrieved from www.cigionline.org/publications/sovereign-debt-crisis-management-lessons-2012-greek-debt-restructuring.

Yellen, J. (2016). *Supervision and regulation. Testimony before the Committee on Financial Services*. Washington, DC: U.S. House of Representatives Retrieved from https://www.federalreserve.gov/newsevents/testimony/yellen20160928a.htm.

Yellen, J. (2017). *The economic outlook and the conduct of monetary policy*. Speech at the Stanford Institute for Economic Policy Research, Stanford University, Stanford, California. Retrieved from https://www.federalreserve.gov/newsevents/speech/yellen20170119a.htm.

Institutions and International Political Economy: Realist Readings of International Regimes

Ilias Kouskouvelis and Kyriakos Mikelis

1   Introduction

International Political Economy (IPE) is, by now, a well established sub-field of International Relations (IR), which functions as a 'bridge' between the latter and Political Economy/Economics. The integration of institutional analysis in that sub-field is equally a given. Within IR, indeed, it is hardly denied that multilateralism exists, while the respective debate seems to be centered upon whether and how multilateralism works and matters (Stein 2008: 201). International institutions were primarily emphasized by the non-Marxist variants of IR and particularly the liberal/pluralist perspective. They largely came to be distinctively understood in terms of 'international regimes' unfolding upon a variety of domains —such as the economy, security, or technology— and they were also notably discussed through realist analytical lenses as well.

I. Kouskouvelis (⊠) • K. Mikelis
University of Macedonia, Thessaloniki, Greece
e-mail: iliaskou@uom.edu.gr; kmikelis@uom.edu.gr

© The Author(s) 2018   191
S. Vliamos, M. S. Zouboulakis (eds.), *Institutionalist Perspectives on Development*, Palgrave Studies in Democracy, Innovation, and Entrepreneurship for Growth,
https://doi.org/10.1007/978-3-319-98494-0_11

Those developments were important. Firstly, within a sizeable and multi-faceted literature, the concept of 'regime' has allowed for a comprehensive analysis of (either successful or failed) international cooperation at both the economic and political realms, including −but not exhausted− to international organizations or agreements. Secondly, it was explored even by (or in the name of) realism, i.e. an IR perspective often criticized for being associated with a conservative or static as well as conflict-prone line of reasoning, in order to elaborate on the potential and dynamics of cooperation. Highly indicatively, it was from its ranks that "the false promise of international institutions" thesis was launched (Mearsheimer 1994/1995), sharply standing for the arguably "minimal influence on state behavior", in the sense that institutions "hold little promise for promoting stability in the post-Cold War world" (7).

In this regard, the chapter addresses the role of regimes in international political economy, as well as international politics, particularly emphasizing the evolution of international cooperation. In specific, it examines how the engagement of realism with institutional analysis and, namely, with the concept of 'regime' has enabled the former to account for cooperative/regulatory dynamics and mechanisms in the international system. Consequently and put succinctly, the aim of the chapter is to expand on realist readings of international institutions and to account for 'what does realism tell us about regimes' and 'what do regimes tell us about realism'? Given the latter's theoretical diversity, it is here understood in terms of 'essential realism', taken to mean a core accepted by all realist versions. This comprises statism (the state as the pre-eminent actor in world politics, along with state sovereignty signifying an independent political community), survival as the supreme national interest and self-help as the impossibility of relying on others for guaranteeing one's survival (Dunne and Schmidt 2014: 107–110). In a similar line of thought, the set of core realist propositions arguably includes groupism, egoism, anarchy and power politics (Wohlforth 2008: 133). To be sure, the incorporation of systemic and structural analysis within IR and particularly realism has long been an important development and has actually and quite soon been reflected in certain strands of regime theory.

With this in mind, the chapter at first presents a series of typologies regarding both the creation and sustainability of international regimes. It subsequently offers a critical appraisal of the multiple understandings of institutions and particularly regimes within the realist perspective, pinpointing the strengths and weaknesses as well as the challenges of realist readings on institutions and the relevance of the latter within international political economy. In this regard, attention is initially given to the role of realism in arguments over international regimes and then to the dynamics of this perspective's 'institutional opening'. Overall, the engagement of realism with an 'originally outsider' concept (in terms more of accommodation rather than resistance) has enabled the former to account for cooperative dynamics in a varied fashion.

2   INTERNATIONAL REGIMES: BASIC CARTOGRAPHIES

Having been depicted as a level of institutionalization particularized in terms of "sets of mutual expectations, generally agreed-to rules, regulations and plans, in accordance with which organizational energies and financial commitments are allocated" (Ruggie 1975: 569), regimes were defined as "sets of governing arrangements" (Keohane and Nye 1977: 11), that consist of "principles, norms, rules and decision-making procedures around which actor expectations converge in a given issue-area" (Krasner 1982: 185). The general principles relate to "beliefs of facts, causation, and rectitude", while norms are the "standards of behavior defined in terms of rights and obligations" (186). The significant challenge for regimes lies in how they enable a mutually beneficial agreement over specific and important issues and in the provision of a framework for an efficient joint action through negotiation, as opposed to an ad hoc joint action, particularly by helping "to make governments' expectations consistent with each other" (Keohane 1982: 334). Consequently, regime variance over time or across cases vis-à-vis strength (degree of compliance), organizational form (design and operation), scope (range of issues) and allocational mode, i.e., mechanisms for resource allocation (Haggard and Simmons 1987: 496–498), has invited a range of relevant questions and answers constituting regime analysis (indicatively Krasner 1983; Rittberger 1993; Levy et al. 1995; Hasenclever et al. 1997; Orsini et al. 2013: 291; Hynek 2017: 21–24).

Equally importantly, equating regimes with institutions depends upon conceptual delineation, which has nevertheless invited diverse choices: "[a]t one extreme, regimes are defined so broadly as to constitute ... all international interactions within a given issue-area ... At the other extreme, regimes are defined as international institutions ... they equal the formal rules of behavior specified by the charters or constitutions ... and the study of regimes becomes the study of international organizations" (Stein 1982: 299–300). Despite the frequent treatment of 'institutions' and 'regimes' as essentially synonymous (see Mearsheimer 1994/1995: 8/n.13), it has also made sense to reflect on institutional analysis and regime analysis as related but distinct, at least as far as the former would get down to the examination of international organizations as actors themselves in terms of what they do (a preferred method in the early Cold-War), while the latter (ever since the 1980s) would go beyond just looking within organizations and expand to their effects and function or their relation with state preferences and behavior, i.e. the differences they make. This is an understanding of regime analysis which views it not as a mere descendant of institutional analysis, but as a both contending and complementary approach (Barkin 2006: 36–37. Cf. Kratochwil and Ruggie 1986: 754–763). In fact, this shift of emphasis was heavily influenced by realism, in respect to the perception of states as the central actors of international politics and to explaining state behavior in terms of power and interest. And yet, another shift was marked by the emergence of new institutionalism, reflecting the enhanced role of the latter within several social sciences: "what began as the study of international organizations and regional integration took a dramatic turn in the early 1980s in what came to be called regime theory, and was subsequently rechristened neoliberal institutionalism" (Stein 2008: 203. See 203–204). Overall, it makes sense to "distinguish international organizations, understood as entities, from international institutions, understood as rules" (Martin and Simmons 2013: 326), while 'institutions' have gained preference of reference instead of 'regimes' on the basis of emphasis to the notion of rules (328–239).

Historiographically, it is intriguing to note varied typologies of theories/perspectives within regime analysis. The path-breaking 1982 issue of the journal *International Organization*, devoted to regimes (and eventually republished in Krasner 1983), involved the identification of three basic orientations towards them, namely (Krasner 1982: 189–194):

(a) a conventional structural view, assigning regimes with a minimal (no independent) impact (e.g. Strange 1982),
(b) a modified structural point of view, acknowledging the importance of regimes under certain conditions (e.g. undesired outcomes of decision-making),
(c) a Grotian (functional) view of regimes as a pervasive and inherent attribute of human behavior's complex patterns.

Soon enough, this typology was followed by an equally illustrative four-fold distinction among: (a) structuralism/'hegemonic stability' (the linkage of regime creation and persistence to international conditions, namely the existence and rise of a hegemon, and vice versa) (b), 'strategic and game-theoretic approaches', emphasizing the linkage of cooperative behavior or exogenously determined preferences to the conditions enabling regime formation, (c) 'functional theories' underscoring the analysis of institutions in terms of their effects, with reference to market imperfection and transactions or information costs as well as uncertainty, and finally (d) 'cognitive theories' focusing on ideology, intersubjective meaning structures and actor's values or beliefs about the interdependence of issues as well as on the relation of knowledge, perception and learning to cooperation (Haggard and Simmons 1987: 498–513). Given the fact that "[m]ost structural, game-theoretic, and functional theories of regimes are state-centered, presuming unified rational actors, even if the assumption is relaxed to gain explanatory leverage" (499), it actually made sense to provide a broader and meta-theory oriented distinction between a 'rationalist' and a 'reflectivist' approach to regime theory, contrasting between the focus on rules, procedures or efficiency and an emphasis on principles, norms and ideas (Barkin 2006: 37. Cf. Kratochwil and Ruggie 1986: 763–771).

Absence of explicit reference to realism in those typologies is certainly not to be confused with the absence of analysis in realist terms or with the undisputed dominance of a liberal worldview. This is after all sharply illustrated by an equally fairly simple, but explicitly realism-related, intellectual move: the juxtaposition of realist and liberal-institutionalist approaches to international regimes. Despite an overall convergence at the perception of states as rational and unitary actors operating in an anarchic international system and the conceptualization of regimes as a means of advancing international order and cooperation, a divergence is emphasized in whether regimes allow state coordination or broader collaboration, whether emphasis should be put to generating differential benefits or to the promotion of the common good, whether their formation is based on power or on a benign hegemon and finally whether their underlying principles or norms reflect the nature of world order, being inherently linked to the rise of globalization and a liberal world order (Little 2014: 295–300. Cf. Grieco 1995a). An also dense but more comprehensive typology of regime theoritization also confirms the distinction between neoliberalism and realism, though emphatically adding cognitivism as a third approach.

Out of the three, the first is characterized as interest-based, with attention in the constellation of interests and in specific political market failure, situation and problem structures as well as institutional bargaining. The second is perceived as power-based, emphasizing power relations and in particular hegemony, distributional conflict and relative gains. The third is presumed to be knowledge-based, pinpointing causal and social knowledge and particularly ideas, arguments and social identities (Hasenclever et al. 1997: respectively ch. 3, 4 & 5; Hasenclever et al. 2000). Then again, it has also made sense to distinguish between consequentialism (unfolding upon the convergence between neorealism and neoliberal institutionalism), cognitivism and radical constructivism/post-structuralism (Hynek 2017). Finally, differences within the liberal institutional approach itself, have given ground for adding to 'realist' and 'epistemic' paradigms of IR two more distinct ones, namely 'institutional' and 'liberal' (presumably emphasizing on the one hand institutions, norms or information and on the other hand exogenous variation of state preferences embedded in domestic and transnational state-society relations (Legro and Moravcsik 1999: 10–11). Evidently, the complexity of regime analysis and the variety of standpoints or arguments, as well as of their intersections, can hardly be captured by a single typology. In this sense, the respective cartographies serve more as heuristic devices enabling the theoretical dialogue, rather than delineating analytical straightjackets.

3   The Role of Realism in Arguments Over International Regimes

The aforementioned cartographies evidently reveal the richness of regime analysis. We propose their reconstruction, focusing on specific arguments and their relation to realism, bearing in mind two central questions which have been raised, in respect to regimes. Firstly, why and how are the latter created? Secondly, why and how are they maintained/sustained? As already noted, those questions have invited several answers.

Regarding the first question, those answers are associated to several IR arguments and corresponding perspectives. Initially, i.e. from the pluralist standpoint, an emphatic argument was made not only about regimes as arrangements leading to the regularization of behavior and to the control of its effects but, most importantly, about how they affect relations of interdependence. They do so, by functioning as intermediate factors between the distribution of power resources among states (power structure of an international system) and the respective bargaining and decision-making occurring within this system (Keohane and Nye 1977: ch. 1). In fact, the characteristics and evolution of regimes were succinctly and extensively used by R. Keohane and J. Nye (1977) as an illustrative case study for understanding the interplay of power and interdependence. Equally importantly, regimes are taken to be about not only form and power in international authority but also content and social purpose (Ruggie 1982). This argument was complemented by others, with the notable example of a game-theoretic/rationalist point of view (Stein 1982), according to which the creation of regimes is the result of inter-state interaction and state decisions taken on the basis of national interest and preferences, addressing collective suboptimality, the dilemma of common interests and the provision of collective goods.

Moreover, from a certain neorealist (structural realist) standpoint, hegemonic stability theory arose, underscoring the connection of uneven power distribution with regimes; namely the association of power economic regimes with the existence of a hegemonic power (Kindleberger 1973; Keohane 1980: 136). In this regard, an imposed regime is one "agreed upon within constraints that are mandated by powerful actors". Power relations and dependence of weaker actors upon stronger ones centrally determine the regime's characteristics (Keohane 1982: 330). However, the mere existence of a hegemonic power doesn't seem to be a sufficient condition for the creation of strong economic regimes, in the sense that historically the power of a hegemon has at certain times – although not always– been reflected on regimes (Keohane 1980: 137). This invites the need of searching causality, i.e. whether and how the existence of the hegemon has actually led (or not) to the creation of a regime.

On the other hand, an amended neorealist argument, the 'voice opportunity thesis' has turned the emphasis from the leader to the less strong, underscoring how institutionalization may serve for relatively weaker states as a second best choice (instead of becoming more powerful in cooperation or of avoiding it), vis-à-vis the handling of a stronger partner and institutionally influence the latter. No reassurance is given though about the success of the respective strategy or the endurance of its successful results (Grieco 1995b, 1996). Indeed, the literature on the international relations of small states provides a wealth of information about this (Pedi 2016). The accommodation of cooperation mechanisms into the neorealist logic took also place in the name of a 'contingent realism' (also associated with 'optimism'), whereby the term stresses the highly conditional nature of state choices between cooperation and competition with the purpose of avoiding a competition-bias as a necessary research premise (Glaser 1994/1995: 57–70). Finally and in contrast to the bias of the hegemonic stability theory for regime supply, attention was brought to the demand for regimes from a rationalist viewpoint and especially constraint choice analysis. The point of focus is on state efforts to overcome institutional problems within anarchy conditions and the competitiveness of the international system. In this context, regime creation is interpreted as an attempt of states to deal with 'market failure' (Keohane 1982: 334–336). The emphasis here is given to preference for regimes over ad hoc agreements and how this presupposes an acknowledgment of the need for a clear legal framework establishing liability regarding action, the need for information and addressing information imperfections (i.e. incompleteness and cost of information) as well as the need for a positive value of transaction costs (Keohane 1982: 337–339, Keohane 1984: 85–88. Cf. Lipson 2004). This line of reasoning was formulated as a version of structural realism, called modified structural realism (Keohane 1986: 190–197. For a case study, see Kuskuvelis 1988), which was heavily influenced by IR pluralism and economic thought.

Interestingly enough, another argument has stemmed as the previous approach's variant, in the name of liberal intergovernmentalism (or intergovernmental institutionalism), linking the evolution of cooperation and institutions particularly in terms of intergovernmental organization of government elites, lowest common denominator bargaining and protection of national sovereignty, i.e. limits of future transfer of sovereignty, evidenced in the case of the negotiation of the Single European Act (Moravcsik 1991) but non-economic cases as well, such as the Common Foreign and Security Policy (Kuskuvelis 1996). In this regard, European integration on the whole was proposed to be understood on the basis that rational choices were made by national leaders and they reflected economic interest's domestic constituents, while the credibility of interstate commitments relates to asymmetrical interdependence and particularly to the relative power of states. In other words, national preferences were driven by issue-specific (generally economic) interests rather than by geopolitical ideas or interests. Substantive bargaining outcomes were shaped by intergovernmental bargaining, on the basis of asymmetrical interdependence, rather than of the manipulation of information by supranational entrepreneurs and information asymmetries. The choice of EU institutions reflected an interest in securing credible member state commitments;

neither ideology (federalism) nor the need for bureaucratic management (Moravcsik 1998).

Moreover, the issue of the sustainability and durability of regimes has also been answered with various arguments. For once, game theory could not directly be used for explaining how regimes are maintained. That's why a realism-inspired interpretation was introduced, according to which the sustainability of regimes depends upon the interests leading to their creation in the first place. Subsequently, changes on those interests will most probably entail regime change. But this is not automatic, in light of costs in interest re-evaluation, vested interests in regime creation and uncertainty regarding the persistence of changed interests (Stein 1982: 321–322). This is also the case with the argument focusing on established legitimacy, i.e. that breaking the rules is more costly than attempting to change them, even if they no more reflect the original respective interests (Stein 1982: 323). Regarding the hegemonic stability argument, the stability of economic international regimes depends upon power concentration and the lack of competition. Just like the case of regime creation, there is the need for illustrating causality, i.e. that hegemonic change actually brings a specific regime change into the fore. The respective limitations of this theory include the collective substitution of the role of the fallen hegemon by middle powers resulting to stability, the choice on behalf of the hegemon not to use her power in light of either domestic or foreign reasons, thus leading to regime change, while finally such a change may occur due to important events which exclude collaboration (Keohane 1980: 135–136). Moreover, if indeed growing interdependence means the blending of the boundaries between international and domestic politics, this then necessities an inquiry on the regime interests of domestic groups and on governments' efforts for preserving the benefits of cooperation and at the same time minimizing the costs on politically important groups, in their choices regarding regime creation and compliance (Haggard and Simmons 1987: 513–517).

Finally, there is the process of learning, emphasized by the cognitive approach but also by pluralism as well. Emphasis is here given to how states may redefine the interests, based upon experience and lessons learned. Learning is not just about responding to structural change in the international system, as neorealism would have it, but also about different understandings of subsequent governments of a state. It may be attributed to domestic power change (e.g. change of political elites), general change of ideas (e.g. abolishment of slavery) and change in available information.

Moreover, it may lead to a redefinition of means and/or ends. Collectivities may well be characterized by institutional memory and processes, but learning is slower and depends upon channels of communication among public opinion, social groups and political elites (Nye 1987: 373, 379–381).

4   The Dynamics of Realism's 'Institutional' Opening

As evidenced at both previous sections, there is no single realist position over institutions and regimes in particular. Indeed, the latter have allowed for a vivid intellectual engagement of realism with contending approaches within IR, but also for internal debates within realism itself. Evidently, the differentiation of realism and a distinct paradigm on institutions seems to have largely made sense, indicatively illustrated in the title of a book devoted to the IR discipline's self-reflection "realism and institutionalism in international studies" (Brecher and Harrvey 2002). To a certain extent, this distinction has indeed reflected one of the major controversies in IR; namely, "realism and the neoliberal challenge" (Kegley 1995). After all, institutional analysis emerged as "largely a response to realism ... and directly challenges realism's underlying logic" (Mearsheimer 1994/1995: 7), insisting on how international institutions have presumably revealed realism's "fallacious logic" particularly in its view of international institutions (Keohane and Martin 1995). Considering a variety of interesting sectors in the evolution of international systems (namely: political, military, economic, social, and environmental. Buzan and Little 2000: 72–77), realism's preoccupation with the first two sectors may at a first glance well explain this predicament. However, it has not at the end of the day prevented attention to the intersection of the economic and political sectors, to which actually regime analysis played a significant role.

The departure from a standard structural position to other versions accommodating for the use and function of institutions either in the form of modified structural realism or contingent realism and the voice opportunity thesis, already mentioned above, indicatively illustrates the realist engagement with 'regimes'. Towards the same direction and departing from the critique that regime theory had underestimated the respective framework of law and norms (Hurrell 1993), lies the incorporation of structural realism into a functional account of the emergence of international society as both a natural product of the logic of anarchy and the legal and political basis (i.e. a sense of community) for regimes, which would then allow for norm reciprocity (Buzan 1993. Cf. Yoshimatsu 1998). In this sense, international society is conceptualized as a "regime of regimes, adding a useful element of holism to the excessively atomized world of regime theory" (350).

On the other hand, R. Schweller and D. Priess (1997), while succinctly agreeing on the need for an expansion on realism's understanding of institutions, characteristically opted for an alternative intellectual move, namely the discussion of such understanding through the division between a neorealist neglect or extremely narrow view of institutions as a mere consequence of the system's structure, exemplified by J. Mearsheimer, and a richer argumentation by what is labeled as 'traditional realism'. To be sure, they simultaneously acknowledge the contribution of modified structural realism, however they prefer to emphasize the respective merits of (neo) classical realism, i.e. a realist version discontent with the systemic overload of structural realism and seeking inspiration on earlier realist writings and premises. This argumentation involves the recognition of institutional arrangements as relevant to actual power distribution but not limited to it, given their potential in influencing outcomes, thus reflecting a "disjunction between the actual power distribution and the existing institutional order–the system's prestige and hierarchy". This is deemed important, as far as instability and conflict eventually require the acknowledgment of a minimal set of rules of the game, after all entailing the restoration of a certain sense of stability through institutions and outcomes which correspond to reformulated power relations (10). An indicative example of this difference refers to the durability of an institution, since a traditional standpoint would emphasize the group-based and dynamic nature of politics, in contrast to the standard neorealist explanation which would stick to predominantly linking institutional endurance to initial structural factors and threats (21). In this regard, this realist version portrays itself as a middle ground between the neorealist disregard of institutions' persistence and the neoliberal overconfidence over the latter, allowing for an examination of the interplay between state characteristics and their varied (i.e. both the persisting and the failed/decaying) interactions (23–25).

Some scholars took a step further, not only by discussing the linkage between participation to institutions and foreign policy (Tziampiris 2000; Kouskouvelis 2004; Karakatsanis 2005) but also by advancing an explicitly stated bridging between realism and institutionalism in the name of a view called "realist institutionalism" (Khoo 2004: 37. Also see Krebs 1999: 344), focusing on negative norms and on the exacerbation of tensions within institutions, or "neorealist institutionalism" as a term coined for describing IR work within a power-based tradition on the distributional effects or consequences of regimes to state interaction's costs and benefits and state choice of advancing multilateralism rather then bilateralism (Aggarwal 1998). In the context of regional integration, 'ideational-institutional realism' was also proposed as a departure from neorealism in respect to the conceptualization of states and their divergence in lieu of variation in either ideational factors or in domestic institutional set-up, allowing margin for co-operative hegemony as a grand strategy, which "implies soft rule within and through co-operative arrangements based on a long-term strategy" (Pedersen 2002: 683). This approach is exemplified by K. He (2006), who succinctly expands upon the notion of "institutional realism" (for another use of the term, see Karakatsanis 2005) as a realist theory concerning institutions based upon classical realism, hegemonic stability theory and arguments such as the voice opportunity thesis and contingent realism. In particular, such a version regards institutions as an intervening variable between power and policy behavior and simultaneously adopts the neorealist assumptions of anarchy, states as unitary actors and the security competition among states. It distinctively and extensively adds the role of economic interdependence, globalization and the information revolution, thus allowing some room for complex interdependence, however without this entailing a change in the nature of international politics. Growing economic interdependence presumably allows states, including middle-sized and small states, to pursue balance of power, through investing on engagement with formal and informal institutions. So, while this version is compatible with hegemonic stability theory's concern with the use of institutions on behalf of stronger states, it distinctively adds how weaker states may rely on institutions for balance of both powers and threats, engaging into a rule-based institutional balancing, notably with norm setting and agenda controlling. This institutional balancing is a two-level process, involving an internal dimension (balancing others within the institution) and an external one (coping with external and especially state-centric threat). In contrast to the liberal emphasis on the value of institutions in facilitating cooperation, attention is here given on how cooperation emerges as a consequence of institutional balancing rather than as the goal of institutions (194–196).

Having the above in mind, the realist-neoliberal debate within regime analysis is not surprising and has actually come close to the formulation of a unified rationalist synthesis, whereby the latter connotes a broader theoretical framework which not only treats actors' interests as exogenously given but is also contextualized, in the sense of including the a priori specification of the conditions for inclusion of various perspectives into it. In fact, margin is also left for the possibility that this framework may comprehensibly include even a weak version of cognitivism, at least as far as it is accepted "that rationalist and cognitive variables represent different links in a causal chain (with cognitive variables either preceding or following rationalist ones". But a grand synthesis with radical or strong cognitivism seems impossible and unnecessary (Hasenclever et al. 2000: 32–33). To be sure, although the focus on regimes proved a useful ground for bridging the gap between realists and institutionalists, it was considered primarily liberal in light of the fact that the linkage of international institutions to mutually beneficial arrangements reflected the liberal economic argument about individuals and firms engaging in mutually beneficial exchanges, while it drew on arguments made by economists to explain the integration of firms. By the same token and despite drawing on microeconomics or using game theory, the new institutional literature is not to be presumed as a mere merge of realism and institutionalism and arguably continues to be characterized by a neoliberal or neoliberal institutionalist connotation (Stein 2008: 204–205).

5   CONCLUDING REMARKS

Certain realist views of international institutions have given ground for critique towards "[t]he fallacious logic of realism" (Keohane and Martin 1995), but this line of reasoning was essentially a criticism of the 'irrelevance of institutions' argument, on the premise that the latter overstates the promising potential of institutions and their prospects as a panacea for conflict, claimed on behalf of institutionalism (50). Our contention here is that the aforementioned kind of critique misses the 'institutional openings of realism', whereby the term denotes varied realist perspectives' engagement with the concept, not reduced to the irrelevance argument. That engagement occurred soon after the coinage of the 'regime' concept, having had an impact in the consolidation of the rationality predicament and the anarchy assumption within regime analysis. As already noted, the 1970s' shift of emphasis from organizations and institutions as entities to institutions as rules and reflections of state preferences was noticeably influenced by realism, in respect to the perception of states as the central actors of international politics and to explaining state behavior in terms of power and interest. In this sense, our specific argument and relevant contribution is that unfolding the role of realism, within the analysis of international regimes, succinctly entails a double reflection on 'what realism tells us, regarding regimes' and 'what regimes tell us, regarding realism', thus revealing that the engagement of this IR perspective with an 'originally outsider' concept has by now taken place in terms more of accommodation rather than resistance, enabling the former to account for cooperative dynamics in a varied fashion.

So answering the question of 'what does realism tell us about regimes', it is evident that a few things may be told from a realist standpoint, but not in a single and comprehensive story. Classical realism and especially neoclassical realism, as its successor, may well leave enough margins for incorporating institutions in a 'realist world' and accounting for cooperation in both economic and security issues. On the other hand, the neorealist treatment of institutions diverges, ranging from the conventional structural realist view, which assigns a minimal impact of institutions and the recognition of their potential with hegemonic stability, to modified structural realism, incorporating more thoroughly insights from economic theory and rational choice as well as to institutional balancing, captured by institutional realism. At the same time, answering the question of 'what do regimes tell us about realism', it is a case of an IR perspective quickly responding to theoretical challenges raised in the name of a particular concept originally stemming outside this approach. This management includes less outright and enduring resistance to the concept rather than efforts of accommodation through some incorporation of certain tenets of the realist logic. After all, the work of a major contributor to regime analysis (R. Keohane) may have been pluralism-oriented, yet it has often left margin for the inclusion of realism. In spite though of this synthetic process, the overall outcome has not been a case of a realist colonization of the respective *problématique* (although from a radical critical standpoint, the pluralist analysis oriented to power and rationality doesn't go far enough).

In a rather ironic tone, the aforementioned institutional openings of realism were identified by J. Legro and A. Moravcsik (1999) as presenting a theoretical problem for realism, with regard to its analytical core being undermined by its proponents and especially the defensive and neoclassical realists' attempt for such reformulations that have eventually ceased to reflect a stable set of core realist premises. By overtly diverging from the latter, the result is presumably 'too much' of a minimal realism emphasizing anarchy and rationality, which yet comes to be not distinctively realist in regime theory, insofar as "nearly all variants of liberal, epistemic, and institutionalist theories share the same three assumptions" (21). The authors see in the recent realist treatment of institutions an undermining of realism's coherence and distinctiveness, without though offering a clear theory of how international institutions affect state behavior (41). In a similar vain, the clarification of the assumptions about state preferences remains crucial, along with elaboration in how material resources shape the outcome of interstate interaction (53). Overall and despite realism's readiness to address international political economy and politics in terms of power politics within anarchical conditions, it has lost control of the notions of 'power' and 'anarchy'.

On the other hand, Keohane's affirmation of institutional liberalism's rise, as a dominant worldview about the role of liberal principles-based multilateralism and three crucial trends (increasing legalization, more legalism and moralism), points to a rather more modest direction, although not to the point of reclaiming a modified structural realist perspective. His rejection of realism as a good moral or practical guide to world politics (particularly, the dictum of 'necessity') was yet followed by the acknowledgement of a declining degree of coherence of international regimes, reflecting a greater divergence of interests, the diffusion of power as well as restraints on learning in the context of domestic politics (Keohane 2012). In this sense, liberalism is mitigated to diverge from optimism about human nature and to function as the last resort taming power through institutions (136). The role of the inter-state relations and bargaining is after all affirmed by liberal intergovernmentalism (Moravcsik 1991, 1998; Kuskuvelis 1996). By the same token, regime complexity affects international interactions as an independent variable, characteristically by creating new and unanticipated constraints or opportunities for actors. In that respect, the enhancement of great powers remains a possibility. So, complexity may at a first glance seem to support an optimist view pointing to the direction of global governance, however this does not automatically entail the transformation of the character of world politics (Drezner 2009: 68). After all, the prospect of regime collapse might not single-handedly be taken out of question, especially in light of an eventual US repositioning vis à vis multilateralism and its leading role (Rudolf 2017: 38–40). A crucial test is thereby indicatively provided by the current US presidency's decision of withdrawing from the 2015 Paris agreement on climate change and by the degree of robustness of the respective regime complex (Orsini 2017) as well as by the eventual course of the World Trade Organization.

Finally, it is noted that, to the extend that IR and realism within it have been characterized by a reduced salience of inter-paradigmatic competition, by a more productive interaction with competing IR perspectives and by the accumulation of new research within the realist line of reasoning (Wohlforth 2008: 145–146), then developments in regime theory reflect this trend. The study of institutions is anyway a fairly progressive line of research, while the call after all to move/go "beyond paradigms in the study of institutions" (Lake 2002) reflects the need for not sticking to academic straightjackets and narrow perceptions. In this regard, it is fair to praise regime theoretical framework for having served as a case of advancing varied analysis on the intersection of the economic and political sectors and promoting dialogue between contending perspectives.

REFERENCES

Aggarwal, V. (1998). Analyzing institutional transformation in the Asia-Pacific. In V. Aggarwal & C. Morrison (Eds.), *Asia-Pacific crossroads: Regime creation and the future of APEC* (pp. 23–64). New York: St. Martin's Press.

Barkin, S. (2006). *International organization: Theories and institutions.* New York: Palgrave Macmillan.

Brecher, M., & Harrvey, F. (Eds.). (2002). *Realism and institutionalism in international studies.* Ann Arbor: University of Michigan Press.

Buzan, B. (1993). From international system to international society: Structural realism and regime theory meet the English School. *International Organization, 47*(3), 327–352.

Buzan, B., & Little, R. (2000). *International systems in world history. Remaking the study of international relations.* Oxford: Oxford University Press.

Drezner, D. (2009). The power and peril of international regime complexity. *Perspectives on Politics, 7*(1), 65–70.

Dunne, T., & Schmidt, B. (2014). Realism. In J. Baylis, S. Smith, & P. Owens (Eds.), *The Globalization of world politics. An introduction to international relations* (5th ed., pp. 99–112). Oxford: Oxford University Press.

Glaser, C. (1994/1995). Realists as optimists: Cooperation as self-help. *International Security, 19*(3), 50–90.

Grieco, J. (1995a). Anarchy and the limits of cooperation: A realist critique of the newest liberal institutionalism. In C. Kegley (Ed.), *Controversies in international relations theory. Realism and the neoliberal challenge* (pp. 151–171). Basingstoke: Palgrave.

Grieco, J. (1995b). The Maastricht treaty, economic and monetary union and the neo-realist research program. *Review of International Studies, 21*(1), 21–140.

Grieco, J. (1996). State interests and institutional rule trajectories: A neorealist interpretation of the Maastricht treaty and european economic and monetary union. *Security Studies, 5*(3), 261–306.

Haggard, S., & Simmons, B. (1987). Theories of international regimes. *International Organization, 41*(3), 491–517.

Hasenclever, A., Mayer, P., & Rittberger, V. (1997). *Theories of international regimes.* Cambridge: Cambridge University Press.

Hasenclever, A., Mayer, P., & Rittberger, V. (2000). Integrating theories of international regimes. *Review of International Studies, 26*(1), 3–33.

He, K. (2006). Does ASEAN matter? International relations theories, institutional realism, and ASEAN. *Asian Security, 2*(3), 189–214.

Hurrell, A. (1993). International society and the study of regimes: A reflective approach. In V. Rittberger (Ed.), *Regime theory and international relations* (pp. 49–72). Oxford: Clarendon Press.

Hynek, N. (2017). Regime theory as IR theory: Reflection on three waves of 'isms'. *Central European Journal of International and Security Studies, 11*(1), 11–30.

Karakatsanis, T. (2005). *A small actor within an institutionalized group of states: Institutional-realism as a framework of analysis.* Paper for the 2nd LSE Symposium on Modern Greece: Current Social Science Research on Greece. LSE/Hellenic Observatory, 10/6/2005.

Kegley, C. (Ed.). (1995). *Controversies in international relations theory. Realism and the neoliberal challenge.* Basingstoke: Palgrave.

Keohane, R. (1980). The theory of hegemonic stability and changes in international regimes. In K. Holsti et al. (Eds.), *Change in the international system* (pp. 131–162). Boulder: Westview.

Keohane, R. (1982). The demand for international regimes. *International Organization, 36*(2), 325–355.

Keohane, R. (1984). *After hegemony.* Princeton: Princeton University Press.

Keohane, R. (1986). Theory of world politics: Structural realism and beyond. In idem (ed.) (Ed.), *Neorealism and its critics* (pp. 158–203). New York: Columbia University Press.

Keohane, R. (2012). Twenty years of institutional liberalism. *International Relations, 26*(2), 125–138.

Keohane, R., & Martin, L. (1995). The promise of institutionalist theory. *International Security, 20*(1), 39–51.

Keohane, R., & Nye, J. (1977). *Power and interdependence.* Boston: Little and Brown.

Khoo, N. (2004). Deconstructing the ASEAN security community: A review essay. *International Relations of the Asia-Pacific, 4*(1), 35–46.

Kindleberger, C. (1973). *The world in depression 1929–1939.* London: The Penguin Press.

Kouskouvelis, I. (2004). Institutionalism and the macedonian question. *Southeast European and Black Sea Studies, 4*(3), 506–515.

Krasner, S. (1982). Structural causes and regime onsequences: Regimes as intervening variables. *International Organization, 36*(2), 185–205.

Krasner, S. (Ed.). (1983). *International regimes.* Ithaca; London: Cornell University Press.

Kratochwil, F., & Ruggie, J. (1986). International organization: A state of the art on an art of the state. *International Organization, 40*(4), 753–775.

Krebs, R. (1999). Perverse institutionalism: NATO and the Greco-Turkish conflict. *International Organization, 53*(2), 344–377.

Kuskuvelis, I. (1988). The method of genetic effectiveness and the future of the military regime of outer space. In T. Zwaan (editor in chief) (Ed.), *Space law: Views of the Future* (pp. 79–97). Leiden: Kluwer.

Kuskuvelis, I. (1996). Intergovernmental institutionalism: An International politics approach to European integration. In *Problems and Prospects of European Integration* (pp. 12–29). Thessaloniki: University of Macedonia.

Lake, D. (2002). Progress in international relations. Beyond paradigms in the study of institutions. In M. Brecher & F. Harrvey (Eds.), *Realism and institutionalism in international studies* (pp. 135–152). Ann Arbor: University of Michigan Press.

Legro, J., & Moravcsik, A. (1999). Is anybody still a realist? *International Security, 24*(2), 5–55.

Levy, M., Young, O., & Zürn, M. (1995). The study of international regimes. *European Journal of International Relations, 1*(3), 267–330.

Lipson, M. (2004). Transaction cost estimation and international regimes: Of crystal balls and sheriff's posses. *International Studies Review, 6*(1), 1–20.

Little, R. (2014). International regimes. In J. Baylis, S. Smith, & P. Owens (Eds.), *The globalization of world politics. An introduction to international relations* (5th ed., pp. 289–303). Oxford: Oxford University Press.

Martin, L., & Simmons, B. (2013). International organizations and institutions. In W. Carlsnaes, T. Risse, & B. Simmons (Eds.), *Handbook of international relations* (2nd ed., pp. 326–351). Los Angeles: SAGE.

Mearsheimer, J. (1994/1995). The false promise of international institutions. *International Security, 19*(3), 5–50.

Moravcsik, A. (1991). Negotiating the Single European Act: National interests and conventional statecraft in the European Community. *International Organization, 45*(1), 19–56.

Moravcsik, A. (1998). *The choice for Europe: Social purpose and state power from Messina to Maastricht.* Ithaca: Cornell University Press.

Nye, J. (1987). Nuclear learning and the US-Soviet security regimes. *International Organization, 41*(3), 371–402.

Orsini, A. (2017). Climate change regime complex. *Academic Foresights, 18.*

Orsini, A., Morin, J., & Young, O. (2013). Regime complexes: A buzz, a boom or a boost for global governance? *Global Governance, 19*(1), 27–39.

Pedersen, T. (2002). Cooperative hegemony: Power, ideas and institutions in regional integration. *Review of International Studies, 28*(4), 677–696.

Pedi, R. (2016). Theory of international relations: Small states in the international system. Dissertation, University of Macedonia. Retrieved from http://thesis.ekt.gr/thesisBookReader/id/38599#page/1/mode/2up.

Rittberger, V. (Ed.). (1993). *Regime theory and international relations.* Oxford: Clarendon Press.

Rudolf, P. (2017). The US under Tramp: Potential consequences for transatlantic relations. In B. Schoch et al. (Eds.), *Peace report. A selection of texts* (pp. 31–41). Zürich: LIT Verlag.

Ruggie, J. (1975). International responses to technology: Concepts and trends. *International Organization, 29*(3), 557–583.

Ruggie, J. (1982). International regimes, transactions, and change: Embedded liberalism in the postwar economic order. *International Organization, 36*(2), 379–415.

Schweller, R., & Priess, D. (1997). A tale of two realisms: Expanding the institutions debate. *Mershon International Studies Review, 41*(1), 1–32.

Stein, A. (1982). Coordination and collaboration: Regimes in an anarchic world. *International Organization, 36*(2), 299–324.

Stein, A. (2008). Neoliberal institutionalism. In C. Reus-Smit & D. Snidal (Eds.), *The Oxford handbook of international relations* (pp. 201–221). Oxford: Oxford University Press.

Strange, S. (1982). Cave! Hic dragones: A critique of regime analysis. *International Organization, 36*(2), 479–496.

Tziampiris, A. (2000). *Greece, european political cooperation and the macedonian question.* Aldershot: Ashgate.

Wohlforth, W. (2008). Realism. In C. Reus-Smit & D. Snidal (Eds.), *The Oxford handbook of international relations* (pp. 131–149). Oxford: Oxford University Press.

Yoshimatsu, H. (1998). Regimes, international society, and regional cooperation in East Asia. *Pacific Focus, 13*(2), 103–124.

.

EU–Russia Antagonism in South-Eastern Europe: The Energy Factor

Andreas Stergiou

1 THE ENERGY PARAMETER OF THE OVERALL EU–RUSSIA ECONOMIC RELATIONSHIP

Following the collapse of the Soviet economic system and especially after the successful overcoming of the 1998 financial crisis, EU–Russia economic relations expanded rapidly, with energy remaining the driver of the overall Russia–EU economic relationship. Energy revenues enable Russia to buy from and invest in the EU, resulting in complex patterns of interdependence, financial ties, and cross-border physical interconnections

The materialisation of this study was made possible thanks to the scholarship granted by the Azerbaijan Development Agency in the framework of which the author was Visiting Research Fellow at the Azerbaijan Diplomatic Academy (ADA University) in July-September 2017. The author also would like to thank Professor Fariz Ismailzade for his precious help as well as all the persons who gave interview to the author. He is also indebted to the anonymous reader for his comments.

A. Stergiou (✉)
University of Thessaly, Volos, Greece
e-mail: snandreas@econ.uth.gr

(mainly pipelines). On balance, however, the increased level of economic interdependence between the EU and Russia has failed to produce the Common Economic Space that was discussed in 2001. An EU–Russia energy partnership never materialized in the terms sketched out in the early 2000s, largely because Moscow was unwilling to play by rules set in Brussels, while the EU lacked the means to compel Moscow to play by these rules (Tiersky and Oudenaren 2010: 82).

As a matter of fact, Russian and EU perceptions of energy security clash. This applies mainly to gas. Coal and oil are traded on a global basis with the result that the price-setting mechanisms are highly liquid and transparent while security of supply is ensured by the multiplicity of potential sources of imports. Beyond that and though opinions are split on the extent to which gas should be part of the EU's decarbonization strategy, natural gas constitutes a basic aspect of *the European Commission's 'Clean Energy for all Europeans' strategy*. Natural gas is considered to be a bridge fuel, which can accompany the transition to renewable energy because gas plants can be easily fired up and down, unlike other types of plants and emits 50 percent less carbon dioxide than coal when burned (European Commission, 30 November 2016).

That's way and despite many serious political conflicts between EU and Moscow resulting in sanctions against Russian economy, the Russian gas sector was essentially exempted. The sanctions have targeted Russian oil but not gas although many EU member states and partnership states claimed that they were subject to bullying tactics by Gazprom, ranging from discriminatory pricing to threats of supply shutoffs, in retaliation for a refusal to allow Gazprom purchases of national distribution assets. Sanctioning Russian gas flows to Europe would have dealt a massive blow to Gazprom, but it would have also hit some other EU members hard (Hedlund 2017).

Therefore, the EU-Russia energy-relationship/competition is tantamount of the EU's incompetence to act as a unitary international actor. Whereas Russia's Putin has increasingly and masterfully been utilising energy diplomacy's soft power, EU has so far been unable to address its fierce bureaucratic structure and its notorious lack of ownership. As a result in many cases EU-countries have followed a different, even opposing course, towards Moscow that the EU-commission has. Therefore, EU–Russia relations on various levels, such as energy, defense, and global politics, went through many transformative phases, ranging from cooperation to overt hostility underlining the need of adopting an energy supply diversification strategy.

Following the Russia–Ukraine gas disputes in 2006[1] and 2009, and given that the main bulk of EU gas and oil imports derived from few suppliers (mainly the Russian Federation, Algeria, and Norway), the necessity of diversifying the routes and sources of gas supplies to the European Union moved to the top of the EU's list of priorities in its external relations. As a matter of fact in 2006 the European Union with the Decision No 1364/2006/EC officially established the Natural Gas route 3 (NG.3.), i.e. the natural gas pipeline network that should connect the EU to the Caspian Sea and Middle East countries.[2] The war in Donbas from 2014 onwards just reinforced this tendency (Stüwe 2017).

In 2016 Europe's overall annual consumption was satisfied by Russia (over a third of its natural gas supply) and secondly by Norway and other countries like Algeria. Gas production in Norway[3] is, however, gradually declining as its fields mature (Coote 2016). In 2015, EU net gas import needs were 194 bcm. In the lowest of demand projections, import needs could be slightly lower (by some 10 bcm) in 2020, but would then be some 20 bcm higher than 2015 levels by 2025. As such, EU gas imports will continue to play a significant role in the future EU gas market and refuel the discussion concerning the diversification of gas supplies (Pisca 2016: 7 and 25–27).

The heavy dependence on so few suppliers urged the European Commission to make the concept of energy supply diversification a cornerstone of its energy policy, with the aim of enabling the EU to "speak with one voice" on the need for sufficient diversity of exporters already in 2008 when the so-called Second Strategic Energy Review was first adopted. Current notable moves are the EU's passage of the Third Energy Package (the legislative foundation for fighting monopolies and promoting

---

[1] The 2005 energy dispute caused a temporary 30 per cent decline in gas flows to European Union states.

[2] European Union: Decision No 1364/2006/EC of the European Parliament and of the Council of 6 September 2006 laying down guidelines for trans-European energy networks and repealing Decision 96/391/EC and Decision No 1229/2003/EC, September 2003.

[3] Norway is regarded as an indigenous (EU) producer, as its gas pipeline exports are seen as 'must flow' volumes.

competition on the European energy market)[4] and the launch of the EU's European Energy Union currently being shaped.

Indeed, on 25 February 2015, the EU adopted the so-called *Framework Strategy for a Resilient Energy Union with a Forward-Looking Climate Change Policy*, the most significant development in plans for an EU-wide Energy Union to date. With the Energy Union, EU countries intend to facilitate cross-border coordination and integration in energy security, trade, regulation, and efficiency, as well as in low-carbon development and research and innovation. It is actually a new model for the European market whereby the EU could unify its gas transportation networks and formulate a single and transparent system of tariffs on imported gas, to be applied at the point of entry into the transportation network and calculated independently of supplier and trader agreements (European Commission 2015a, b).

The new EU energy strategy had serious geopolitical and security implications, ushering in a new, antagonistic approach to dealing with Russia's monopoly practices in European gas markets. Paradoxically, although the annexation of the Crimean peninsula by Russia in 2014 along with an already existing Russia–Ukraine gas price dispute reinforced fears of disruptions to EU gas supplies, EU dependence on Russian supplies increased and broke all records in autumn 2016, raising worries in Eastern European countries, which notably are unfavourably disposed towards Russia, about the increasing Russian clout within the European Union (EU-Parliament 2016).

Normally, energy diversification, a prime concern of developed energy markets, does not make up a factor of friction. Multiplying one's supply sources reduces the impact of a disruption in supply from one source by providing alternatives, thereby serving the interests of both consumers and producers (Yergin 2006). In this case, however, the efforts for diversification that Brussels has undertaken in recent years have not emerged out of the enormous European demand for the relatively cleaner power of natural gas. They have been politically motivated by the long-pursued aim

---

[4]According the EU-official announcement the Third Energy Package covers five main areas: unbundling energy suppliers from network operators, strengthening the independence of regulators, establishment of the Agency for the Cooperation of Energy Regulators (ACER), cross-border cooperation between transmission system operators and the creation of European Networks for Transmission System Operators, increased transparency in retail markets to benefit consumers.

of putting an end to Moscow's tactic of using its natural gas exports to exercise economic and political influence (Sartori 2013: 2).

Indeed, energy strategy is seen by many analysts as an important element of Russia's economic strategy, but also—and not least—as a tool of foreign policy, of security strategy and, by extension, of the so-called Russia's Grand Strategy. The Russian government and its state-controlled energy company Gazprom act as one, united, and coherent actor, with the Kremlin as the decision-making centre.[5] It is not only the system of 'guided democracy' in Russia that fosters potential manipulations, but also the gas sector structure, namely Gazprom's export monopoly, that allows for rapid, coherent, and thought-out activities. Consequently, the Russian gas strategy can be characterized as highly consistent, as the decision makers have the capacity to identify long-term and overall aims and interests, as well as means to achieve them (Nowak 2016: 23–26).

The inception of the 3rd Energy Package by the EU Commission, however, heavily challenged Russia's gas interests. Consider, for example, issues like the *Gazprom antitrust case* and the reluctance of the EU towards the South Stream and Turkish Stream projects. More precisely, with reference to Gazprom, the omnipresent Russian energy company, in 2011 the EU decided to conduct two investigations against Gazprom, concerning alleged breaches of Article 101 of the Treaty on the Functioning of the European Union (TFEU) and in 2012 concerning possible breaches of Article 102 of the TFEU. In turn, in April 2014 Russia commenced proceedings against the EU before the World Trade Organisation, arguing that EU certification, especially article 11 of the Third Gas Directive provisions adopted in the framework of the Third Energy Package, violates the organisation's regulations. The respective article, known as the 'Gazprom clause', is believed to have been adopted for 'fear that ownership unbundling—the separation of integrated energy companies' production assets from their transmission assets—would lead to the indiscriminate acquisition of EU energy grids by third countries and, more specifically, by Russia. Eventually the European Commission, filed charges against the company in April 2015, accusing it of breaking regional antitrust rules (European Commission 2015a, b).

---

[5] Interview with Alexander Sotnichenko, Former Russian Diplomat in Israel and currently Associate Professor at the Saint Petersburg State University, School of International Relations (Jerusalem July 2013) and Yuri Kvashnin (Head of Section of the EU Studies of the Institute of World Economy and International Relations of the Russian Academy of Sciences).

After fitful negotiations spanning nearly two years, in March 2017 Gazprom reached an amicable solution in the EU antitrust case by committing itself to address the Commission's charges. It seems that the high level of mutual dependence between the two sides helped pave the way for a settlement that could prove to be very temporary (Stanic 2016: 37–46; Kanter, Kramer and Reed 2017).

The same outcome is very likely in another disputed deal pertaining EU–Russia energy relations. Despite serious security concerns of some member states about the controversial energy Nord Stream 2 pipeline project (the pipeline's route running from Russia's Leningrad Oblast under the Baltic Sea to Greifswald in Germany), the materialisation of the deal looks meanwhile likely. In previous years and under pressure from about a dozen governments led by Poland, the EU had been attempting to block the project which would provide a second gas link from Russia to Germany and allow Russia to divert its gas shipments to Europe away from Ukraine, thereby doubling the Baltic Sea export capacity of Gazprom to EU markets (Peker 2017). In addition, the EU Commission had stated that the project was not consistent with the objectives of the Energy Union, because it did not give access to new sources of gas, and strengthened the position of Russia as the largest supplier in the European market. In the given situation in the European market, the Commission was also unable to see any demand for the construction of new gas pipelines of the size of Nord Stream 2 (Łoskot-Strachota, Kardaś, Szymański 2017).

On the contrary, Germany has been vividly supporting the project providing for two additional pipelines with a capacity of 55 bcm. If they one day will be built, Russia could pump up to 70 percent of its total European gas exports through just one route, though its exports could rise further increasing Europe's dependency on Russian gas. In this context, Germany's energy and foreign policies regarding Russia seem contradictory, as Berlin has become the most important defender of the West's sanctions against Russia (Umbach 2017).

In September 2017, the legal service of the Council of the European Union proposed on the issue a special legal framework for the Nord Stream 2 gas pipeline and hence turned down the numerous concerns regarding the possible compliance of the new infrastructure's operation with the rules of European law (including, in particular, the so-called Third Energy Package). Contrary to the European Commission's initial assessments, the opinion by the EU Council's legal service meets the expectations of those parties, which are most interested in implementing the project; in particular, it is consistent with the position of Germany and Russia. Permission to proceed would mean that a number of restrictions arising from the so-called Third Energy Package, such as the principle of third-party access, the principle of unbundling (separating the ownership of the infrastructure from the transmission and distribution of gas), certification requirements and setting transmission tariffs, would not apply automatically to the Nord Stream 2 gas pipeline. This would allow Gazprom and Western European companies to set the conditions for operating the planned pipeline in a free and unrestricted manner. In its opinion the EU Council's legal service has defined the security of gas supplies in a way that conflicts with the predominant interpretation and the hierarchy of priorities set out in the EU's strategic documents (Kardaś and Bajczuk 2017).

Regardless of the outcome of the negotiated project, the Nord Stream 2 case has already strategic implications for the EU's energy policy indicating EU's disability to speak with one voice toward Moscow and became tantamount of the EU's incompetence to act as a unitary international actor. Whereas Putin's Russia has increasingly and masterfully been utilising energy diplomacy's soft power,[6] EU has so far been unable to address its fierce bureaucratic structure and its notorious lack of ownership. As a result, in many cases EU-countries have followed a different, even opposing course, towards Moscow that the EU-commission has.

2   THE SOUTH-EASTERN EUROPEAN FIELD OF THE EU-MOSCOW ENERGY-ECONOMIC COMPETITION

Regarding South-Eastern Europe and following the disintegration of the Soviet Union, relations between Russia and the EU have mainly been marked by geo-political and geo-economic rivalries and competition. Russia's influence in South-Eastern Europe is real and easily observed

---

[6] The Russian domestic energy industry is organized in two legal regimes. Unlike the oil-companies that should be private, gas companies (Gazprom) should be state-run companies for two reasons: first, in order to control gas prices on which so many people depend (Gazprom controls about 90% of the Russian market), and second, Gazprom's activities are fully intertwined with Russia's foreign policy. Interview with Alexander Sotnichenko, Former Russian diplomat in Israel and currently Associate Professor at the Saint Petersburg State University, School of International Relations, personal communication, Jerusalem, July 2013 and Yuri Kvashnin, Head of Section of the EU Studies of the Institute of World Economy and International Relations of the Russian Academy of Sciences, Moscow 4 September 2015.

affecting the region in a multitude of ways. The Russian oil and gas companies still play an enormous role in the local energy markets, despite the obstacles they face and the beefed-up EU-legislation aimed at encouraging competition and diversifying supplies (Bechev 2017: 238).

The region constitutes a particularly antagonistic terrain in the EU–Russia energy and economic relations because of its special position in the Euro-Asiatic energy map. Especially Greece, Cyprus and Turkey have a twofold function in the European and Asian energy architecture: they are in a very delicate position as energy consumers dependent on Russian energy exports and of supreme importance as energy hubs or potential energy producers. Their real or assumed geo-political and geo-economic potential as energy hub and energy producing countries elevates them to a valuable alternative source for energy imports for the energy-deprived EU, still heavily dependent on Russian gas. Their heavy energy dependence on Russian energy supplies, gas supplies in particular, in combination with their fragile and volatile politico-economic state and sensitive geo-strategic, geo-economic location, renders them very susceptible to foreign political and economic manipulation. Notably, natural gas supply, unlike oil, is particularly vulnerable to political influences because of the direct and long-term nature of natural gas supply relations. Decisions on natural gas projects are especially likely to be affected by political considerations, because they can be quite risky.

Against this background, ensuring security of supply of natural gas to states located in the periphery of the EU looks quite challenging. In European energy security architecture, geography matters. States located at the centre of Europe have access to more supply options and lower prices than those located on Europe's periphery. In addition, for states on Europe's geographic periphery, which are primarily small markets, it is unlikely that even if excellent market rules are established and observed, those states on the periphery will represent attractive investment destinations for additional suppliers due to commercial considerations. Thus, many markets may remain singularly supplied by Russia (Shaffer 2015: 184).

In this context the so-called Southern Gas Corridor, i.e. the supply routes running from the Caspian basin (so far Azerbaijan but potentially other countries in the future), have been an apple of discord between the EU and Russia and are therefore haunted by difficulties and political rivalries.

3   THE IMPACT OF THE SOUTHERN GAS CORRIDOR ON THE EU-RUSSIA RELATIONS

In the late 1990s the EU had already identified the Caspian and Central Asian regions as key targets for its energy diversification initiatives. With the Interstate Oil and Gas Transport to Europe (INOGATE) program first, launched in 1997, as well as the 2004 Baku Initiative, the EU attempted to establish stable energy ties with the region's countries, thereby promoting the security of the EU's energy supply by increasing the number of energy sources and building new transport infrastructures. The INOGATE Programme's mandate was supposed to support the development of energy co-operation between the European Union, the littoral states of the Black and Caspian Seas and their neighbouring countries. The co-operation framework covered the areas of oil and gas, electricity, renewable energy and energy efficiency (Sartori 2012: 5–7).

The Southern Gas Corridor's main route is the 10 billion cubic metre (bcm) capacity Trans Adriatic Pipeline (TAP), the project's end piece, joining up with the Trans Anatolian Pipeline (TANAP) at the Turkish border, then crossing Greece and Albania to reach Italy.[7] The pipeline scheme has the capacity to transport gas also from other Caspian countries—though the latter have made the choice so far to sell their gas to the Russians or to the Chinese or to both of them—as well as from Iran, Iraq and even from the Mediterranean via Turkey to Europe. The last but at the same time most unlikely option[8] would coincide with Turkey's geo-economic ambitions, whereas Greece and Cyprus aspire to use alternative gas pipeline schemes to bring it to the Europe maybe with the prospect to use Liquefaction Natural Gas terminals in Greece (by Athens and in northern Greece).

The realisation of the Southern Gas Corridor, however, has revealed the incompatibility of the strategic interests between the European Commission and the single EU-member states and the lack of ownership haunting EU-energy policy. The European Commission and the pro-Atlanticist member-states of the EU who are either not dependent on Russian natural gas (UK) or over-dependent on Russian gas imports

---

[7] TANAP and TAP are different legal entities. TANAP ends in the territory of Turkey and TAP begins in the territory of Greece and ends in Italy. According a mutual agreement commercially the connecting point of TANAP-TAP is in the middle of Evros river.

[8] Interview with Bakhtiyar Aslanbayli, Vice President of the BP Azerbaijan (Baku, August 2017).

(Poland, Baltics, Bulgaria, Central Europeans) followed an energy policy in the Caspian Sea region that aspired to consolidate the geopolitical independence of the former Soviet states by securing them both export markets for their hydrocarbon resources and transit routes bypassing Russia. This has been the case since the early 1990s and the completion of the Baku-Tbilisi-Ceyhan oil pipeline (BTC) and later on with Nabucco project. The original Nabucco plan was also predestined to drive a hole in Russia's ability to dominate the post-soviet economies of its hydrocarbon-rich "comrade" colonies. It also would not only "open up" Turkmenistan to Western influence, but also allow Ukraine to limit its dependence on Russian gas imports thereby facilitating a more pro-western orientation of Kiev's foreign and defense policy. At the same time Russia's ambassador to NATO indirectly threatened Ukraine with the possibility of Crimea's separation (Rzayeva & Tsakiris 2012: 7–8). Notably, in January 2007 the Ukrainian President Viktor Yushchenko stated during his visit to Romania and Turkey officially Ukraine's intentions to join the Nabucco project.[9]

European Commission's particular support to the realisation of Nabucco, a 3893 km pipeline running from Turkey to the European gas hub of Baumgarten in Austria, via Bulgaria, Romania, and Hungary was meant to thwart Russia's soft power in the region. Nabucco could indeed address the energy security supply problem of the EU, if, as initially planned, were connected to a possible trans-Caspian pipeline providing access to the huge Turkmen gas resources. Additionally to the Azeri energy resources Nabucco needed to secure 10 billion to 15 billion cm gas from Turkmenistan and Iraq in order to fill the promised pipeline's capacity (31 billion cubic metre a year) (Petroleum Economist 2011). To the extend to such an option really did exist, it would have been a real challenge against Moscow that has been trying for many years to prevent the construction of the trans-Caspian pipeline exercising its political leverage in Turkmenistan.[10]

Therefore, given its limited capacity (10 bcm a year) the TAP project was clearly the underdog in the competition to deliver Shah Deniz II gas to Europe and lacked political support from the EU-institutions. The

[9] Web-Portal of Ukrainian Government, "Ukraine to participate in tenders for construction of Nabucco gas pipeline, as alternative to Russian gas suppliers", 18 January 2007: http://www.kmu.gov.ua/control/publish/article?art_id=63077434.

[10] Interview with Canus Abushov, Russia-Expert and Professor at the ADA University (Baku, August 2017).

Commission's choice, however, did not take into account some key factors, such as the diverging, and sometimes conflicting, interests of individual South-European EU member states as well as the commercial constraints on Nabucco. The Commission's preference also did not meet the criteria Shah Deniz II consortium had set out for the selection process, *commerciality, project deliverability*, etc. Eventually and according to the main shareholders of the consortium[11] various legal and commercial aspects such as the cost of shipping Azeri gas, the expected prices and demand forecasts in the respective markets, as well as potential access to Western Balkans' transmission systems and not political criteria determined Shah Deniz II consortium's preference for TAP.

Especially the exemption from *Third Party Access* legislation granted by the EU to TAP appears to have been more attractive than the scheme agreed for Nabucco. Through TAP, in fact, the Shah Deniz II consortium is offered an initial (first phase) export capacity of 10 bcm for a period of 25 years, while in the second phase the new volumes (a further 10 bcm) is to be allocated through an open auction process. On the contrary Nabucco-shareholders was confirmed a total of 5 bcm in the first phase and another 6.5 bcm in the second phase. Last but not least, the commercial interests of SOCAR—the Azerbaijani state-run energy company—in the Greek gas market seem to have played also an important role. During the evaluation phase, SOCAR reached an agreement with the Hellenic Republic Assets Development Fund for the acquisition of a 66% stake in the Greek natural gas grid operator DESFA company. For SOCAR, controlling DESFA meant entering the European gas transmission and distribution sector for the first time.

While some labeled the result as a victory of Europe, the truth of the matter is that the main beneficiaries are of course Azerbaijan and SOCAR as well as Italy, Greece and Albania. The three countries after initial hesitations made significant diplomatic efforts resulting in the signature of the Memorandum of Understanding and the Trilateral Intergovernmental Agreement used as vehicle for promoting their preferences for the new pipeline architecture in the region. Through Nabucco EU interests as bloc would be certainly better served. As contradictory as it may sound, Russia has also an indirect benefit from the Shah Deniz II consortium's decision, because the TAP route provides much less competition for the Russian

---

[11] Interview with Bakhtiyar Aslanbayli, Vice President of the BP Azerbaijan and Vitaliy Baylarbayov, Deputy Vice-president of SOCAR (Baku, August 2017).

economic and probably also political interests in Europe. Nabucco, on the contrary, was expected to supply the same countries as those reached by the Gazprom-led South Stream pipeline and challenge more seriously Russia's long-term interests around the Caspian Sea.[12] Given the fact that in Shah Deniz Consortium also comprises a Russian company LUKOIL[13] (10% share), it is not surprising at all that the decision for the investment in the TAP made by unanimous consensus between the shareholders.[14]

Notwithstanding, though the project has minor value for the EU energy security (the volume of the pipeline in its first phase of development corresponds to about 3% and in its second phase to approximately 8% of the whole EU-markets gas consumption) its political repercussions might change the energy and geopolitical map of the region radically and for good. Once TANAP and TAP pipelines are completed, Gazprom will lose its prevalent position as energy supplier in southern Europe and may have to resort to price dumping to stay competitive.

The Southern Gas Corridor, however, though it has progressed adequately so far and is to be finalized by Azerbaijan in 2020, the full materialisation of the project, i.e. to transform it into a really alternative gas route to Europe, is also subject to some unpredictable variables.

First, the security aspect of the project should not be underestimated, possible PKK actions are Islamic terrorist attacks cannot be ruled out for the near future. Ankara has taken over the full responsibility of the security of the TANAP pipeline but this was agreed at a different time, before the coup d'état of July 2016 resulting in extensive purging in the military and police and more importantly before the Kurdish referendum of September 2017 adding one more factor of uncertainty.

---

[12] Gazprom has devised a strategy aimed at hindering Caspian and Central Asian gas export to Europe by routes other than through Russia. Gazprom has its own network of pipelines in Central Asian countries (the Central Asia Centre gas pipeline system), which allows it from time to time to import Central Asian gas and then re-export it further to Europe. Although the strategy itself is not as profitable as Gazprom producing the gas itself in Russia, due to its near-monopolistic position in a large part of the European gas market, Gazprom can make up for this loss by charging its European consumers higher prices than they would pay if they had direct access to Central Asian gas supplies (Cohen 2014: 9).

[13] PJSC LUKOIL has been operating in the Azerbaijani oil-and-gas industry since 1994, when the Company joined its first international development project for the Azeri-Chirag-Gyuneshli oil field, one of the largest in the Azerbaijani sector of the Caspian Sea. LUKOIL was the first among Russian major business enterprises to start operations in Azerbaijan.

[14] (Sartori 2012, 2013); Interview with Bakhtiyar Aslanbayli Vice President of the BP Azerbaijan (Baku, August 2017) Interview with Bakhtiyar Aslanbayli, Vice President of the BP Azerbaijan and anonymous source of the Azeri Foreign Ministry (Baku, August 2017).

Some analysts (Kanter 2015) believe that also the Greek route[15] might turn out to be a source of problems, because Athens and the TAP-company have allegedly not yet been able to come to terms on the financial portion of the deal, because the DESFA-deal that has been an incentive for SOCAR, has been canceled. According the Shah Deniz consortium, however,[16] the agreement signed has covered all the aspects of the deal and no outstanding issues exist between Greece and TAP. Moreover, except some minor problems with some communities (land issues) the consortium expresses a general optimism about the progress of the project so far and indicates a supporting attitude of the Greek government.

In Italy, however, the project faces serious reactions from the Civil Society and some political figures in the government that rose in power in 2018. Various ecologist organisations have raised serious concerns about environmental damages the pipeline is supposed to cause (replanting of the olive trees during the construction in a distance of about 8 kilometers). Though the consortium attributes those problems to disagreements between the central and the regional governments, diplomatic sources of the Azeri Foreign Ministry suspect Russian interference behind some radical leftist groups that raised the major objections so far.[17]

Secondly, the only identified gas source for the pipeline so far is Azerbaijan. It is highly uncertain whether other countries such as Turkmenistan, Kazakhstan, Iran and Iraq will be joining the scheme. Kazakh gas, though voluminous, is very difficult to be pumped into the pipeline scheme, because there is not infra structure enabling its transport to the Caspian shore. Turkmenistan has enormous gas resources and needs desperately cash, as it sells its gas only to China and to Iran at the moment.[18] The main snag and real challenge simultaneously with this option is the transport of Turkmen gas until Baku, i.e. to build the so-called Trans-

---

[15] In 2007, Greece became the first EU-country to receive directly through a pipeline Azerbaijani gas. The Turkey–Greece pipeline is a 296 kilometres long pipeline connecting Turkish and Greek gas grids. The pipeline begins in Karacabey in Turkey and runs to Komotini in Greece. The length of Turkish section is 210 kilometres, of which 17 kilometres are under the Sea of Marmara. The length of Greek section is 86 kilometres. The diameter of pipeline is 36 inches (910 mm) and the capacity is 7 billion cubic meters (250 billion cubic feet) of natural gas per year.

[16] Interview with Vitaliy Baylarbayov, Deputy Vice-president of SOCAR (Baku, August 2017).

[17] Interview with Bakhtiyar Aslanbayli, Vice President of the BP Azerbaijan and an anonymous diplomat of the Azeri Foreign Ministry (Baku, August 2017).

[18] China, however, pays only a part of the gas it receives and it considers the rest as credit for the pipeline it is constructing in Turkmenistan. Iran also does not provide any cash but only some chemical products in return.

Caspian pipeline, since there is infra structure to bring it until that point from the Eastern Turkmenistan where the energy field are located. But, as already mentioned, this scenario is subject of diametrically opposed geopolitical and geo-economic interests. The energy resources of Northern Iraq can under given political circumstances quite easily be an additional source of gas, when a small gas pipeline will be constructed to join to the TANAP-TAP system. It is theoretically feasible to include gas from Iran into the project as well, if the sanctions were one day terminated but Iran needs to increase its production because its existing current gas volume barely covers domestic demand. What Iran sells abroad is actually what it buys from Turkmenistan. East Mediterranean gas could also be pumped into the TANAP-TAP system but only through pipelines crossing the Cyprus' Economic Exclusive Zone into Turkey. Nevertheless, this project presupposes a sub-sea pipeline that is very expensive and a resolution of the Cyprus conflict, which is rather unlikely in the foreseeable future and that's way it is prioritised by the consortium as the last option.[19]

Moscow's attitude is difficult to appraise at the moment. In recent years, Gazprom has been developing a masterfully strategy, seeking to defend its market share in the region using economic and political tools at a whim. In the case of TANAP-TAP, what Gazprom appears to do is to use EU-regulations in order to avoid EU-regulations. More precisely, the Russian company has already made public that it was considering to access the TAP by pumping gas through the link under one auction system giving equal access to any would-be supplier. It is the so-called *Open Season Auctions* prescribed in the TANAP-TAP agreement for the second phase of its operation. In this way, the Russians will probably bypass the obstacles of the EU legislation (Third Party access) designed to prevent them in particular from acquiring a monopolistic position in the European energy market! All of the companies participating in the TAP with the exemption of the SOCAR, which but controls only 20% of the pipeline, greeted this option as there are doubts on Azerbaijan's ability to pump more gas into the pipeline. Also the states involved in the project are well disposed to the undertaking. This however could yield various geopolitical complications.[20]

The consortium downplays it as media speculation, as there is no agreement of mutual understanding or letter of intention indicating this devel-

[19] Interview with Bakhtiyar Aslanbayli Vice President of the BP Azerbaijan and Vitaliy Baylarbayov, Deputy Vice-president of SOCAR (Baku August 2017).

[20] Interview with international diplomat involved in the development accredited to Greece, (Athens, May 2017) and diplomatic source of the Greek Foreign Ministry (Athens, July 2017).

opment. Both BP and SOCAR people point out, that the second phase of the project is still not clear neither for the quantity nor about the timing. So there is no rush to determine such details. Secondly, they heavily disagree that Azerbaijan do not possess enough gas. Beyond Shah Deniz II field, which is about to be exploited, there is also Absheron,[21] Shah Deniz III, ACG, Umid Babec and Shafag-Asiman fields as potential resources, i.e. five projects that could be developed further in the coming years.[22]

Furthermore, since 2015, the Kremlin has been pursuing some other pipeline schemes. The first was the promotion of the *Interconnector Turkey-Greece-Italy Poseidon* (ITGI) for its own use. Poseidon, the marine part of the Southern Gas Corridor project from Turkey to Italy through Greece (Ionian Sea) had once been backed by the EU to transport Azerbaijani gas to Italy as an alternative to Russian imports but was eventually replaced by the TAP pipeline. A more serious geo-strategic gambit has been Russia's attempt to resurrect the Russian-sponsored South Stream project (the construction of a natural-gas pipeline under the Black Sea, consisting of one link serving the Turkish market and another one possibly to southern Europe via Greece) under a new name, Turkish Stream. This could be a project of geostrategic magnitude, which would not only by-pass Ukraine, "a difficult transit partner" for Russia, but also ensure Russia's energy and economic expansion in South-Eastern Europe for good (Łoskot-Strachota 2016: 174–175).

In spring 2015, Moscow appears to have managed to persuade the newly elected left-wing government in Athens to negotiate a possible multibillion-dollar pipeline deal. To that end, Russians offered the possibility of 47 billion cubic meters of Russian gas, which could arrive through Turkish Stream to the Greek border. This amount is obviously much more profitable than the 10 billion cubic meters of Azeri gas to be pumped through the TAP pipeline, whose construction would of course not be stopped but its profitability heavily undermined. What began as a rumour circulated by various Greek media reports was in July 2017 confirmed by the former energy minister Panayotis Lafazanis, who negotiated the deal with Kremlin. According Lafazanis, the Tsipras administration

---

[21] The development of the Absheron field, however, is currently expected to extract 1.5 billion cubic meters of gas a year, which will fully flow to the domestic market of Azerbaijan (Camal 2017).

[22] Interview with Bakhtiyar Aslanbayli Vice President of the BP Azerbaijan (Baku, August 2017).

indeed appeared to be positive to this option, expecting Russian financial assistance in return that in turn would be used in order to circumvent the conditions laid down by EU institutions for a new bail-out package for Greece and to finance Greece if it left the euro (Kathimerini 2017b).

The idea behind the request seems to have five to 10 billion US dollars advance on the construction of the Greek branch of the Turkish Stream gas pipeline. The deal that came across the provisions of the Third Energy Package, did not work out, as it first of all would jeopardise Greece's relations with the United States. The latter seem to have pushed the leftist government in Athens to resist Russia's energy overtures (Kanter 2015). It would also pose Moscow's relations with the EU in a manner that even the Kremlin could not afford. Apparently, as Moscow is led by pragmatic *realpolitik* motives, it prefers not to give money to anybody, unless it can get something tangible in return, which Athens was unable to do. There is also another very plausible interpretation for the Kremlin's behaviour in line with Moscow's penetration history in the region. Russia acted this way just to gain political benefits from the Greek crisis, by trying to exploit rifts and fissures in European unity. Such kind of overtures, together with various cordial statements Putin has made in his frequent visits to Greece in recent years, are apparently meant to be sowing division and discord among the EU states in order to undermine the sanctions regime against Russia. In this respect, Moscow might have let the Europeans look weak and bad so as to have a Russia friendly country within the EU to use as a lobbying and communication channel (Stergiou 2017: 114–115).

As some experts have noted, the Southern European states had many times to face the bitter reality that cashing in on Russia's friendship does not always work. Russia's hard-nosed pragmatism and absence of ideological scruples differentiates it from both the Soviet Union and the Tsarist Empire. Its soft power strategy never goes far beyond a low-cost approach that neither puts Russia's resources under strain nor generates much risk. When Moscow is indeed prepared to spend vast amounts of money for projects such as South Stream, it does so from the premise, that it will take the lion's share of the expected benefits (Bechev 2017: 21–22).

Indeed, recent surveys show that Russia's nationalist foreign policy, with its emphasis on its own sovereignty, meets with sympathy within much of the Greek population, as many Greeks sense some kind of Christian Orthodox solidarity with Russians and many regard Russia as a state that upholds its sovereignty and defies the EU diktat. Vladimir Putin, in particular, enjoys great popularity among the Greeks, essentially more than Angela Merkel or Donald Trump (Kathimerini 2017a).

This perception has been reinforced by the social repercussions of the Greek debt crisis and the EU's severe austerity measures at home. This rosy view, which is mostly centred on the idea of dignity, overlooks Russia's aggression against Ukraine and the annexation of Crimea. At the same time, the EU is suffering a massive loss of respect. Meanwhile, Greece belongs to the countries where anti-Europeanism rose so abruptly (DiaNeosis 2016). Recent comparative polls in many countries also indicate that even more Greeks see their biggest security threat coming from Turkey and they cannot rely on NATO to protect them, so they look to Russia (Bloomberg 2017).

Since 2016, Turkey also turned out to be another unpredictable variable for the EU and the US energy diplomacy.[23] Capitalizing on the recent improvement in Russia–Turkey relations, in October 2016 Gazprom undertook a new attempt to resurrect the project, clinching with Turkish Botas Petroleum a preliminary deal on the project, that could be up and running by the end of 2019. Talks on this project had in fact been suspended in December 2015 due to the Russian-Turkish political crisis, although Gazprom did not back down from plans to build a gas pipeline. The revived project provides for the construction of two lines of the pipeline (each with a capacity of 15.75 bcm), one of which is to be used for the supply of gas to the Turkish market, and the other for the transit of Russian gas via Turkey to European customers. The current plan is less ambitious in relation to the original assumptions, foreseeing a smaller capacity. Thus, on one side there exist the unfavourable provisions of the Third Energy Package and possible EU countries' reluctance to consume the Russian gas, due to the serious deterioration in EU–Turkey relations. Greece gets about three-quarters of its gas from Russia, but for Gazprom, it is a relatively small customer. Even Turkey, despite being the second-largest market for Russian gas in the region after Germany, would not be a big enough buyer on its own for all the gas Gazprom would eventually plan to send through a Black Sea pipeline.

On the other side, however, and given the recent strained EU-Turkey relationship, Ankara might feel free from any commitment towards Brussels. At least the line designed to bring gas to the Turkish market, should be taken for granted. Turkish Stream, which could use the gas

---

[23] Former US President Obama's final foreign trip to Greece in November 2016 apparently served to demonstrate, somewhat belatedly, American engagement in Greece in the face of Russian meddling in the region. Jason Horowitz and Liz Aldermanaug, "Chastised by E.U., a Resentful Greece Embraces China's Cash and Interests", New York Times 26 August, 2017. Retrieved 27 August 2017 from https://www.nytimes.com/2017/08/26/world/europe/greece-china-piraeus-alexis-tsipras.html.

infrastructure and pipes that were originally used for the construction of the South Stream gas pipeline, would create another direct channel for gas imports from Russia, after Blue Stream, via a new pipeline under the Black Sea (Chudziak et al. 2016).

Turkey's importance as a future European natural gas hub, or even a transit country, might be highly dependent on Russia's ability to exert market power. Turkey's role may be stronger if European gas demand is higher than expected and Russia exerts greater market power. From a European perspective, these conditions would not be preferable as they would lead to higher gas prices and a corresponding worsening in general welfare levels (Schulte and Istemi 2017: 15). In geopolitical analytical terms, Moscow's ambition to remain a key energy producer and Ankara's ambition to ascend to a key energy transit hub seem very likely to have precipitated in summer 2016 the rapid improvement in Russia–Turkey relations, which had been damaged because of a series of incidents in recent years. It is no accident that Erdogan's first foreign trip since the abortive July 15 putsch in Turkey was to Russia, just as Turkey's relations with traditional allies like the United States and Europe showed increasing strain once again.

Athens has also not rejected the idea to participate in the project. In June 2017, the Russian Gazprom, Greek DEPA, and Italian Edison companies inked a Cooperation Agreement on southern route for Russian gas supplies to Europe. The document envisages joint efforts aimed at implementing both the Turkish Stream and the Poseidon project in the area from the Turkish-Greek border to Italy in full compliance with applicable legislation (Gazprom 2017).

Gazprom, the main provider for DEPA until 2026 also managed to break DEPA's monopoly in the Greek market and to export additional gas to Greece through the Prometheus Gas company, a joint company parity (50–50) owned by Kopelouzos Group and GazpromExport (100 percent subsidiary of Gazprom). Using to its advantage the EU-antitrust legislation compelling Greece to reduce state-run DEPA company's share in the Greek market in 2014, began importing directly gas into Greece laying the foundations for remaining after 2016 main gas supplier in the country and further undermining EU-diversification policy.

Furthermore, the Greek Conglomerate Kopelouzos Group and GazpromExport have shaped a joint venture, the Greek private limited company Gastrade. The latter has been licensed to develop a floating storage and regasification unit (FSRU) off the coast of Alexandroupolis, aimed at importing liquefied natural gas from various sources to North-Eastern

Greece and to the so-called Vertical Corridor, the energy scheme to be constructed for bi-directional natural gas transport, interconnecting the networks of Bulgaria, Greece, Romania and Hungary.[24]

As Gazprom has the advantage of being a low-cost producer, and it can reduce its prices below that of the available competitors, could try, in compliance with the Third Party Access directive of the EU's Third Energy Package, to flood cheap Russian gas to the countries in South-Eastern Europe, seriously affecting the profitability of the Southern Gas Corridor (Rzayeva 2017). Gastrade is also one of six companies—including Greek DEPA, the State Oil Company of Azerbaijan Republic (SOCAR), as well as Edison and Noble—that have already booked capacity in the Greece-Bulgaria Interconnector (IGB) pipeline to transport the imported LNG from the Alexandroupolis FSRU north to the Bulgarian market.

The FSRU in Alexandroupolis is included on the European Union's list of Projects of Common Interest and therefore was supported by the Obama administration.[25] Once again, Gazprom is using the loopholes or the possibilities included in the EU-legislation to oppose a significant energy strategy pursued by the EU.

4   Conclusion

All things considered, one can conclude that the EU-Russia energy antagonism in South-Eastern Europe that has been raging for years, is very likely to continue because of the highly variable relations among countries and the many and still unresolved tensions, as well as the heterogeneous needs and interests of the regional actors involved. Russia is a traditional energy supplier in the region with a prevalent, yet nearly monopolistic position in the local market. Therefore, it has been trying to render projects undermining Russian dominance uncompetitive. It seems that in some cases Moscow's energy policy is determined by political considerations as well. The competition becomes even stronger when the availability of gas is growing and new suppliers come into emergence. Therefore, Gazprom is trying to keep away potential alternative suppliers.

---

[24] The Vertical Corridor concept is not a single pipeline project but a gas system consisted of national grids, underground gas storage facilities, interconnectors (Greece-Bulgaria Interconnector), LNG terminals that will connect existing national gas grids and other gas infrastructure in order to secure easy gas transiting from South to North.

[25] Vitaliy Baylarbayov, Deputy Vice-president of SOCAR (Baku August 2017).

Russia, however, through Gazprom appears to be in an advantageous position, because it is full supported by the Russian government, whereas its rival, the EU, is a huge bureaucratic institution plagued by the so-called lack of ownership handicap, i.e. the contradictory and opposing interests among its members.

REFERENCES

Bechev, D. (2017). *Rival power. Russia's influence in Southeast Europe.* New Haven and London: Yale University.
Bloomberg. (2017). Four NATO Nations would pick Russia to defend them if threatened Poll. Retrieved February 18, 2017, from https://www.bloomberg.com/politics/articles/2017-02-17/melania-trump-s-slovenia-would-pick-russian-over-u-s-protection.
Camal, G. (2017). Total steps up work to launch gas production at Absheron field. In *Azernews.* Retrieved October 10, 2017, https://www.azernews.az/oil_and_gas/114520.html.
Chudziak, Mateusz, Kardaś, Szymon, Rodkiewicz, Witold. (2016). Turkey-Russia: partnership of convenience. The Centre for Eastern Studies. Retrieved December 20, 2016, from https://www.osw.waw.pl/en/publikacje/analyses/2016-10-12/turkey-russia-partnership-convenience.
Cohen, A. (2014). Caspian Gas, TANAP and TAP in Europe's energy security, Istituto Affari Internationali Working Papers. Retrieved November 20, 2015, from http://www.iai.it/en/pubblicazioni/caspian-gas-tanap-and-tap-europes-energy-security.
Coote, B. (2016). *Surging liquefied natural gas trade how US exports will benefit European and global.* The Atlantic Council of the United States. Retrieved June 30, 2016, from http://www.atlanticcouncil.org/publications/reports/surging-liquefied-natural-gas-trade.
DiaNeosis. (2016). Survey on what Greeks believe (In Greek). DiaNeosis. Retrieved February 20, 2017, from http://www.dianeosis.org/wp-content/uploads/2017/03/ti_pistevoun_oi_ellines_final_version.pdf.
EU-Parliament. (2016). Parliamentary questions 15 November 2016: Subject: Increase in EU gas imports. Retrieved November 25, 2016, from http://www.europarl.europa.eu/sides/getDoc.do?type=WQ&reference=P-2016-008554&language=EN.
European Commission. (2015a). *Energy Union: Secure, sustainable, competitive, affordable energy for every European.* Retrieved July 20, 2016, from http://europa.eu/rapid/press-release_IP-15-4497_en.htm.
European Commission Press Release. (2015b, April 22). Antitrust: Commission sends Statement of Objections to Gazprom for alleged abuse of dominance on Central and Eastern European gas supply markets. Retrieved November 20, 2015, from http://europa.eu/rapid/press-release_IP-15-4828_en.htm.

European Union. (2003). Decision No 1229/2003/EC, September 2003. Retrieved January 20, 2017, from http://eurlex.europa.eu/LexUriServ/LexUriServ.do?uri=OJ:L:2006:262:0001:0001:EN:PD.

European Union. (2006). Decision No 1364/2006/EC of the European Parliament and of the Council of 6 September 2006 laying down guidelines for trans-European energy networks and repealing Decision 96/391/EC. Retrieved January 20, 2017, from http://eurlex.europa.eu/LexUriServ/LexUriServ.do?uri=OJ:L:2006:262:0001:0001:EN:PD.

Gazprom. (2017). Press Release. Retrieved August 10, 2017, from http://www.gazprom.com/press/news/2017/june/article335060/.

Hedlund, Stefan. (2017). Another twist in the Gazprom saga, Geopolitical Intelligence Service. Retrieved October 10, 2017, from https://www.gisreportsonline.com/another-twist-in-the-gazprom-saga,energy,2344,report.html.

Kanter, J. (2015). U.S. Urges Greece to reject Russian energy project, New York Times. Retrieved September 19, 2016, https://www.nytimes.com/2015/05/09/business/international/greece-us-russia-energy-pipeline.html.

Kanter, J., Kramer, A., & Reed, S. (2017). Gazprom Makes concessions in E.U. Gas deal, but trouble looms for Russian giant, *New York Times*. Retrieved August 10, 2017, from https://www.nytimes.com/2017/03/13/business/eu-russia-gazprom.html.

Kardaś, S., & Bajczuk, R. (2017). A gas pipeline 'above the law'? The EU Council's legal service gives its opinion on Nord Stream 2. The Centre of Eastern Studies. Retrieved October 10, 2017, from https://www.osw.waw.pl/en/publikacje/analyses/2017-10-04/a-gas-pipeline-above-law-eu-councils-legal-service-gives-its-opinion.

Kathimerini. (2017a). Are the Greeks Russia – or Europe-friendly? Survey carried out by the University of Macedonia (PAMAK) (In Greek). Retrieved September 6, 2017, from http://www.kathimerini.gr/929821/article/epikairothta/politikh/ellhnes-rwsofiloi-h-eyrwpaistes.

Kathimerini. (2017b). Lafazanis claims Russian cash could have helped with Grexit. Retrieved September 8, 2017, from http://www.ekathimerini.com/220304/article/ekathimerini/news/lafazanis-claims-russian-cash-could-have-helped-with-grexit.

Łoskot-Strachota, A. (2016). Winds of change. Challenging future for Russia's gas. In S. Colombo, M. El Harrak, & N. Sartor (Eds.), *The future of natural gas. Markets and geopolitics* (pp. 159–180). Rome: Istituto Affari Internazionali and OCP Policy Center and Lenthe Publishers.

Łoskot-Strachota, A., Kardaś, S., & Szymański, P. (2017). The European Commission is ready to talk to Russia about Nord Stream 2. Centre for Eastern Studies. Retrieved October 10, 2017, from https://www.osw.waw.pl/en/publikacje/analyses/2017-04-05/european-commission-ready-to-talk-to-russia-about-nord-stream-2.

Nowak, Z. (2016). Russia's energy policy: The EU case. In: Gürel A. et. al. (eds.) Global energy debates and the Eastern Mediterranean. PRIO Cyprus Centre-Friedrich Ebert Stiftung-Atlantic Council, Nicosia, p. 23-28

Peker, E. (2017). EU Says It can't block Russia-backed Nord Stream 2 Pipeline. *World Street Journal*. Retrieved April 1, 2017, from https://www.wsj.com/articles/eu-says-it-cant-block-russia-backed-nord-stream-2-pipeline-1490906474.

Petroleum Economist. (2011). Trans-Caspian gas pipeline vital to Nabucco. Retrieved July 25, 2017, from http://www.petroleum-economist.com/articles/midstream-downstream/pipelines/2011/trans-caspian-gas-pipeline-vital-to-nabucco.

Pisca, I. (2016). *Outlook for EU gas demand and import needs to 2025.* Clingendael Institute: Den Haag.

Rzayeva, G. (2017). Russian Gazprom shows renewed interest in Greek Natural Gas Infrastructure. *Eurasia Daily Monitor Journal, 14*(12), 1.

Rzayeva, G., & Tsakiris, T. (2012). Strategic imperative: Azerbaijani gas strategy and the EU's southern corridor. The Collapse of Nabucco Classic and the Elusive "Turkmen Connection". Center for Strategic Studies. Retrieved August 10, 2017, from http://www.eliamep.gr/wp-content/uploads/2012/08/tsakiris.pdf.

Sartori, N. (2012). *The European Commission's policy towards the Southern Gas Corridor: Between National Interests and Economic Fundamentals.* Istituto Affari Internazionali Working Papers 12. Retrieved October 20, 2016, from http://www.iai.it/en/pubblicazioni/european-commissions-policy-towards-southern-gas-corridor.

Sartori, N. (2013). *Energy and politics: Behind the scenes of the Nabucco-TAP Competition.* Istituto Affari Internazionali Working Papers 13. Retrieved May 20, 2017, from http://www.iai.it/sites/default/files/iaiwp1327.pdf.

Schulte, S., & Berk, I. (2017). *Turkey's role in natural gas – Becoming a transit country?* Institute of Energy Economics at the University of Cologne (EWI) Working Paper, No 17/01.

Shaffer, B. (2015). Europe's natural gas security of supply: policy tools for single-supplied states. *Energy Law Journal, 36,* 179–201.

Stanic, A. (2016). EU-Russia relations through the prism of EU energy law. In A. Gürel et al. (Eds.), *Global energy debates and the Eastern Mediterranean* (pp. 29–42). PRIO Cyprus Centre-Friedrich Ebert Stiftung-Atlantic Council Report: Nicosia.

Stergiou, A. (2017). Russia's energy and defense strategy in the Eastern. *Mediterranean Economics World Journal, 5*(2), 101–119.

Stüwe, R. (2017). EU external energy policy in natural gas: A case of neofunctionalist integration? In Center for European Integration Studies (ZEI) Discussion paper C 241. Retrieved September 20, 2017, from https://www.zei.uni-bonn.de/news/2017/zei-discussion-paper-c-241-2017.

Tiersky, R., & Oudenaren, J. V. (2010). Europe and Russia strategic partnership and strategic mistrust. In R. Tiersky et al. (Eds.), *European foreign policies: Does Europe still matter?* (pp. 69–92). New York: Rowman & Littlefield Publishers.

Ukrainian Government, Web-Portal. (2007). Ukraine to participate in tenders for construction of Nabucco gas pipeline, as alternative to Russian gas suppliers. Retrieved August 20, 2017, from http://www.kmu.gov.ua/control/publish/article?art_id=63077434.

Umbach, F. (2017). The risks of German unilateralism on Nord Stream 2. In: Geopolitical Intelligence Services. Retrieved May 11, 2017, from https://www.gisreportsonline.com/the-risks-of-german-unilateralism-on-nord-stream-2,energy,2213.html.

Yergin, Daniel (2006). Ensuring energy security. *Foreign Affairs*, vol. 85, 69–82.

INTERVIEWS

Alexander Sotnichenko. Former Russian Diplomat in Israel and currently Associate Professor at the Saint Petersburg State University, School of International Relations (Jerusalem, July 2013).

Bakhtiyar Aslanbayli, Vice President of the BP Azerbaijan (Baku August 2017).

Diplomatic Source of the Azeri Foreign Ministry (Baku August 2017).

Diplomatic Source of the Greek Foreign Ministry (Athens, July 2017).

International diplomat accredited to Greece (Athens, May 2017).

Kavus Abushov, Professor at the ADA University: Russia-Expert (Baku August 2017).

Vitaliy Baylarbayov, Deputy Vice-president of SOCAR (Baku August 2017).

Yuri Kvashnin (Head of Section of the EU Studies of the Institute of World Economy and International Relations of the Russian Academy of Sciences) (Moscow, September 2015).

Declining Activity of the European Commission in Legislative Initiatives: Is the Commission Losing Its Influence?

Jerzy Ząbkowicz

1   INTRODUCTION

Proponents of the 'new intergovernmentalism' approach clearly point out that in the post-Maastricht days the Member States consistently avoid transferring more powers to traditional supranational EU bodies (the Commission and the Court), also because of the strong resistance from the public and difficulties of justifying such decisions in terms of legitimacy (Bulmer 2015). If such delegation occurs, it is more likely that the addressee will be a *de novo* body,[1] a newly created institution that enjoys considerable autonomy—rather than the Commission (Bickerton et al. 2015; Hodson 2015). Such a scenario means much more shared authority

---

[1] Such as the European Central Bank (ECB), the European Stability Mechanism (ESM), the European External Action Service (EEAS) etc. Not all of them are created within the EU treaties.

J. Ząbkowicz (✉)
Forum for Institutional Thought (FIT), Cracow, Poland

© The Author(s) 2018   235
S. Vliamos, M. S. Zouboulakis (eds.), *Institutionalist Perspectives on Development*, Palgrave Studies in Democracy,
Innovation, and Entrepreneurship for Growth,
https://doi.org/10.1007/978-3-319-98494-0_13

at the EU level and implies increased legislative activity of the political leaders in the European Council (de Schoutheete 2012). In other words, a relative importance of the traditional supranational bodies (first of all—the Commission) in determining the character and direction of the European integration process is increasingly questioned and the EU is a subject to ongoing institutional change (Puetter 2014; see also Peterson 2015a; Wallace and Reh 2014).

The 'new supranationalists'—the main protagonists of the 'new intergovernmentalists', who look to be fully convinced that the European Council, more active than before, is on the best way to retake control over the EU governance (Costello and Thomson 2013)—continue to see the Commission and the Court as the bodies still driving integration through their greater role in policy design and enforcement (Schmidt 2016). In their opinion it is worth pointing out to the fact that, for example, the initiatives launched by political leaders—confirming (according to the 'new intergovernmentalists') an unprecedented leadership role in the EU they now exercise—have been developed in detail not by themselves but, paradoxically, mainly by the Commission's bureaucrats. One can risk claiming that the latter did their job without any particular enthusiasm, but this gave them the opportunity to discreetly sneeze a number of legal solutions favorable to the position of traditional supranational EU bodies.

Both the 'new intergovernmetalists' and the 'new supranationalists'—unlike the "new parliamentalists"—treat the European Parliament (EP) as second-rate player (Tsebelis 1994; Tsebelis and Garrett 2000). This is mainly due to their conviction that the co-decision process of the Community method is the great looser in the shift to the new EU governance as it is no longer the *sine qua non* condition of possible processes of deeper integration. However, there are researchers who do not share these views. According to Vivien A. Smith, such a conclusion is too far-reaching. The EP remains a player to be reckoned with, in the first place because of the greater involvement in intergovernmental negotiations. At the same time, in areas that are not subject to intergovernmental and supranational policymaking, the Parliament has gained increasing influence in decision-making (Schmidt 2016; Häge 2011; Hix and Høyland 2013). The possibility of vetoing or slowing down the co-decision procedure by the EP is, in fact, the most likely to strike the Commission. Equally annoying for the latter is the enhanced exercise of oversight over the supranational bodies, increasingly used by the Parliament in the form of hearings, committee reports and direct criticism.

The only common view shared by all sides—the 'new intergovernmentalists', the 'new parliamentarists' and the 'new supranationalists'—is that one can observe the ongoing process leading to gradual changes in powers and responsibilities of the main EU actors (Bauer and Becker 2014; Naurin and Rasmussen 2011). For the first two of the above aforementioned sides such situation means, in particular, that the Commission loses its influence as the driver of European integration, in favor of the Member States pursuing their national/domestic interests via the European Council, the European Parliament or the *de novo* bodies (Puetter 2015), more and more frequently operating through informal decision-making (e.g. 'early agreements' between the Parliament and the Council, prior to first reading of a legislative act (Reh 2014)). In this context, it is often stated that a declining activity of the Commission in legislative initiatives appears to be one of the most significant signals confirming the fact that a political 'new hand' in the EU takes place.

This chapter argues that it is entirely wrong to draw the final conclusions on the Commission's position on statistics showing changes in its activity in legislative initiatives.

2   STATISTICS SEEM TO SPEAK AGAINST THE COMMISSION ...

Indeed, given the statistical data alone, it is hard to disagree with the assessment that the activity of the Commission in new legislative initiatives has recently undergone a significant weakening. Several years ago, the number of such initiatives exceeding a hundred per year was the norm. So far, the last "fruitful" year has been 2012. The number of 141 forthcoming initiatives we can find in the Commission Work Programme 2012, announced under the significant title 'Delivering European renewal', is quite impressive (European Commission 2011). Of these, 76 proposals were legislative, and the other 13 were a mixture of legislative and non-legislative action. The Commission committed to deliver them in the course of 2012 as a significant contribution to the response of the European Union to 'the challenge of a generation' it faced.

EU statistics clearly point to a sudden decline of the legislative activity of the Commission, which is happening from 2013. According to the Commission Work Programme 2013 the list of forthcoming initiatives 2013–2014 was limited to 25 legislative actions (together with the other

13 being a mixture of legislative and non-legislative initiatives) (European Commission 2012). Only eight of them the Commission committed to deliver in the course of 2013. This very modest result, however, can be explained by the fact that bearing in mind the end of the legislature the outgoing Barroso Commission focused, to a great extend, on finalizing negotiations on earlier initiatives. Just to note President Barroso's statement at that time: "We will work hard to accelerate implementation on the ground. (...) There is a lot on the table and the Commission will push to finalize it." (European Commission 2013).

Statistical data from recent years on the Commission's activity in the field of legislature initiatives seem to confirm its loss of powers and influence. In its first Work Programme (2015) the current Commission presented a modest number of 23 new initiatives (only five of them were legislative and another nine combined legislative and non-legislative action) (European Commission 2014). The same number of such initiatives were included in the Work Programme 2016 (none of them was purely legislative and 18 were a mixture of legislative and non-legislative action) (Commission 2015), and even smaller number of new initiatives in the Work Programme 2017 (altogether only 21 of them) (European Commission 2016).

The question is, to what extent the above change in the legislative activity of the Commission has been forced by the overall situation of the European Union, and to what extent by the possible weakening of the Commission itself? Let us remember that we are analyzing the period in which the Commission is headed by Jean-Claude Juncker, a politician with great experience in running a bureaucratic apparatus,[2] and with a concrete vision of the Commission as a key EU institution.

3   ... But Should They Be Interpreted Only as a Sign of the Weakness of the Commission?

While the end of 2014 may be considered as a transitional period ('inherited' after the Barroso Commission), the legislative activity of the current Commission's in 2015–2017 must undoubtedly be recognized as a result of its own approach and capabilities. It was clear from the outset that the rules governing the functioning of the Juncker Commission would be

---

[2] The longest-serving head of any national government in the EU and the first permanent President of Eurogroup.

fundamentally different from the Barroso Commission. This was explicitly announced in the first sentence of the introduction to the Commission Work Programme 2015 by stating that "This Commission was voted into office with a commitment to make a difference: to do different things and to do things differently", and then specifying that "(...) we [the Commission] will apply political discontinuity and will take off the table pending proposals that do not match our objectives or which are going nowhere, because we want all institutions to focus on delivering what really matters." (European Commission 2014).

Indeed, the Commission Work Programme 2015 gives the impression of surgical cutting. Just compare a limited number of new proposals (23) with the list of initiatives from the previous Commissions (speaking precisely—the Barroso Commission) which were proposed to withdraw or amend (80), and a list of existing legislation which the Commission intended to review "to see if they are still fit for purpose" (around 450) (European Commission 2014).

It is difficult to have a more convincing confirmation of Frans Timmermans' call for "clearing the decks" (European Commission 2014a) than the reasons given by the Juncker Commission for the decisions to withdraw or modify a number of pending proposals. Some of these reasons are in use for years ('obsolete proposal', 'no foreseeable agreement' etc.), but there are also clear expressions that the Commission does not intend to limit itself to the role of passive observer of endless negotiations between the EP and the Council, and to act only as their notary. Apparently the Commission decided to recall that it should be treated as a heavyweight player to be reckoned with, and that is why in a number of cases a much less frequently used instrument—'political' withdrawal—appears. Firstly, as a way of exerting time pressure on both co-legislators by giving them six months to finalize the procedure, under the threat of withdrawal of the initiative (or replacing it by another one). Secondly, as a warning that the Commission is not going to give the co-legislators *carte blanche* to make unlimited modifications to its projects. Hence, by example, justifying the withdrawal of the proposal for a Council Directive COM/2011/0169 2011/0092/CNS the Commission stated that "Council negotiations have resulted in a draft compromise text that has fully denatured the substance of the Commission proposal" (European Commission 2014).

4   COALITION: BUT WITH WHOM, AND ON WHAT TERMS?

Let us assume as our starting point that Juncker's opening statement in the European Parliament Plenary Session on 15 July 2014 was sufficiently clear and unambiguous to outline his vision of the Commission's position among EU institutions (Juncker 2014). We should take this speech very seriously, not as a courtesy to the EP, especially as the presented then approach was confirmed in another Juncker's speech of the same day (Juncker 2014a).

Juncker had no doubt that the European Parliament should be the key partner of the Commission, even for the sake of the fact that these bodies "are both Community institutions par excellence". And that means that "they should have a special working relationship with each other" (Juncker 2014). However, these relations are not intended to be simply a continuation from the previous Commission's term. Juncker explicitly stated that he is interested in a political dialogue with the EP, not a technocratic one. And so as no one doubts, it is said that although the President of the Commission is elected by the European Parliament's assembly "that does not mean he is at your [EP's] beck and call; I'm [President of the EC] not going to be the European Parliament's lackey" (Juncker 2014).

Equally important is the reference made by Juncker to the future relations of the Commission with the European Council. He did not deny the fact that the President of the Commission is proposed by the European Council, "but that does not mean he is its secretariat" (Juncker 2014a). On behalf of the Commission he declares that the EC is ready to be a member of the EU team, since "in Europe we should play as a team". But he also does not hesitate to point to the Council as an example that not everyone fully understands what teamwork means: "If you said 'yes' in Brussels, don't say 'no' elsewhere. And never again say after a Council meeting that you won and the others lost." (Juncker 2014a)

In Junker's vision, the Commission is no longer bureaucratic. This in turn means that its purpose is to co-decide on the political future of the European Union, not to remain merely "a technical committee made up of civil servants who implement the instructions of another institution" (Juncker 2014). Juncker is not afraid to say straight: "We will be Community players (…)". There is no doubt that one word—"political"—repeated several times in both speeches, plays a key role. The Juncker guidelines for the new Commission were to be at the same time a clear signal to the European Parliament and to the Council: "The Commission is political. And I want it to be more political. Indeed, it will be highly political." (Juncker 2014) The next few years have shown that these were not words that could just go into the agenda (see also Peterson 2015b; Peterson 2017). Such approach clearly demonstrates the ambition of the Juncker Commission. The question is whether it is not vaulting and whether the current EU rules of the game allow the Commission to gain a sufficiently strong position to achieve its objectives.

5   THE COMMUNITY METHOD V. THE INTERGOVERNMENTAL METHOD

At least on one point Juncker is absolutely consistent with his predecessor. Three years after the Barroso Commission expressed in the Work Program 2011 its conviction that "To succeed (...) we need to work through the Community method of decision as the basis for this true Union" (European Commission 2011), Juncker was even more pressing to call the European Parliament: "Let us apply the Community method. Yes, it is demanding, but it is effective, it is tried and tested and it is more credible than inter-governmental wrangling. We need to restore the Community method." (Juncker 2014)

Is the call for restoration of the Community method to be understood as giving the right to those who claim that such method is—and therefore the Commission—in reverse, as indicated by the ever-decreasing number of Commission legislative initiatives? It is true that the Community method involving the use of the ordinary legislative procedure is the only one that gives a key role to the traditional supranational bodies—first of all to the European Commission with its sole right to initiate legislation[3] (Nugent and Rhinard 2015). Independence in making legislative and policy proposals is crucial for the EC as without it has no ability to effectively execute policy that reflects the approach taken (Ząbkowicz 2013).

In case of the intergovernmental method the rules of the game are set by the European Council in the first place. In the light of the EU law, the position of the Commission is much weaker—it has to share its right of initiative with the EU countries or confine it to specific areas of activity.[4] And such situations are considered by the Member States to be an excellent opportunity to counterbalance the power of the Commission, for

---

[3] Defined in Article 294 of the Treaty on the Functioning of the European Union.
[4] The European Parliament has a purely consultative role.

instance, by setting up ad hoc bodies with powers only parsimoniously allocated to them (Dehousse 2013).[5] Such a solution is simply treated by public authorities as a lesser evil, as it is the Commission that is most often the symbol of the 'unlimited' and 'unacceptable' expansion of EU powers. Doing so, the authorities easily gain the support from their own citizens, who—under the pressure of demagogic slogans—fear the 'uncontrolled' authority of the traditional supranational bodies.

However, it is important to realize that possibilities of 'taking over' the European Union by intergovernmental bodies are still very limited, in a purely practical dimension (de Schoutheete 2012). Some policies have retained a predominantly intergovernmental character, this is not, however, a sufficient argument to define the current EU power sharing system as 'intergovernmental' (Schimmelfennig 2015). The intergovernmental method of operation is used in decision-making mainly on Common Foreign and Security Policy. The Member States may initiate laws only in one policy area—some aspects of police and judicial cooperation. In other areas all concerned can only address their requests for new initiatives to the Commission, which is not formally obliged to act upon such requests. It is difficult to define Article 241 of the Lisbon Treaty as a special restriction on the freedom of action of the Commission. According to this provision of the treaty, if the Commission does not submit a proposal in response to the request from the Council then "it shall inform the Council of the reasons" (Nugent and Rhinard 2016).

During Barroso's term of office, a number of signals pointed to readiness of the Commission to adapt to the situation in which the European Council is taking steps towards broadening its steering power, just as the European Parliament is increasingly exercising its control powers (see also Ponzano et al. 2012). The Juncker Commission also declared its openness to teamwork with the co-legislators, however, it clearly stated at the outset that it will not be done at the expense of limiting the use of the classic Community model, which is (again, Juncker's words) "tried and tested and it is more credible than intergovernmental wrangling" (Juncker 2014).

The past years are, in fact, a period of constant threat of unstable equilibrium between supranational and intergovernmental bodies (Christiansen 2015). A good example of conflicting interests seems to be the Commission's power of withdrawal of proposals submitted under the

---

[5] Such as the Eurogroup.

ordinary legislative procedure. According to the Court (another traditional supranational body) it "cannot confer upon that institution a right of veto in the conduct of the legislative process, a right which would be contrary to the principles of conferral of powers and institutional balance." At the same time, however, the Grand Chamber of the Court in its judgment of 2015 has taken a position according to which "where an amendment planned by the Parliament and the Council distorts the proposal for a legislative act in a manner which prevents achievement of the objectives pursued by the proposal and which, therefore, deprives it of its *raison d'être*, the Commission is entitled to withdraw it." (Court 2015).

The above power of withdrawal accompanies the Commission's right to initiate legislation, both being crucial to the whole legislative procedure (Ponzano et al. 2012). Nothing has changed in this respect, the above judgment even reinforced this principle. The Court stated explicitly that "the Commission's power does not come down to submitting a proposal and, subsequently, promoting contact and seeking to reconcile the positions of the Parliament and the Council." Such approach fully supported Juncker's Opening Statement in the European Parliament Plenary Session on 15 July 2014, which was a clear signal that the Commission intends to make full use of the power of withdrawal, if necessary.

At the same time, however, the Juncker's Commission wants to be effective instead of wasting time on endless disputes with co-legislators. Hence the declining number of 'old type' new legislative initiatives included in the Commission Working Programmes gives the impression of a weakening legislative activity of the European Commission. However, proposals which follow on from regulatory fitness and performance reviews (REFIT), updating and improving existing legislation, are undoubtedly their full value equivalents. Taking into account only two years (2015–2016), 119 REFIT actions were included in the Commission programmes. 93 proposals in the legislative procedure have been identified for withdrawal (European Commission 2016).

As a clear signal of the Commission's attitude to cooperate constructively with partners, priority is given to work in all areas covered by the opinions of the REFIT Platform. What connects all these activities is the fact that they implement the Commission's own concept that focuses primarily on evaluating and reviewing existing laws, including the repeal of a series of pieces of legislation that have been considered obsolete. The Commission is interested in the smooth implementation of these modifications, that is why it has committed in Paragraph 7 of the Interinstitutional

Agreement on Better Law-Making of 13 April 2016 to agree each year with the EP and the Council on a number of proposals to which all these bodies want to give priority treatment in the legislative process (European Union 2016).

6   CONCLUSIONS

The lines of action taken by the European Parliament and the Council are usually the resultant of particular interests of the Member States, which often contradict each other (see also Bulmer and Joseph 2016; Häge and Naurin 2013). In comparison, the Commission is a determined, bureaucratically efficient body with a concrete action plan and clearly defined objectives. This is above all the strength of the Commission (especially in times of crisis), even more than any rules favorable to it. It was said straightaway by Barroso in his State of the Union Address 2011 calling for more than ever the independent authority of the Commission "to propose and assess the actions that the Member States should take. Governments, let's be frank, cannot do this by themselves. Nor can this be done by negotiations between governments" (Barroso 2011).

In view of the above, it seems reasonable to argue that, in the sense of intergovernmental action, the position of the European Commission can be severely weakened only by two dominant members of the EU, Germany and France, adopting jointly the political plan, in its assumption limiting the role of the European Commission solely to the tasks of a technocratic contractor. However, it seems unlikely, as the Commission with its current powers seems to be a very useful tool for both countries.

REFERENCES

Barroso, J. M. (2011). European reneval. State of the Union Address 2011. Speech 11/607. Strasbourg, 28 September. Retrieved from http://europa. eu/rapid/press-release_SPEECH-11-607_en.htm.

Bauer, M. W., & Becker, S. (2014). The unexpected winner of the crisis: The European Commission's strengthened role in economic governance. *Journal of European Integration, 36*(3), 213–229. https://doi.org/10.1080/07036337 .2014.885750.

Bickerton, J., et al. (2015). The new intergovernmentalism: European integration in the post-Maastricht era. *Journal of Common Market Studies, 53*(4), 703–722. https://doi.org/10.1111/jcms.12212.

Bulmer, S. (2015). Understanding the new intergovernmentalism: Pre- and post-Maastricht EU Studies. In C. Bickerton et al. (Eds.), *The new intergovernmentalism: States and supranational actors in the post-Maastricht era* (pp. 289–303). Oxford: Oxford University Press. https://doi.org/10.1093/acprof: oso/9780198703617.003.0014.

Bulmer, S., & Joseph, J. (2016). European integration in crisis? Of supranational integration, hegemonic projects and domestic politics. *European Journal of International Relations, 22*(4), 725–748. https://doi.org/10.1177/135406 6115612558.

Christiansen, T. (2015). Institutionalist dynamics behind the new intergovernmentalism. The continuous process of EU Treaty Reform. In C. Bickerton et al. (Eds.), *The new intergovernmentalism: States and supranational actors in the post-Maastricht era* (pp. 90–107). Oxford: Oxford University Press. https:// doi.org/10.1093/acprof:oso/9780198703617.003.0004.

Costello, R., & Thomson, R. (2013). The distribution of power among EU institutions: Who wins under codecision and why? *Journal of European Public Policy, 20*(7), 1025–1039. https://doi.org/10.1080/13501763.2013.795393.

Court. (2015). Judgment of the Court (Grand Chamber) of 14 April 2015. Case C-409/13.

Dehousse, R. (2013, February 11). The Community method, the EU's "default" operating system. Notre Europe, Synthesis.

European Commission. (2011). Delivering European renewal. Commission Work Programme 2012. COM(2011) 777 final.

European Commission. (2012). Commission Work Programme 2013. COM(2012) 629 final.

European Commission. (2013). Commission adopts Work Programme for 2014: A year of delivery and implementation. Press Release, 22 October.

European Commission. (2014). A New Start. Commission Work Programme 2015. COM (2014) 910 final.

European Commission. (2014a). A New Start: European Commission work plan to deliver jobs, growth and investment. Press Release, 16 December.

European Commission. (2015). No time for business as usual. Commission Work Programme 2016, COM(2015) 610 final.

European Commission. (2016). Delivering a Europe that protects, empowers and defends. Commission Work Programme 2017, COM(2016) 710 final.

European Union. (2016). Interinstitutional Agreement between the European Parliament, the Council of the European Union and the European Commission of 13 April 2016 on Better Law-Making. OJL 123, 12.5.2016: 1–14.

Häge, F. M. (2011). Politicising Council Decision-making: The Effect of European Parliament Empowerment. *West European Politics, 34*(1), 18–47. https://doi. org/10.1080/01402382.2011.523542.

Häge, F. M., & Naurin, D. (2013). The effect of codecision on Council decision-making: informalization, politicization and power. *Journal of European Public Policy, 20*(7), 953–971. https://doi.org/10.1080/13501763.2013.795372.

Hix, S., & Høyland, B. (2013). Empowerment of the European Parliament. *Annual Review of Political Science, 16,* 171–189. https://doi.org/10.1146/annurev-polisci-032311-110735.

Hodson, D. (2015). De novo bodies and the new intergovernmentalism. The case of the European Central Bank. In C. Bickerton et al. (Eds.), *The new intergovernmentalism: States and supranational actors in the post-Maastricht era* (pp. 263–285). Oxford: Oxford University Press. https://doi.org/10.1093/acprof:oso/9780198703617.003.0013.

Juncker, J.-C. (2014). A new start for Europe. Opening Statement in the European Parliament Plenary Session. Strasbourg, 15 July.

Juncker, J.-C. (2014a). A New Start for Europe: My Agenda for Jobs, Growth, Fairness and Democratic Change Political Guidelines for the next European Commission. Strasbourg, 15 July.

Naurin, D., & Rasmussen, A. (2011). New external rules, new internal games: How the EU institutions respond when inter-institutional rules change. *West European Politics, 34*(1), 1–17. https://doi.org/10.1080/01402382.2011.5 23540.

Nugent, N., & Rhinard, M. (2015). *The European Commission.* London: Palgrave Macmillan.

Nugent, N., & Rhinard, M. (2016). Is the European Commission really in decline? *Journal of Common Market Studies, 54*(5), 1199–1215. https://doi.org/10.1111/jcms.12358.

Peterson, J. (2015a). The Commission and the new intergovernmentalism. Calm within the Storm? In C. Bickerton et al. (Eds.), *The new intergovernmentalism: States and supranational actors in the post-Maastricht era* (pp. 185–207). Oxford: Oxford University Press. https://doi.org/10.1093/acprof:oso/9780198703617.003.0009.

Peterson, J. (2015b). The Juncker Commission: Partner or partisan?. 14th Biennial Conference of the European Union Studies Association, Boston, 5–7th February 2015.

Peterson, J. (2017). Juncker's political European Commission and an EU in crisis. *Journal of Common Market Studies, 55*(2), 349–367. https://doi.org/10.1111/jcms.12435.

Ponzano, P., Hermanin, C., & Corona, D. (2012). The power of initiative of the European Commission: A progressive erosion? *Notre Europe, Studies & Research, 89.*

Puetter, U. (2014). *The European Council and the Council. New intergovernmentalism and institutional change.* Oxford: Oxford University Press.

Puetter, U. (2015). The European Council. The Centre of new intergovernmentalism. In C. Bickerton et al. (Eds.), *The new intergovernmentalism: States and supranational actors in the post-Maastricht era* (pp. 166–184). Oxford: Oxford University Press. https://doi.org/10.1093/acprof:oso/9780198703617.003.0008.

Reh, C. (2014). Is informal politics undemocratic? Trilogues, early agreements and the selection model of representation. *Journal of European Public Policy, 21*(6), 822–841. https://doi.org/10.1080/13501763.2014.910247.

Schimmelfennig, F. (2015). What's the news in the "New Intergovernmetalism"? A critique of Bickerton, Hodson, and Puetter. *Journal of Common Market Studies, 53*(4), 723–730. https://doi.org/10.1111/jcms.12234.

Schmidt, V. (2016). The new EU Governance: New intergovernmentalism, new supranationalism, and new parlamentarism. Instituto Affari Internazionali Working Papers 16/11.

Schoutheete de, P. (2012). The European Council and the community method. Notre Europe, Policy Paper 56.

Tsebelis, G. (1994). The power of the European Parliament as a conditional agenda setter. *American Political Science Review, 88*(1), 128–142. https://doi.org/10.2307/2944886.

Tsebelis, G., & Garrett, G. (2000). *Legislative politics in the European Union.* European Union Politics.

Wallace, H., & Reh, C. (2014). An institutional anatomy and five policy modes. In H. Wallace, M. A. Pollack, & A. Young (Eds.), *Policy-making in the European Union* (pp. 72–112). Oxford: Oxford University Press.

Ząbkowicz, J. (2013). Limits to the European Commission. Managing services of general interest. *Oeconomia Copernicana, 3*, 23–48. https://doi.org/10.12775/Oec.2013.021.

Amendments to Legal Regulations in the Field of the Enterprises Restructuring Procedures in Poland

Sylwia Morawska and Joanna Kuczewska

1 Introduction

The EU has focused on the institutional and economic problems, especially after the recent global economic crisis and while the EU single market seems to become less and less popular. The Small Business Act for Europe (SBA) (as the main programme of simplifying the business environment conditions) has also been reconsidered in the context of delivering the positive effects of economic integration. One of the SBA's principles is the second chance policy. Current research frequently concerns the insolvency and restructuring procedures.

S. Morawska (✉)
Warsaw School of Economics, Warsaw, Poland
e-mail: smoraw@sgh.waw.pl

J. Kuczewska
University of Gdańsk, Gdańsk, Poland
e-mail: j.kuczewska@ug.edu.pl

S. Vliamos, M. S. Zouboulakis (eds.), *Institutionalist Perspectives on Development*, Palgrave Studies in Democracy, Innovation, and Entrepreneurship for Growth,
https://doi.org/10.1007/978-3-319-98494-0_14

249

The aim of this paper is the assessment of the amendments to legal regulations in the field of the enterprises restructuring procedures in Poland. This study will attempt to answer the following questions: Are the Polish restructuring procedures of companies in financial difficulties align with the entrepreneurs' requirements? And were there any strategic amendments to legal regulations in the field of enterprises restructuring procedures in Poland?

In order to solve the research problems, the following research methods will be used: analysis of the legal acts and the EU strategic documents and presentation of the data collected in selected Polish courts concerning the implementation of the enterprises restructuring procedures in 2016. The tasks of the paper are the following: analysis of the SBA principles concerning the second chance policy in Poland over the period 2008–2016 and the analysis of the amendments to legal regulations in the field of enterprises restructuring procedures in Poland in 2016.

2   EU POLICY FOR ENTERPRISES: REALIZATION OF THE SECOND CHANCE PRINCIPLE

The main priorities of the contemporary EU enterprise policy have been adopted in European Council's 2000 "Lisbon Strategy" (Budzyńska et al. 2002). The key problem in the strategy mentioned above is the issue of increasing business dynamics in Europe, which is supported by the dominant small and medium-sized enterprises (SMEs) sector. Ensuring a friendly business environment is a guarantee of their harmonious development, which in turn results in the growth of sectors, branches, regions and finally the whole economy.

The European Community launched a series of activities to improve the business environment, the most important being the adoption of the European Charter for Small Business (June 2000) by the European Council in Feira (European Commission 2004). The aim of the Charter was to improve the situation of European companies (especially SMEs) by stimulating entrepreneurship and better matching existing instruments to the needs of the sector (Stępniak and Kuczewska 2004). The European Commission's Programme Small Business Act for Europe (SBA) (European Commission 2008), is another strategic document that shaped the European policy of supporting entrepreneurship. The strategic objectives of the Act were "... *to improve the overall policy approach to entrepreneurship, to irre-*

versibly anchor the "Think Small First" principle in policy-making from regulation to public service, and to promote SMEs' growth by helping them tackle the remaining problems which hamper their development" (European Commission 2008, p. 3). According to the SBA's guidelines, strategic business support policies focus on the implementation of the 10 principles that serve as guidelines for the development and implementation of policies at EU and Member State levels. These include: second chance principle, responsible administration, *"Think Small First"* rule, public aid and public procurement, access to financing, entrepreneurship, effective internal market, skills and innovation, environment, and internationalization.

The European Commission aimed the permanent monitoring and assessment of the SBA's principles implementation using cross-countries and cross-principle approaches. A set of indicators measuring effectiveness of implementation of each SBA's principle has been both recognised and agreed (more about indicators: European Commission 2017). The average results of measuring the principles compared across countries deliver an opportunity for identification the strengths and weaknesses of SBA implementation among all Member States. Of course, this analysis does not constitute a comprehensive assessment of country policies. Some other relevant in-depth studies concerning the policy actions and regulations should contribute the effective assessment process.

The second chance principle has content five indicators since 2016 (European Commission 2016; European Commission 2017):

- Strength of insolvency framework index (0–16)—the strength of insolvency framework index is the sum of the scores on the commencement of proceedings index, management of debtor's assets index, reorganization proceedings index and creditor participation index.
- Fear of Failure Rate—percentage of 18–64 population with positive perceived opportunities who indicate that fear of failure would prevent them from setting up a business;
- Degree of support for allowing for a second chance—share of responders who strongly agree and agree with the opinion that "people who have started their own business and have failed should be given a second chance" (Flash Eurobarometer on Entrepreneurship);
- Costs to resolve insolvency (% of debtor's estate)—the costs of the proceedings are recorded as a percentage of the value of the debtor's estate. The cost is calculated based on the survey responses and

includes court fees and government levies; fees of insolvency administration, auctioneers and lawyers; and all the other fees and costs;

- Time to resolve insolvency—it measures the time needed by creditors to recover their credit and is recorded in calendar years.

Practically of the beginning of the process of monitoring implementation of Small Business Act for Europe, regarding the progress of the second chance law, Poland belongs to the group of countries with one of the lower indicators, next to Malta, Hungary, Italy, Luxemburg, Slovakia, Lithuania, and Croatia. Invariably, leaders in this area, which have the highest indicator of progress regarding implementation of second chance rule, remain: Finland, Netherlands, Germany, and United Kingdom (Fig. 1).

The biggest problem during the implementation of the second chance principle in Poland has been and currently is a long time of proceedings related to insolvency of enterprises, high costs of bankruptcy procedures, a high rate of fear of failure and lack of appropriate restructuring procedures for many years up to 1 January 2016. In 2014, the Ministry of Economy introduced the "*New Opportunity Policy*" (Ministry of Economy

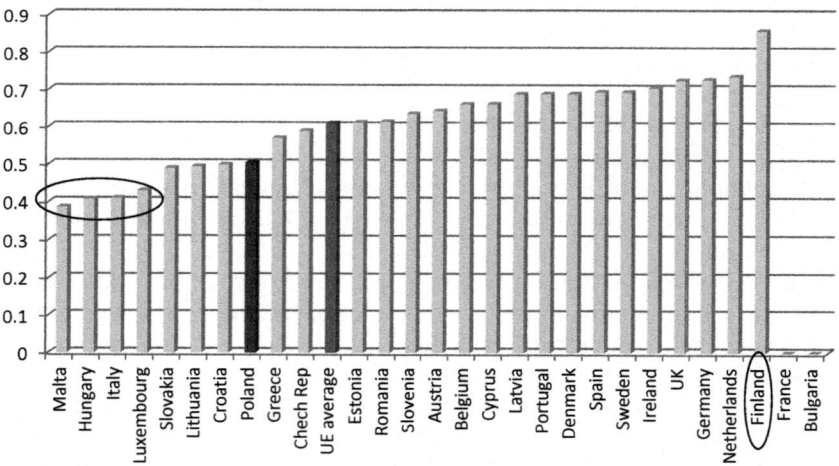

Fig. 1 Implementation of the second chance principle in Poland and the EU countries with the most favourable environment in 2016. Source: own calculation based on European Commission SBA database

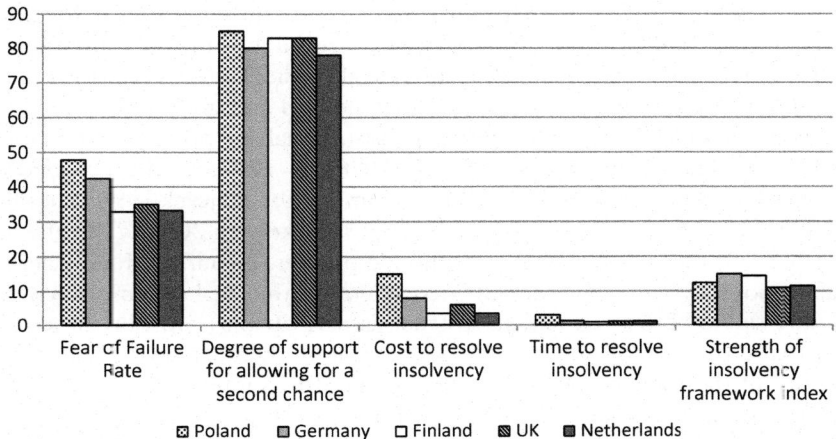

Fig. 2 Implementation of the second chance principle in Poland and the EU countries with the most favourable environment—detailed indicators 2016. Source: own calculation based on European Commission SBA database

2014). Its main activities included: preventing bankruptcy, limiting the risk of premature insolvency, efficient liquidation proceedings and assistance in resuming operations. Since 2016, a new restructuring law has been introduced covering several restructuring paths, and its efficiency will probably be reflected in next year's presentation of the SBA implementation profile (Fig. 2).

3 AMENDMENTS TO LEGAL REGULATIONS IN THE FIELD OF THE ENTERPRISES RESTRUCTURING PROCEDURES IN POLAND

A comprehensive regulatory framework governing the issues of insolvent entrepreneurs has a pivotal role in the functioning of bankruptcy institution. The quality of the law and its efficiency is crucial when it comes to adopting insolvency practices in the economy. Properly set targets in the insolvency procedure, responsive to the needs of the economy, can facilitate business activities, guaranteeing an immediate return of production means in case of underperformance on one hand, and favouring actions aimed at debt restructuring or corporate restructuring on the other.

The lack of efficiency of legal institutions causes the legislation to lose its importance. The need for cross-disciplinary research is mainly caused due to the need for entrepreneurship. Empirical studies on institutions in the economy blend with the institutional economics and are crucial when it comes to emphasize the importance of institutional and political factors for the economic growth (Coase 1937; Demsetz 1997; Godłów-Legiędź 2005; Hodgson 2004; North 1990; Ostrom 1990; Ratajczak 1994; Rudolf 2005; Stankiewicz 2012; Williamson 1998; Ząbkowicz 2003). The effectiveness of the coordination of economic policies, favouring the efficient allocation of resources, is directly dependent on the legal system, which is addressed to both active and passive market participants (in the broad sense of that term). It not only must serve the role of the guarantor of the certainty of the transactions, but is also required to stimulate entrepreneurship—to make Europe the most competitive economy in the world.

As of January 1, 2016, the Act on Restructuring Law entered into force in Poland, which essentially changed the approach to entrepreneurs experiencing financial difficulties. The new law is in line with the new approach to business failure and insolvency contained in the Commission Recommendation of 12 March 2014 published in 14 March 2014 in Official Journal of the European Union L 74 of 14 March 2014 (European Commission 2014). The purpose of The Recommendation is to ensure that viable businesses, regardless of where they are located in the Union territory, have access to early-stage restructuring regulations to prevent their insolvency, therefore maximizing total value for creditors, employees, owners and for the entire economy. The new law fundamentally changed the notion of entrepreneurs' insolvency and introduced several restructuring pathways for them.

Insolvency—is the basis under the Restructuring Law for the opening of restructuring proceedings. The law introduces two grounds for insolvency. Both bases of insolvency are independent of each other. In a particular case, both the basis of the insolvency may come true, or only one of them. The first and widespread basis for insolvency is the failure of the debtor to pay his due obligations (loss of liquidity). This applies both to private and public law obligations. The current wording of the provision limits the state of non-performance of liabilities only to monetary liabilities, those in which the object of the provision is money. It is presumed that the debtor has lost the ability to perform his/her pecuniary obligations if the delay in performing monetary obligations exceeds three months. The liability requirement is the condition in which the creditor has the legal right to demand satisfaction of his claim. The second basis for insolvency (so-called over-indebtedness) concerns a narrower group of debtors: a legal entity and an organizational unit without legal personality, whose separate law grants legal capacity.

A debtor who is a legal entity or an organizational unit without legal personality, whose separate law grants legal capacity, is also insolvent when his / her monetary obligations exceed the value of his/her assets and this condition persists for more than twenty-four months. The premise of insolvency in the form of excessive debt is sometimes referred to as the so-called "Bankruptcy". As a rule, bankruptcy occurs when the debtor's balance sheet shows a negative value in the "equity" position (Adamus 2015, p. 30).

What is also important is that the new law separates insolvency proceedings from restructuring, and we now have separately the Act on Restructuring Laws of 2015 and the Bankruptcy Act of 2003. By 1 January 2016, one act regulated with bankruptcy and restructuring and bankruptcy proceedings. This caused the entrepreneur—the debtor both the one to whom the restructuring proceeding was conducted and the one to whom the bankruptcy proceeding was conducted, was in bankruptcy. The basic differences between the new regulations and the non-binding ones are presented in Figs. 3 and 4.

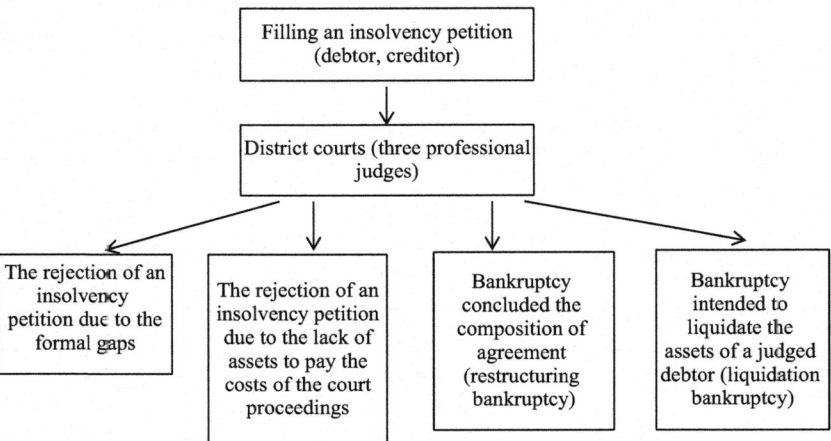

Fig. 3 Proceeding in case of entrepreneurs' bankruptcy when the Act on Insolvency Law dated 2003 was in effect. Source: Self-study

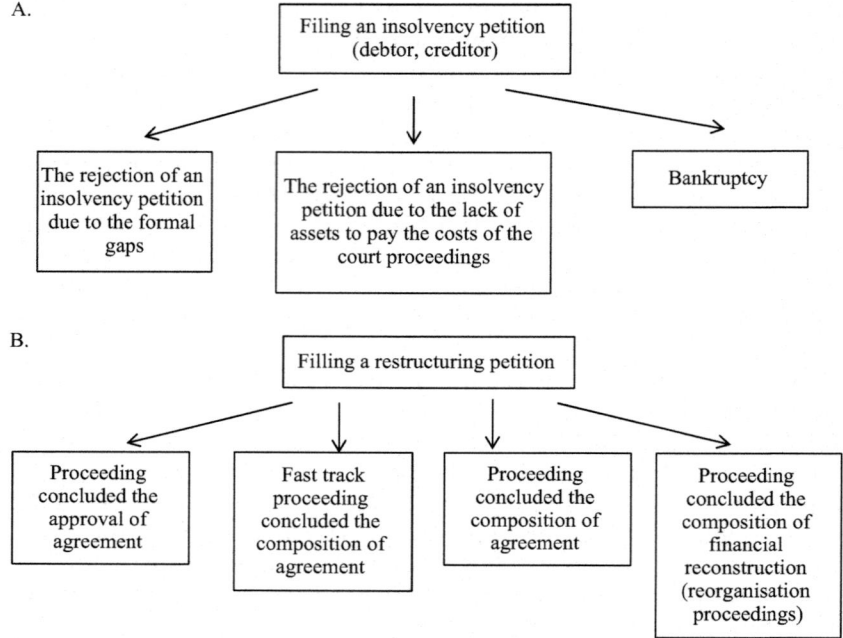

Fig. 4 Proceeding in case of entrepreneurs' bankruptcy when the Act on Restructuring Law dated 2015 and the revised Act on Insolvency Law dated 2003 have been in effect. Source: Self-study

A solution, that is no longer in force which assumed that the court decides which procedure will apply to the entrepreneur with problems, will discourage entrepreneurs from submitting motions for bankruptcy proceedings. This is proved by statistical data showing the number of restructuring bankruptcy proceedings in 2004–2015 (Fig. 5). Nowadays, the entrepreneur experiencing financial difficulties decides which procedure to choose—restructuring or bankruptcy. In addition, in situation when a creditor requests a bankruptcy and the debtor wants restructuring proceeding, the court must first identify the restructuring request.

The current regulation means a return to the legal solution already known in Poland and binding before 2003. The process of changes in the Polish restructuring and bankruptcy law is shown in Fig. 6.

The current, basic objectives of the restructuring law are the following:

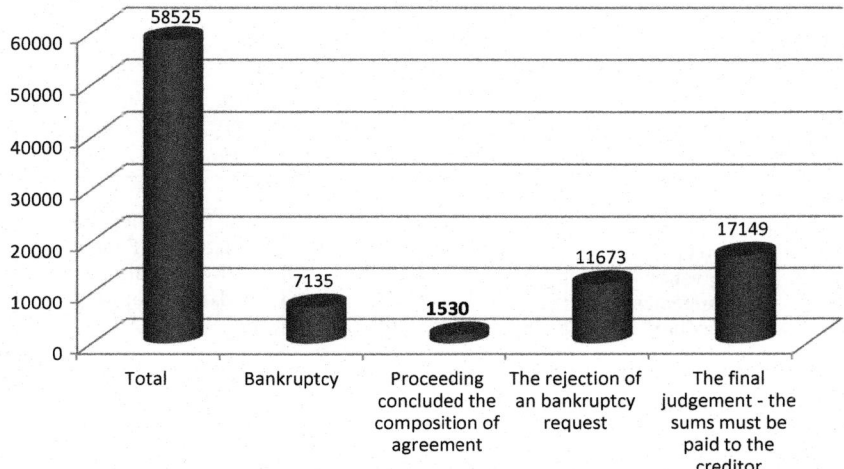

Fig. 5 Number of bankruptcy/restructuring proceedings in Poland in the years 2004–2015 against other kinds of proceedings. Source: Self-study based on data from Ministry of Justice

1. Provide entrepreneurs and their contractors with effective instruments for restructuring while maximizing the protection of creditors' rights,
2. Ensure institutional autonomy of restructuring procedures in isolation from staggering bankruptcy proceedings,
3. Introduce the principle of subsidiarity in insolvency proceedings as an ultima ratio to the economic failure of restructuring,
4. Increasing the privileges of active creditors,
5. Maximizing the speed and effectiveness of restructuring and bankruptcy,
6. Uniformalised procedures and a broader use of modern ICT tools in them,
7. Increase the liability of untrustworthy debtors and bankrupts.

The Restructuring Law Act regulates the insolvent or threatened with insolvency debtors' ability to conclude an agreement with the creditors, the effects of the arrangement and the carrying out of reorganization measures.

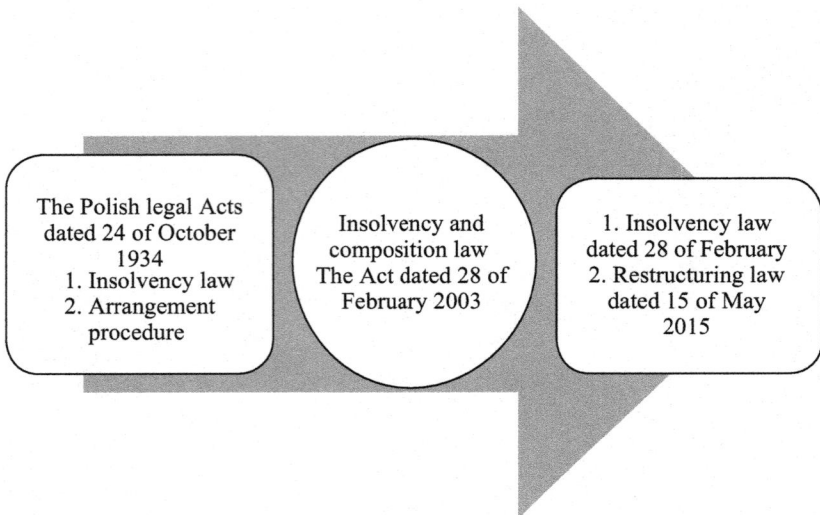

Fig. 6 The process of changes in the Polish restructuring and bankruptcy law. Source: Self-study

Restructuring is carried out in the following restructuring proceedings:

1. Proceedings for approval of the agreement
2. Fast track to the arrangement proceedings
3. Arrangement proceedings
4. Reorganization proceedings.

The purpose of the restructuring process is to prevent the debtor from being declared insolvent by allowing him to restructure by way of an agreement with creditors and, in the case of remedial proceedings, also by conducting reorganization activities, with secured rights of creditors.

Proceedings for approval of the agreement:

1. Allows you to conclude an arrangement as a result of self-collection of creditor's votes by the debtor without court involvement;
2. It may be conducted if the sum of the disputable liabilities giving right to voting on the arrangement does not exceed 15% of the sum of the claims giving right to voting on the arrangement.

Fast track to the arrangement proceeding:

1. Allows the debtor to enter the arrangement after the simplified insolvency table has been drawn up and approved;
2. It may be conducted if the sum of the disputable liabilities giving right to voting on the arrangement does not exceed 15% of the sum of the claims giving rise to voting on the arrangement.

Arrangement proceedings:

1. Allows the debtor to enter an arrangement after the insolvency table has been drawn up and approved;
2. It may be conducted if the sum of the disputable liabilities giving right to voting over the arrangement exceeds 15% of the sum of the claims giving right to voting on the arrangement.

The reorganization procedure enables the debtor to carry out reorganization activities and to conclude the arrangement upon the drawing up and approval of the insolvency table. Reorganization activities are legal and factual actions aimed at improving the economic situation of the debtor and aimed at restoring the debtor's ability to perform obligations, while protecting against the execution.

In order to determine how much the new Restructuring Law Act is being used in practice by entrepreneurs experiencing financial difficulties, there was conducted research in courts dealing with restructuring proceedings in Warsaw, Gdansk and Wroclaw—the biggest cities in Poland located in different Polish regions. In order to establish nationally relevant research results, the courts of Northern, Central and Southern Poland were selected for analysis. The results of the study indicate that the new restructuring pathways, including reorganization, proposed by the new law are not attractive to entrepreneurs experiencing financial difficulties (Table 1). The data presented in Table 1 shows that the procedure for approval of the arrangement—in fact the simplest, informal procedure has not been used by entrepreneurs ever.

The question arises, why this happens? Preliminary results indicate that in Poland there is a lack of demand for restructuring in court. Polish entrepreneurs do not trust that the court will perform an effective restructuring in economic terms. The reason for this is the lack of substantive preparation of the judges to carry out the restructuring and even more,

Table 1 Number of proceedings under the New Restructuring Law in 2016 in the courts of Warsaw, Gdansk and Wroclaw

The Polish district courts	Number of open fast track to the agreement proceedings	Number of completed fast track to the agreement proceedings	Number of open reorganization proceedings	Number of completed reorganization proceedings	Number of open arrangement proceedings	Number of completed arrangement proceedings
Warsaw	13	4 (cancellation)	15	1 (cancellation)	1	0
Gdańsk	3	2	0	0	0	0
Wrocław	9	3	4	0	3	0

Source: Self-study on basis of data collected from courts in Warsaw, Gdansk and Wroclaw

the reorganization of the company. Economic restructuring consists of building a new system of connections with the environment and shaping the resources of production factors, organizational structures, and management systems in the area of economics and the market (Jarka 2008, p. 152).

Restructuring is just a tool for achieving a specific purpose. It enables the company to improve its functioning, development and maintaining a level of competitiveness that is in line with the owners' expectations in a changing environment. Adaptive changes are, in principle, primarily to protect the indebted company from bankruptcy and to take the path of development (Cenkier 2007, p. 455). Restructuring takes place both in businesses in a good financial situation and in companies that have lost or are at risk of losing their liquidity and creditworthiness. For this reason, it is possible to distinguish between remedial restructuring and development restructuring. Often, these two forms of restructuring are interrelated in an enterprise under restructuring and there are no clear boundaries between them. Remedial restructuring is when a company is in financial difficulty (loss of liquidity, lack of creditworthiness, real threat of collapse) associated with the loss of existing outlet markets. It primarily serves to eliminate the negative effects of the current or imminent crisis. It then takes the nature of stabilizing measures to restore a lost business efficiency and treat it as an attempt to formulate a rescue program and then implement it (Suszyński 1999, p. 110). Remedial restructuring in enterprise is imperative, and action is focused on achieving rapid results. Therefore, the time horizon of such changes should not exceed 1–2 years. Developmental restructuring is intended to ensure long-term stability and development of the company. This process covers several years and is holistic.

4 Conclusions

In Poland, in 2008, since when the implementation of the Small Business Act for Europe was under continuous monitoring, measures have been consistently implemented to improve the business environment. Analysis of Poland's profile in terms of SBA implementation in 2008–2015 shows a systematic improvement in nearly all the rules, but this profile is still unbalanced and several areas must be improved, for example: skills and innovation, second chance law, internationalization, internal market or Think small first principle. There is also no leading area that would far outperform the average EU country. On the contrary, many positions are far below this level, and Poland today, despite many changes is in the group of countries with the weakest level of implementation of the Program rules.

The biggest problem in the implementation of the principle of the second chance law in Poland has been and still is a long time of proceedings related to insolvency of enterprises, high costs of bankruptcy procedures, a high rate of fear of failure and ongoing for many years to 1 January 2016 the problem of lack of appropriate restructuring procedures for enterprises experiencing financial difficulties.

As a result, in 2016 new restructuring law has been introduced, covering four restructuring routes. It guarantees the entrepreneur experiencing financial difficulties to decide which procedure to choose—restructuring or insolvency. In addition, when a creditor requests bankruptcy and the debtor apply for a restructuring proceeding, the court is required to first identify the restructuring request. It is therefore possible to respond to the second research question and to state that in Poland, strategic amendments to legal regulations were introduced in the field of enterprise restructuring procedures.

Nevertheless, the results of studies conducted in selected Polish courts indicate that the four restructuring pathways proposed by the new law, including reorganization, are not attracting entrepreneurs experiencing financial difficulties and are lacking in demand of restructuring in court proceedings. Polish entrepreneurs do not trust that in court they will perform an effective restructuring in economic terms. The reason for this state of affairs is the lack of substantive preparation of the judges to carry out the restructuring, and even more the rehabilitation of the entrepreneur. Economic restructuring consists of building a new system of connections with the business environment and shaping the resources, production factors, organizational structures, and management system in the area of economy and the market. This arrangement is not yet fully created and will not develop without a thorough change of approach and implementation of new attitudes, behaviours and skills of people involved in the restructuring process (judges, trustees). It can therefore be stated that the Polish restructuring procedures of companies in financial difficulties are not aligned with the entrepreneurs' requirements.

References

Adamus, R. (2015). *Prawo restrukturyzacyjne*. CH Beck, Warszawa: Komentarz.

Budzyńska, A., Duszczyk, M., Gancarz, M., Gieroczyńska, E., Jatczak, M., & Wójcik, K. (2002). *Strategia Lizbońska – droga do sukcesu zjednoczonej Europy. Wyzwania członkostwa*. Warszawa: Urząd Komitetu Integracji Europejskiej.

Cenkier, A. (2007). Restrukturyzacja finansowa przedsiębiorstwa. In J. Szczepański & L. Szyszko (Eds.), *Finanse przedsiębiorstwa* (pp. 453–454). Warszawa: PWE.

Coase, R. H. (1937). The nature of the firm. *Economica, 4*, 386–405.

Demsetz, H. (1997). The firm in economic theory: A quiet revolution. *American Economic Review, 87*(2), 426–429.

European Commission. (2004). Europejska Karta Małych Przedsiębiorstw. Available via European Commission. Retrieved March 22, 2017, from http://ec.europa.eu/DocsRoom/documents/2148/attachments/1/translations/pl/renditions/native.

European Commission. (2008). Think Small First. A Small Business Act for Europe. COM, 394 final, Brussels.

European Commission. (2014). Commission recommendation of 12 March 2014 on a new approach to business failure and insolvency, Official Journal of the European Union, L 74/65.

European Commission. (2016). Definitions of Small and Medium-sized Enterprises Performance Review (SPR) indicators. Available via European Commission. Retrieved December 10, 2016, from http://ec.europa.eu/growth/smes/business-friendly-environment/performance-review/index_en.htm.

European Commission. (2017). SME Performance Review. Available via European Commission. Retrieved March 22, 2017, from https://ec.europa.eu/growth/smes/business-friendly-environment/performance-review-2016.

Godłów-Legiędź, J. (2005). Transformacja ustrojowa z perspektywy nowej ekonomii instytucjonalnej. *Ekonomista, 2*, 171–189.

Hodgson, G. M. (2004). *The evolution of institutional economics: Agency, structure and Darvinism in American Institutionalism*. London and New York: Routledge.

Jarka, S. (2008). Restrukturyzacja przedsiębiorstwa. In E. Weiss (Ed.), *Podstawy i metody zarządzania* (pp. 98–100). Warszawa: VIZJA PRESS&IT.

Ministry of Economy. (2014). Polityka Nowej Szansy. Available via Ministry of Economy. Retrieved November 16, 2016, from, http://kancelaria-pmr.pl/site/images/Polityka%20Nowej%20Szansy%20PNS_RM_ver_7.pdf.

North, D. (1990). *Institutions, institutional change and economic performance*. Cambridge: Cambridge University Press.

Ostrom, E. (1990). *Governing the Commons: The evolution of institutions for collective action*. Cambridge: Cambridge University Press.

Ratajczak, M. (1994). Nurt instytucjonalny we współczesnej myśli ekonomicznej. *Ruch prawniczy, ekonomiczny i socjologiczny, 1,* 27–39.

Rudolf, S. (2005). *Nowa ekonomia instytucjonalna. Teoria i zastosowania praktyczne.* Kielce: Wyższa Szkoła Ekonomii i Prawa w Kielcach.

Stankiewicz, W. (2012). *Ekonomika instytucjonalna. Zarys wykładu.* Warszawa: Wydawnictwo Prywatnej Wyższej Szkoły Businessu, Administracji i Technik Komputerowych.

Stępniak, A., & Kuczewska, J. (2004). *Polskie przedsiębiorstwo na rynku Unii Europejskiej.* Gdańsk: Fundacja Rozwoju Uniwersytetu Gdańskiego.

Suszyński, C. (1999). *Restrukturyzacja przedsiębiorstw.* Warszawa: PWE.

The Act on Restructuring Laws, Ustawa z dnia 15 maja 2015 r. Prawo restrukturyzacyjne (t.j. Dz. U. z 29 września 2016, poz. 1574 ze zm.).

The Bankruptcy Act, Ustawa z dnia 28 lutego 2003 Prawo upadłościowe (tj. Dz. U. z 2016, poz. 2171 ze zm.).

Williamson, O. E. (1998). *Ekonomiczne instytucje kapitalizmu. Firmy, rynki, relacje kontraktowe.* Warszawa: PWN.

Ząbkowicz, A. (2003). Współczesna ekonomia instytucjonalna wobec głównego nurtu ekonomii. *Ekonomista, 6,* 795–824.

Index[1]

[1] Note: Page numbers followed by 'n' refer to notes.

© The Author(s) 2018
S. Vliamos, M. S. Zouboulakis (eds.), *Institutionalist Perspectives on Development*, Palgrave Studies in Democracy, Innovation, and Entrepreneurship for Growth, https://doi.org/10.1007/978-3-319-98494-0

Printed by Printforce, the Netherlands